PAYCHECKS:
WHO MAKES WHAT

PAYCHECKS: WHO MAKES WHAT

by David Harrop

HARPER COLOPHON BOOKS
Harper & Row, Publishers
New York, Cambridge, Hagerstown, Philadelphia, San Francisco
London, Mexico City, São Paulo, Sydney

A hardcover edition of this book is published by Facts On File under the title *America's Paychecks: Who Makes What?* It is here reprinted by arrangement.

First HARPER COLOPHON edition published 1980.

ISBN: 0-06-090790-8

80 81 82 83 84 10 9 8 7 6 5 4 3 2 1

Contents

2116254

Introduction

A MERICANS ARE MORE concerned than ever before about their economic security as they watch the purchasing power of their paychecks being sapped daily by inflation. Moreover, while the nominal amounts listed as gross earnings on these paychecks keep rising impressively for most people, actual take-home pay inches up far more slowly. Thanks to the structure of progressive income tax brackets legislated in less inflationary times, the well-off are taxed as if they were extraordinarily rich, the middle class as if they were well-off and blue-collar workers as if they were middle class.

Nevertheless, all around are the signs of unprecedented abundance and prosperity. Shop windows overflow with luxurious merchandise, and the commercial din is exuberant and incessant. Advertisements extoll 20 different styles of designer "jeans," formerly the farmer's dungarees, and each pair costs as much as a good suit did, not many years ago. A perplexed citizen may wonder how people can afford the dime-thin watches, the suede suitcases, the ubiquitous fur coats and the high-priced restaurant dinners when the weekly food bill alone brings tears to the eyes.

He looks at his paycheck and wonders whether he is missing something. Is he in the wrong career? Are others in his line of work making much more than he is? How can other people buy these things that are so obviously out of his financial reach given today's prices? Who is making "real" money anymore? In these times nearly everyone is asking himself these questions and this book attempts to answer them.

Other people's salaries and incomes, of course, have always been an object of insatiable curiosity as well as a source of envy and awe, or from another point of view, perhaps sympathy and even compassion. Americans are considered an uncommonly materialistic people. One consequence of this weakness has been to equate a person's intelligence and significance with how much he makes. Because of this ingrained attitude, many Americans are driven to try to learn or guess how much someone else earns, to see, in effect, how they measure up. The same people are usually just as anxious to prevent other people from discovering how much they themselves make. Almost everyone denies playing this game at the very moment they are playing it most. High-minded denials aside, the game is played at every level of society and affords no end of recreation, amusement, chagrin, malice and food for thought.

The game of discovering incomes has numerous variations and unstated rules, some long established, others of recent and practical origin. The rich pretend to be less rich so that they will be less resented; the almost rich act rich; the middle class, the artists and the intellectuals pretend to be indifferent, although it hurts; and the poor, or those unaware of their limitations, simply lust to be rich.

To ask a friend how much he makes is to court suspicion and rejection; to ask a stranger is considered extremely rude and invites hostility, even a punch in the nose. These responses are understandable when the size of one's income is considered to reveal so much about a person's place on the social, economic and even intellectual ladder. The best course is to say nothing specific, but to imply with a shrug or a smile that you are making more than you do if you think you are underpaid, and less than you do if you think you are overpaid. And how many people think they are making neither more nor less than they deserve?

The most recent addition to the rules of this ancient game, an American variation, is that the rich, the almost rich, the middle class, and the artists and intellectuals do not want the government for obvious tax reasons to know any more about how much they make than is absolutely necessary. Therefore, only public servants, politicians holding office under the scrutiny of the public eye and the media and top executives who must answer for their usually generous salaries to stockholders are legally bound to openly declare their incomes.

As most readers go through this book, they will be astounded and possibly enraged by some of the incomes for "top earners" in various fields. Lest they become too despondent, it is worth considering how relative these numbers are as demonstrated by a rather awesome projection made by the Social Security Administration. If inflation continues but gradually drops off to about one-half the present rate, the average annual wage in the year 2025 will be $162,000. Of course, what such a salary will buy is another question.

In this book I've attempted to throw some light on what a great number of people in many different walks of life earn. The purpose is both to entertain and to inform. While I hope that the book will satisfy healthy human curiosity, I also hope that it will clarify some of the complexities and values of the American economy by comparing the history and scale as well as the monetary rewards of different occupations. Which occupations employ the most people now and in the past, which have the greatest economic output, the highest average wages, the lowest average wages, the greatest growth and fastest decline, which get the most and why? These and many other questions are considered.

Since this book was not written primarily as economic analysis but rather to entertain, most of the space and effort have been given to occupations that are interesting as well as vital.

Part One deals with jobs that entertain, divert and inform the public. These jobs, which sometimes seem more like play than work to those in the audience, are among the most cherished and important in society. The actor, novelist and sports superstar fulfill the essential role of making life truly pleasurable and comprehensible for a while. If they are good at their work, the financial rewards for these glamour jobs can be staggering.

Part Two covers the men and women who govern the nation and who ostensibly work for the taxpayer in positions high and low. It reports how much they are paid for their public service today and how this compares with what their counterparts were paid throughout the history of the Republic. It also demonstrates that the financial payoff for the power and responsibility exercised while in public office usually comes later.

Part Three considers three professions that are generally regarded as representing the country's trained elite: lawyers, doctors and educators. These occupations vary greatly in historical development, degree of specialization, and remuneration when examined in detail. The image each has in the public's eye has an equal or greater impact on the incomes of their practitioners than what they actually do.

Part Four looks at the main arteries of the economy: the farming, mining, producing, selling and financing of goods for profit that constitute the essential core of capitalism. This section deals with the widest range of activities and the broadest segments of the economy. Consequently, it includes an immense variety of different jobs and incomes.

Part Five examines the earnings of people outside the mainstream of the regular employee-employer job-salary relationship. People born into wealth are discussed, along with those who have made their own wealth in recent years through entrepreneurial skills and persistence. The fact that these people are beholden to no one for paychecks makes them both heroes and villains in popular opinion. Criminals are also entrepreneurs in the sense that they too are highly risk-oriented. The rewards, while they may come more swiftly, are usually less stable and the consequences of failure more severe than those faced by legitimate entrepreneurs, who may lose their shirts but rarely their freedom.

Each of these parts attempts to fit the occupations it covers into a general national and historical perspective and to give the reader an overall sense of the salary pattern of the industries covered. There are, of course, intangible rewards in almost every job. Some are economic; some are psychic; some are indefinable. Frequently, these cannot be is covered in a general work of this sort even though they add to the total value and prestige of a position. In many cases, the information is simply not available, or is so particular to a specific job or person that it would have no meaning to the reader. For example, some college presidents have a house that goes with the job, some do not; some executives have the use of a company box at the theater or stadium, some do not.

In numerous cases monetary figures for salaries and incomes are estimates. Moreover, whenever one uses average or median income figures, it must be remembered that by nature they are composed of many separate figures, some far above and some far below those cited. Also, this book is about incomes, jobs and economic situations that are continually changing; what was as accurate as possible when written will always be less accurate when read. Given the natural upward pressure of inflation, the reader can fairly assume that almost every income figure in this work will be higher when he reads it than when I wrote it.

I've made every reasonable effort to verify the truthfulness of the information upon which this book is based. Most of the information comes from sources in the public record or from other sources with a reputation for veracity. Despite these precautions, I cannot guarantee the absolute accuracy of the information. Salaries are, as this book points out, by their very nature often difficult to pin down. Therefore, neither I nor the publisher can accept responsibility for any loss or injury resulting from factual inaccuracies.

One problem that confronted me while writing this book is that the value of a dollar is constantly changing. Throughout, I have used the standard Department of Labor Consumer Price Index, which puts the dollar at $1.00 in 1967 and then rates it up and down in numerical value from that year. Everytime that a historical dollar value is used in this book for incomes, an equivalent contemporary value of that dollar is given.

Another problem inherent in the subject matter is the great disparity between incomes earned by men and women for the same job. Nearly all the average wages or salaries quoted are for both sexes, but many of the median and top salaries given in cases when the recipient is not named are based on what men earn. This treatment throws little or no light on what women have been earning for many jobs or on how much less it is on average than the earnings of men. Only in the education section are the comparisons between male and female faculty members shown, and this is mainly because that profession has committed itself to making the information available. It is interesting to note that while women have extremely few full professorships, they are equally or better represented in the beginning faculty jobs, a statistic that bodes well for the future of sexual equality in at least the education profession.

Sources for this book were magazines, newspapers, books, independent studies, government publications and many interviews. A great number of people helped me, while at the same time guarding the secret of their income from me. I talked with hundreds of people during the work on this project; some were encouraging and enthusiastic, a few offended and even offensive, one or two supercilious, and many suspicious.

Only one person in all this time ever voluntarily, without a second thought, even cheerfully, told me what his paycheck was, although he works for a private company that is quite secretive about such matters. He was the only person who seemed genuinely indifferent to the game mentioned earlier. He was not boasting about his salary, nor was he complaining about it. He simply told me the amount because our conversation was lagging a bit and he wanted to put me at ease. I swore then never to reveal his name, and I was so moved that I even forgot the figure he mentioned for some time. He is in the book, but which one he is I will never tell.

A great many people helped me organize and write this book. Jo Lynn Sanders found invaluable and esoteric information for me; so did Carl Sifakis. Joseph Reilly did a marvelous copyediting job, and Nancy Fishelberg was supportive all the time. I am most grateful to Marjorie Bank who did a very fine index for the book. By far the most and best help came from Edward Knappman, who is a superb editor and a gentle but very effective taskmaster. The original idea was proposed to Facts On File by Lawrence Benenson, to whom I am also grateful.

Part One
GLAMOUR JOBS

CHAPTER 1
Professional Sports

PAYCHECKS ARE BIG news in the field of professional sports. The sports sections of newspapers, magazines and television news resemble accounts of stock and commodity market transactions. What a player makes, how much a horse wins, how a franchise fares in the financial "won-lost" column are as important as the athletic achievements.

Yet, total revenues for the four major spectator sports in 1978-79 came to somewhat more than $1 billion. The average annual gross of a National Football League team in 1977 was $8.9 million, of a National Basketball Association team only $4.3 million—pocket change by the standards of American industry. Why, then, is so much attention paid to the financial ups and downs—mostly ups—of the players?

Most Americans think that they could have been great athletes, or perhaps will be someday. By the millions, we identify with the stars, heroes and villains in our favorite games. Because we imagine our-

3

selves out there, as one sports agent put it, "the colossal growth in athletes' salaries has caused a frenzy of outrage and envy among the fans that sells more and more tickets and makes possible greater and greater profits of all kinds in professional sports."

When baseball star Pete Rose signed a contract in 1979 to play with the Philadelphia Phillies, he was 37 years old. The contract guaranteed him a four-year minimum of $2,980,000 and a maximum of $4,035,000 over five years. The ink was hardly dry on the paper when it was revealed that the publicity and clamor over these terms immediately had brought in enough new income through increased ticket and TV sales to pay Rose's salary for the entire length of the deal.

Interest in sports statistics has long been a theme in American popular culture. Who pitched the most complete games? Who hit the most triples in one year? What man and what horse ran the fastest mile? Who caught the most passes in Superbowl X? And now a new chapter has been added to the record book and is getting more attention all the time.

Who got the largest contract in football for 1978? Who won the most money on the Professional Golf Association circuit in 1974? What are the terms of Jim Rice's baseball contract with the Boston Red Sox? How many years does it run?

These questions are much closer to home to the average American than how much the board chairmen of various corporations make or what a famous opera singer earns per performance. Most of us have swung bats, kicked or aimed balls in one way or another, skated or played tennis and golf. Moreover, we think of being industrialists, financiers, doctors, lawyers, truck drivers, farmers, waiters, hotel managers and other "serious" occupations as work. Sports remains a form of play. (Or, at least, we think of it that way.) And it's entertaining. No one buys tickets or sits through interminable TV commercials to observe a stockholders' report being written, a budget balanced, a person washing dishes.

Of course interest in sports money has always been there, and there have always been outstanding cases of extremely well-paid athletes and sensationally lucrative events. The second largest boxing gate in history after the $4,806,675 receipts for the Ali-Spinks fight in 1978 was the $4,658,660 take for the Tunney-Dempsey fight in 1927. Babe Ruth was paid $80,000 a year by the Yankees in 1930-31. Consider that the dollar was worth somewhat more than four times then what it is now, and that income taxes were negligible in those days compared to today, and you can see that Ruth was making the equivalent of about $800,000. When Ruth was asked how he felt about making more money than the president of the United States, he replied, "I had a better year than he did."

This year, dozens and dozens of baseball, basketball, football, hockey, tennis, golf and other players as well as horses are making more than the President, and many more look forward to having a better year than he does next year.

Professional sports are currently more popular and accessible than ever for two reasons: larger audiences attending events at ever bigger stadiums and television. In 1920 nine million people attended baseball games, a record for that time. In 1978 almost five times as many people bought tickets to see baseball games. In 1980, 102 million people watched the Superbowl on television, and advertising time for that game sold for $450,000 per minute.

Tickets and television are the principal sources of income (there are also concessions and rentals) for the four major professional spectator sports in America, and this is how they break down by sport:

PRO SPORTS INCOME (1978-79)

Sport	Attendance	Average Ticket Price	Approximate Ticket Income
Baseball*	40,800,000	$3.99	$163,200,000
			Television Income $92,800,000
			$256,000,000 total
Basketball	9,875,000	$6.78	Approximate Ticket Income $66,952,000
			Television Income $74,000,000
			$140,952,000 total
Football	16,057,000	$9.75	Approximate Ticket Income $156,555,000
			Television Income $656,000,000
			$812,555,000 total

PRO SPORTS INCOME (1978-79)

Sport	Attendance	Average Ticket Price	Approximate Ticket Income
Hockey	8,526,000	$7.87	$67,099,000 total
			Television Income
			(Little network,
			small local income
			for individual teams.)

*Television and ticket revenues from the playoffs and World Series games plus estimated concession incomes bring the 1978 baseball figure total to $278.7 million. Concession figures for the other sports are not available.

Each sport has its superstars, its run-of-the-mill players and its rookies. And for every player that makes it big, there are hundreds of thousands who tried but did not make it at all. In professional basketball, to take the best example, there are literally one million people in the United States for each player—242 in all—who succeeds in getting into the top competition.

The best way to understand how the stars and the others are paid, including some who do not play but are paid for supporting roles, is to look at each of the major sports separately.

BASEBALL

In 1975 the New York Yankees, owned by the ebullient and wealthy George Steinbrenner, blew the lid off free-agent contracts and started the great salary race in baseball. The Yankees signed Jim "Catfish" Hunter to a contract worth $2,892,000 for a period of five years; payment was broken down into a number of categories—partly for tax reasons. Since Hunter's contract was both a landmark and a model for contracts signed since 1975, its details are worth examining.

CATFISH HUNTER'S CONTRACT, NEW YORK YANKEES (1975-79)*

Five Years' Playing Salary ($100,000 per year)	$500,000
Cash Bonus	$100,000
Deferred Bonus	$250,000
Deferred Salary	$1,500,000
Insurance	$500,000

Scholarships	$36,000
Buick	$6,000
	$2,892,000 total

*Hunter retired when his contract expired in 1979.

(There was no extra charge for the nickname Catfish, which had been given to Hunter by George Finley, the owner of his previous team. It was actually invented by Finley to give the pitcher some Southern color and "liven up his public image.")

Hunter's salary perked up the interest of the fans, the press, the Internal Revenue Service, other baseball players and their agents. Four years after Hunter signed his contract, there were at least a dozen players making $500,000 a year or more and another dozen or so making over $400,000. Who knows what fat salaries the future will bring?

Two contracts signed in 1979 represented the greatest amount of money ever paid to baseball players. Many in the baseball business felt that the heights attained by Rod Carew and Dave Parker would be the earnings peak in the sport, after which baseball salaries would level off and possibly even start a slow decline. But who really knew? (In 1979 Nolan Ryan signed with the Texas Rangers for $1 million a year for four years plus a $500,000 bonus.) In any case, it is worthwhile to examine the Carew and Parker agreements; they represent the finest financial flowering of a great sports civilization.

ROD CAREW'S CONTRACT, CALIFORNIA ANGELS (1979-83)

Playing Salary,	1979	$800,000
" "	1980	$800,000
" "	1981	$800,000
" "	1982	$1,000,000
" "	1983	$1,100,000
		$4,500,000 total
		$900,000 per year

DAVE PARKER'S CONTRACT, PITTSBURGH PIRATES (1979-83)

Five Years' Playing Salary ($625,000 per year)	$3,250,000
Signing Bonus	$625,000
	$3,875,000 total
	$775,000 per year

In addition, Parker receives $100,000 for any year he is elected Most Valuable Player, $50,000 if the Pirates finish second or $25,000 if they finish third. He does not receive financial incentive for winning first place. He gets an additional $15,000 for any year he wins the Golden Glove fielding award, plus $150,000 for any year the Pirates' attendance exceeds two million, $100,000 for a year of 1.75 million or $50,000 for a year of 1.5 million. The maximum incentive pay he can earn in any one year is $265,000. Added to his regular annual salary of $775,000, this means he could make $1,040,000 in one season.

Listed below are the 21 top money earners in baseball for 1979. In several cases the total value of the contract has been divided by the number of years it covers to average out bonuses given in addition to salary and reach a simple per annum amount. Income made off the field in advertising and sponsoring products, lecturing and appearing before fans offseason is not included here.

BASEBALL'S TOP MONEY EARNERS (1979)

Player	Team	Earnings
Dave Parker	Pittsburgh Pirates	$1,000,000
Nolan Ryan	Texas Rangers	$1,000,000
Rod Carew	California Angels	$900,000
Pete Rose	Philadelphia Phillies	$745,000
Jim Rice	Boston Red Sox	$700,000
Vida Blue	San Francisco Giants	$700,000
George Foster	Cincinnati Reds	$700,000
Catfish Hunter	New York Yankees	$670,000
Ted Simmons	St. Louis Cardinals	$665,000
Mike Schmidt	Philadelphia Phillies	$560,000
Reggie Jackson	New York Yankees	$532,000
Larry Hisle	Milwaukee Brewers	$526,000
Bert Blyleven	Pittsburgh Pirates	$500,000
Bobby Bonds	Cleveland Indians	$484,000
Sparky Lyle	Texas Rangers	$484,000
Oscar Gamble	New York Yankees	$475,000
Tommy John	New York Yankees	$472,000
Robin Yount	Milwaukee Brewers	$470,000
Rich Gossage	New York Yankees	$458,000
Joe Rudi	California Angels	$440,000
Johnny Bench	Cincinnati Reds	$420,000

In 1980 new names will be added to the list, including that of the Boston Red Sox outfielder Carl Yastrzemski, who will earn a reported

$600,000 this year and in 1981. Yastrzemski's salary history is a veritable Horatio Alger story, symbolizing the rise of a great star in rhythm with the upward financial spiral of the game. His pay record is as follows:

CARL YASTRZEMSKI, BOSTON
RED SOX (1962-81)

1962	$25,000
1967	$65,000
1972	$160,000
1977	$230,000
1979	$375,000
1980	$600,000
1981	$600,000

Not all players in the major leagues make staggering sums. However, dozens made $200,000 a year or better in 1979 and many more than that were over the $100,000 mark. In fact, in 1979 seven teams paid an average salary of over $100,000. The Philadelphia Phillies and the Yankees were the highest with averages of about $150,000. The lowest were Minnesota and Toronto with average salaries of less than $40,000. Together the 26 baseball teams carried 650 players under contract and the average salary was nearly $121,000 per year, up from $19,000 in 1967. The minimum salary in 1979 was $21,000, up from the minimum of $5,000 that Willie Mays earned in 1951. This represents a great deal of money paid out in players' salaries, and yet it comes to only 26% of the total revenue for teams, the lowest proportion of the four major sports.

The managers of professional baseball teams are hired to master-mind the strategy for the season and the tactics of each game and to handle the high-priced talent. As one says, "It's not an easy job to make a multimillionaire, one of the highest paid humans in the world, go to bed at curfew time and generally behave himself if he doesn't want to." There are only a handful of managers who have kept the same job for more than two or three years. Furthermore, managers average a mere $60,000 a year in salary, peanuts in terms of baseball salaries. The explanation for this state of affairs was given by Buzzy Bavasi, executive vice president of the California Angels, who said, "It's a lot easier to get a new manager than a shortstop." However, recently certain managers have become superstars in their own right. Sparky Anderson

signed in 1979 to manage the Detroit Tigers for about $160,000 a year
and Billy Martin signed a $125,000 contract to manage the Oakland A's
in 1980.

Farther down the list, we come to the umpires, whose decisions are
final and who frequently decide the outcome of a game in a furor of
controversy and a storm of abuse. The minimum salary for umpires in
1978 was $16,500. After a lengthy strike in 1979, umpires now get
$22,000 after the first year and $50,000 after 20 years. Batboys make
$17.50 per game, groundkeepers $24,000 per year, gate attendants
$35.00 per game and ushers $18.50 per game before tips.

BASKETBALL

The National Basketball Association (NBA) has 22 teams and
carries 242 players under contract during the season, by far the smallest
number of performers in any major team sport. The average salary of
these players is $148,000 a year, making them the highest paid within
the four major spectator sports. There are two reasons for this: the
individual stars in basketball are highly visible, and one superstar
frequently makes the difference between a championship or a losing
season. More than 30 basketball players earn over $250,000 a year, and
the ranks of the highly paid are expanding. Even more remarkable is
that first-year men in basketball can and often do start at the top of the
salary scale. David Thompson of Denver made $500,000 in his first
year and Ernie DiGregorio started at Buffalo for $450,000 way back in
1973. Recent years have seen the starting salary drop and a top rookie
now begins at about $250,000. However the 1979-80 season was the
"Year of the Bird," when superstar rookie Larry Bird began with the
Boston Celtics at $650,000 a year, an all-time record for neophytes in
the world of professional sports.

The salary figures cited below are the latest available for 1979-80.
But basketball contracts and incomes are subject to volatile change,
moving up and down, but mostly up. Furthermore many contracts have
special clauses added to them. These can stipulate that a star will make
so much extra for number of points scored, free throws made, shots
blocked, rebounds pulled down etc.

BASKETBALL'S TOP MONEY EARNERS 1979-80

Player	Team	Earnings
Moses Malone	Houston Rockets	$1,000,000
Bill Walton	San Diego Clippers	$1,000,000

David Thompson	Denver Nuggets	$800,000
Larry Bird	Boston Celtics	$650,000
Kareem Abdul-Jabbar*	Los Angeles Lakers	$650,000
Julius Erving	Philadelphia 76ers	$600,000
Magic Johnson	Los Angeles Lakers	$600,000
Bob McAdoo	Detroit Pistons	$500,000
Bob Lanier	Detroit Pistons	$450,000
George McGinnis	Denver Nuggets	$450,000

*The Los Angeles Lakers have reportedly agreed to a new contract that will pay Jabbar more than $1 million a year for 1980-84.

The minimum player salary in the NBA is now $35,000. Once again the coaches are relatively underpaid, earning on average about $60,000 for masterminding the games, handling the talent, fighting with the referees and enlivening the crowds. Referees make more than umpires in baseball, going up to the $60,000 in 1979 that Jake O'Donnell made for using the whistle in 95 games during his 10th season on the job. Ushers make $18.50 for five hours of work, not including tips.

FOOTBALL

The gross revenue of the National Football League in 1978-79 was over three times that of its next highest competitor, baseball. Yet both in terms of highest and average salaries, football players are easily the lowest paid performers in the four major spectator sports; the average annual salary in 1978-79 was a mere $55,288. The total salaries paid out represent 31% of the game's gross, which is more than the percentage paid out in baseball, but because of the large number of players on each team, the individual football salaries are much lower than those in baseball.

There were only a few players earning $250,000 or more in 1979-80. (Overall, quarterbacks were once again the best paid, averaging $113,932, but the two top earners were running backs.) The number of big money earners in football was extremely small compared to the number in basketball and baseball. It is interesting to note that the highest NFL salary in 1979-80 was nearly twice as much as the next highest in the league.

FOOTBALL'S TOP MONEY EARNERS (1979-80)

Player	Team	Earnings
O. J. Simpson (retired 1979)	San Francisco 49ers	$806,668

Player	Team	Earnings
Walter Payton	Chicago Bears	$450,000
Bob Griese	Miami Dolphins	$400,000
Dan Pastorini	Houston Oilers	$379,000
Ken Stabler	Oakland Raiders	$342,000
John Riggins	Washington Redskins	$300,000
Bert Jones	Baltimore Colts	$275,000
Franco Harris	Pittsburgh Steelers	$250,000

Football salaries are less in the public eye than those of the other sports because the salaries are not as high and they are quite strictly grouped according to position. It is therefore informative to examine the high, low and average pay by position.

FOOTBALL SALARIES BY POSITION (1978-79)

Position	Low	High	Average
Quarterback	$22,000	$350,000	$102,606
Running Back	$20,000	$733,358	$66,516
Defensive Lineman	$20,000	$183,000	$66,063
Offensive Lineman	$20,000	$139,951	$60,241
Receiver	$20,000	$175,000	$59,824
Linebacker	$20,000	$200,000	$58,061
Defensive Back	$20,000	$118,750	$54,838
Kicker	$20,000	$72,600	$48,354

One of the reasons for the relatively low salaries in professional football (as noted earlier) is the fact that in 1978-79 there were 1,485 players under contract, more than twice as many as in baseball. This means that the average money paid out for salaries by football teams ($3,319,340), while considerably larger than the average for baseball ($1,907,350), resulted in a smaller paycheck in each player's pocket. The minimum salary in football is $20,000.

But football is the most generous of the pro sports when it comes to paying coaches. For example, the New England Patriots paid their coach and general manager, Chuck Fairbanks, $150,000 per year on a multiyear contract until he left in a dispute in 1979, and other coaches generally make higher sums for their work than their counterparts in baseball and basketball.

The grounds keepers, gate attendants and ushers make approximately the same as they do in baseball; waterboys work for free, plus an occasional team jacket thrown their way. Referees also work mainly as a hobby or for the dubious distinction of being snarled at by millions of fans at the stadium and on television; they earn between $350 and $800 per game depending on seniority and can earn extra for officiating at playoff and championship games. Dallas Cowgirls make the disappointing salary of $15.00 per game and pay their own expenses (except travel) on the road. It is the exposure and the chance to meet people that counts.

HOCKEY

The National Hockey League (NHL) had almost the same paid attendance in 1978-79 as the National Basketball League, but there is one striking difference. Professional hockey has been unable to stir enough national interest to get regular TV network contracts for the games, and the local telecasts of games yield much less revenue in comparison to the TV money earned by the other sports. Hockey Night on the Canadian Broadcasting System brought the three Canadian teams about $3.5 million a year in 1978-79, with the Toronto Maple Leafs getting the largest share, $1.5 million. For the NHL as a whole, the main source of income is the box office.

However, in 1978-79 the 425 players carried by the league's 17 teams earned an average salary of $100,000 per year (up from $22,000 in 1972), second only to basketball. Even in the minor leagues there are a number of hockey players making over $50,000 while waiting for their chance in the big time. The minimum NHL salary is $30,000. It is not surprising that nearly 60% of the gross revenue in hockey goes into the players' paychecks. One reason for this high figure is the superstar who is almost as important in hockey as he is in basketball.

The first really grand salary in hockey was the $1 million cash bonus and $250,000 per year salary that induced Bobby Hull to jump from the National Hockey League to the newly formed World Hockey Association in order to give it credibility. The new league folded after the 1978 season, but not before its intense competition had caused the NHL to substantially raise the salaries of players at every level.

HOCKEY'S TOP MONEY EARNERS (1979-80)

Player	Team	Earnings
Anders Hedburg	New York Rangers	$500,000
Ulf Nilsson	New York Rangers	$500,000
Gil Perreault	Buffalo Sabres	$350,000

Player	Team	Earnings
Phil Esposito	New York Rangers	$325,000
Mike Bossy	New York Islanders	$300,000
Brad Park	Boston Bruins	$265,000
Denis Potvin	New York Islanders	$250,000
Marcel Dionne	Los Angeles Kings	$240,000
Walt Tkaczuk	New York Rangers	$225,000

Hockey has a large number of players whose paychecks fall just below these high levels, which accounts for the sport's generous average salary considering the number of players involved. There are 60 players who make $120,000 or more per year.

Once again the coaches are back in the $60,000-a-year league; referees and goal judges are paid $75 to $150 per game. The men who clean and make fresh ice average $17,500 per year and ushers and attendants in hockey make about the same as they do in basketball.

Of course there are other profitable team sports, including soccer, but generally competitions based on individual performance bring the biggest paychecks of all to athletes. And the greatest money makers of these, by far, are boxers and golf stars, who stand out in the list that follows of the richest sports performers.

In most sports based on individual achievement, however, it is also true that the minimum earnings can be very low indeed, in some cases nothing at all for a year's work. This is true, for example, in bowling and tennis. In golf, the lowest recorded winnings in 1977 were $30, in harness racing $546 and in skiing $133. In sports, all roads are not paved with gold.

AUTORACING

Autoracing is run internationally before larger crowds every year and is destined to make more and more money for the drivers.

AUTORACING'S TOP MONEY EARNERS (1978)

Driver	Earnings
Al Unser	$591,396
Cale Yarborough	$530,000
Darrell Waltrip	$343,000
Tom Sneva	$340,396

BOWLING

Highest 1978 Income: Mark Roth $124,517;
Marshall Holman $107,255.

Bowling is breaking into the big money more significantly than before. The sport has the advantage of being popular and playable by great numbers of Americans at all economic levels, more so than most other individual sports. This gives it a growing mass appeal as a professional sport.

BOXING

Muhammad Ali's $5.75 million earnings in 1977 were the greatest single amount of money ever made by one athlete in one year. However the following year, Ali earned a million dollars more from his two fights with Leon Spinks. Ali retired in June 1979 and some of the luster—and gate appeal—of heavyweight boxing went with him. Nevertheless, three months later heavyweight Larry Holmes made $2.5 million for successfully defending his World Boxing Council crown against Ernie Shavers, who got $300,000 for his losing efforts. Also in 1979 the welterweight fight between challenger Ray "Sugar Ray" Leonard and champion Wilfredo Benitez earned $2.2 million, the highest amount ever paid for a nonheavyweight title bout. Leonard, who won the fight, made $1 million and Benitez, the defeated champion, took home $1.2 million. Below are listed the two top money makers and the sums they earned for major title matches during 1977, 1978 and 1979.

BOXING'S TOP MONEY EARNERS

Year	Fighter	Earnings
1977	Muhammad Ali	$5.75 million
	Ken Norton	$2.20 million
1978	Muhammad Ali	$6.75 million
	Leon Spinks	$4.00 million
1979	Larry Holmes	$2.50 million
	Wilfredo Benitez	$1.20 million

GOLF

Golf is a game requiring enormous skill, discipline and athletic ability. Every year hundreds of ambitious young players join the pro tour in hopes of making their way; few succeed. Professional golf is one of the most money-conscious of all sports. Accounts of tournaments frequently center as much or more on the amount of winnings as on the quality of play. But the high stakes involved and the publicity surrounding them make golf all the more exciting.

The Professional Golfers Association has entered into television contracts to show 26 of the 41 major tournaments over the next three years. The contracts are worth $30 million. Additional money comes from the sponsorship of individual tourneys by companies interested in promoting their own name.

It must be remembered that golf stars can earn great sums in off-the-course promotional and advertising activities. Arnold Palmer's total earnings from all the facets of his career as a golfer are the highest of any one athlete in history. He made an estimated $55 million between 1955 and 1977 in golf earnings and nonsports income. As the most recent example, he made $27,073 in tour earnings in 1978, but approximately $3.5 million in other related income.

GOLF'S TOP MONEY EARNERS

All-Time Winners, PGA Tours		*1979 Winners, PGA Tours*	
Jack Nicklaus	$3,408,827	Tom Watson	$462,636
Lee Trevino	$2,088,178	Larry Nelson	$281,022
Arnold Palmer	$1,798,431	Lon Hinkle	$247,693
Tom Weiskopf	$1,741,155		
Bill Casper	$1,683,618		

All-Time Winners, Ladies PGA		*1979 Winners, Ladies PGA Tours*	
Kathy Whitworth	$858,461	Nancy Lopez	$197,489
Judy Rankin	$761,130	Sandra Post	$178,751
Jane Blalock	$708,937	Amy Alcott	$144,839
JoAnne Carner	$649,980		
Donna C. Young	$602,809		

HORSERACING

Man has been betting on racing horses for thousands of years. Every year fortunes are won and lost wagering on the animal, and more money changes hands in this sport than any other. Staggering sums have been won on a $2.00 bet. Here are the two highest $2.00 straight mutual ticket bets in history.

TWO BIGGEST ALL-TIME $2.00 BETS

Year	Horse	Track	Amount
1912	Wishing Ring	Latonia	$1,885.50
1933	Augeas	Agua Caliente	$840.00

Here are the top money-winning thoroughbreds of the last five years:

TOP MONEY-WINNING RACEHORSES (1975-79)

Year	Horse	Earnings
1975	Foolish Pleasure	$716,278
1976	Forego	$491,701
1977	Seattle Slew	$641,370
1978	Affirmed	$901,541
1979	Spectacular Bid	$1,285,000

Here are the top money earning jockeys of the last five years:

TOP MONEY-EARNING JOCKEYS (1975-79)

Year	Jockey	Earnings
1975	Braulio Baeza	$369,520
1976	Angel Cordero	$470,950
1977	Steve Cauthen	$615,175
1978	Darrell McHargue	$602,986
1979	Laffit Pincay	$800,000

SOCCER

The North American Soccer League (NASL) has grown to 24 teams in America and Canada. With a paid attendance of 5,351,499 in 1978, it was the fifth largest spectator sport. The first great money earner in the NASL was the Brazilian star Pele. He was lured out of retirement by the New York Cosmos in 1975 for approximately $1 million a year for three years to spread the popularity of the game in the United States.

On a worldwide basis, soccer (also called association football) is the most popular sport by far, and hundreds of millions watch it each year on every continent. Soccer stars are also the highest paid athletes in the world.

In recent years many European, Latin American and other foreign stars have been signed by teams in the United States and Canada offering high salaries in return for their box-office appeals. Many believe that when soccer increases its TV network contracts, it will surpass the other spectator sports in both its following and income. This is speculation, of course, and depends on whether the sport can develop indigenous stars. At present, foreign-born players, usually near the end of their careers, are generally paid significantly more than Americans. This is a source of discontent and unrest among the native-born Americans. Below are listed the three top salaries for soccer players in 1978. All three are foreign born.

SOCCER'S TOP EARNERS (1978)

Player	Team	Earnings
Giorgio Chinaglia	New York Cosmos	$283,333
Franz Beckenbauer	New York Cosmos	$250,000
Dennis Tueart	New York Cosmos	$200,000

The average salary in 1978 for players in the NASL was $17,500, strikingly below that for players in the other spectator sports and indicative of the serious imbalance of pay that exists between native- and foreign-born players. All the teams in the NASL hire foreign stars when they can afford them, but the New York Cosmos have been the most successful at this. Not coincidentally, the Cosmos are also the most lucrative team. A rule requiring each team to start at least three American-born players may encourage the development of more native talent.

TENNIS

Professional tennis is another sport that has grown by leaps and bounds. First gaining broad popularity just 10 years ago, tennis is now frequently shown on both local and network television. Like golf, it is generously financed in many tournaments by ticket sales and corporate sponsors. Landmarks in the game are constantly being set. At the new National Tennis Center in New York in 1978, 57,000 more fans than ever before paid to watch the U.S. Open, played for the largest purse to that date, $558,310. Below are the big money winners, both men and women, for 1977-79; the highest earnings made in a single season for the past two years; and the five highest male and female all-time earners on the pro circuit as of 1978.

TENNIS'S TOP MONEY EARNERS

(Male) Player	Year	Earnings
John McEnroe	1979	$585,238
Bjorn Borg	1978	$691,886
Jimmy Connors	1977	$922,657

(Female) Player	Year	Earnings
Martina Navratilova	1979	$525,248
Martina Navratilova	1978	$500,000
Chris Evert	1977	$503,751

ALL-TIME CAREER EARNERS (Men)

Player	Year	Earnings
Jimmy Connors	1972-79	$3,194,002
Bjorn Borg	1973-79	$2,620,516
Ilie Nastase	1969-79	$2,316,461
Guillermo Vilas	1974-79	$2,028,024
Arthur Ashe	1969-79	$1,810,018

ALL-TIME CAREER EARNERS (WOMEN)

Player	Year	Earnings
Chris Evert	1973-79	$2,550,639
Martina Navratilova	1974-79	$1,670,767
Billie Jean King	1968-79	$1,246,035
Virginia Wade	1968-79	$1,205,246
Rosemary Casals	1971-79	$825,083

The wealth among tennis players is not shared with the umpires, who make $27.50 a day. This discrepancy was particularly noticeable at the 1979 U.S. Open, where the much-publicized prize money was $536,000. Ball boys and girls made the minimum wage, $2.90 an hour in 1979.

SUBSIDIARY EARNINGS IN PROFESSIONAL SPORTS

The superstars in professional sports frequently make as much, and sometimes a great deal more, off the field as on. By lending their names to products, sponsoring goods and services, advertising, lecturing, making movies and becoming entertainment personalities, great sums are added to the salary sweepstakes. Two dramatic examples illustrate this point.

O. J. Simpson, who retired at the end of the 1979 playing season, was his own agent, and a very good one as well. He negotiated his annual $733,358-a-year playing contract. Furthermore he has made more than $200,000 for every movie he played in and has a five-year sportscasting and jack-of-all-trades contract with NBC-TV. He continues to make money by hurdling for Hertz; advertising and sharing in the profits of the Tree Sweet orange juice company; plugging Shindana toys (Shindana makes an O. J. Simpson doll); recommending Dingo boots; and promoting Wilson Sporting Goods and Hyde Spot-Bilt athletic shoes.

In 1977 Simpson made approximately $800,000 with his off-the-field running and, adding in his playing salary, grossed about $1.5 million that year.

Another example of cashing in on athletic ability is Bjorn Borg. His tennis outfit on the court is a showcase of different commercial products that can be bought and used by many people for many things. In 1978 he made $50,000 for wearing his renowned headband advertising Tuborg beer and $200,000 for his shorts, shirts, socks and warming suits by Fila. He was paid $100,000 for using Bancroft rackets and $2,000 more for having them strung with VS gut. His tennis shoes by Tretorn earned him $50,000 and his shoulder patch advertising the Scandinavian Airlines System brought him $25,000. The name Bjorn Borg was also used on statues, games, cereals, sheets, jeans, towels, cars, comic books and games. Altogether he netted between $1.5 and $2 million off the court in one year.

Admittedly these two examples are striking, but golf pro Arnold Palmer does better then either Simpson or Borg, and there are many other stars bringing in big money away from the sports arena. Consider the sums made by Reggie Jackson for putting his name on a candy bar, or Chris Evert for pushing Borden's cheese and Puritan sportswear or Jack Nicklaus for selling Hathaway shirts. Muhammad Ali could sell virtually anything, but does rather limited promotional work considering the commercial potential of his name. When he was an active player, Fran Tarkenton made $350,000 a year on the football field and at least another $700,000 endorsing Delta Air Lines, General Mills, AT&T and Eastman Kodak, among other goods and services. This former quarterback is a millionaire many times over and, given his business acumen, probably would have been one in almost any line of work.

Sports superstars bring in the big bucks when they are riding high. But who can fault a person for cashing in on such perishable commodities as youthful appearance, exceptional physical skills and fame.

AGENTS

While O. J. Simpson was his own agent, this is rare in the present era of incredibly lucrative and complex contracts for sports performers. There have always been agents, but they are now more important than ever to both athletes and owners. The club owners may groan about the greed of agents and vice versa, but everybody seems to come out better when all parties are clearly and legally protected. In the past 10 years, the number of agents has risen, and there are now 208 lawyers and agents listed in the directory published by the Association of Representatives of Professional Athletes.

The usual commission for agents is 6 to 7% of their clients' sports incomes and higher, sometimes up to 20% on money made from endorsements etc. Well-known agents include Jerry Kapstein, who earned more than $1 million representing baseball players during the first free-agent draft; Alan Eagleson and Arthur Kaminsky, who mainly represent hockey players; Tom Reich, who handles baseball players; Robert Wolff, who is Larry Bird's agent, and Irwin Weiner, who has athlete clients in a number of sports, but mostly in basketball.

CHAPTER 2
Book Publishing

P RINCESS DAISY IS a romantic novel about the daughter of a white Russian prince and a Hollywood actress. Daisy is, not unexpectedly, young and beautiful and the tale is set against the steamy background of the cosmetics and television advertising industries. The author of this book is Judith Krantz, whose first novel, *Scruples*, sold 220,000 copies in hardcover at $10.00 and over three million copies in paperback at $2.75. When Krantz finished a 29-page outline of *Princess Daisy*, Morton Janklow, her agent, sold the hardcover rights for $400,000 to Crown, which was about to come out with *Scruples*. Negotiations for the paperback rights to the new novel were not completed at that time, however, and when Miss Krantz finished the manuscript over a year later, it was shown to nine leading paperback houses so that they could bid on it. (About 150 paperback novels a month are published in America, and the amount of money a publisher is willing to or can spend on a given title indicates his estimation of its profitability more than his savoring of its plot.)

At the time, *Scruples* was doing enormously well in sales. This success and the skillful combination of action, love, lust, and greed in *Princess Daisy* led to a rush of bidding that culminated in what may stand as the record for a prepublication book sale. Bantam Books agreed to pay a $3.2 million advance on sales for paperback reprint rights to *Princess Daisy*; 30% of the money will go to Crown and 70% to author Krantz (along with her agent). Bantam intends to publish the paperback version in March 1981.

To break even, or pay off the advance, Bantam will have to sell at least seven million copies, according to some, and will probably have to spend a million dollars in advertising and promotion. However the company's publisher, Marc Jaffe, thinks that a sale of four to six million copies will put his company ahead, thanks to the rising retail prices of paperback books. Furthermore the publicity stemming from the sale will increase the value of the book to Bantam, in the same way that the furor over the size of Pete Rose's contract generated enough TV and ticket revenue for the Philadelphia Phillies management to pay it off.

This deal incorporates many components that characterize the world of mass paperback publishing today. Bantam Books is now the American paperback division of Bertelsmann, a vast communications conglomerate that derives income from worldwide book publishing and numerous other sources. The enormous payment for rights, the elaborate advertising and promotion campaigns, the emphasis on the "big blockbuster book" and access to a more sophisticated and centralized distribution and merchandising apparatus than ever before (partly due to the growth of large bookstore chains) are all aspects of contemporary publishing. These developments have also been spurred by larger and more lucrative sales of literary properties to TV, movies, serializations, book clubs and foreign publishers.

Finally, there is the ingredient that always accompanies large outlays of money—large risks. This is particularly true now when the paperback market shows signs of softening. There is fear that too many books at too high a price will glut the outlets, turn off the customers and damage the industry. (When a Bantam official was asked in late 1979 how the advance money for *Princess Daisy* would be recouped, he said, "$3.50 may be a totally acceptable cover price"—when the paperback edition is published in 1981.)

RECENT PAPERBACK ADVANCES

Book and Author	Year of Negotiation	Advance
Princess Daisy Judith Krantz	1979	$3.2 million
Love Signs Linda Goodman	1978	$2.25 million
Fools Die and The Godfather (reissue) Mario Puzo	1978	$2.25 million
The Bleeding Heart Marilyn French	1979	$1.91 million
The Thorn Birds Colleen McCullough	1978	$1.9 million
Ragtime E. L. Doctorow	1977	$1.85 million
The Investigation Dorothy Uhnak	1977	$1.6 million

The Final Days
    Bob Woodward and
    Carl Bernstein
	1977	$1.55 million

Oliver's Story Erich Segal	1977	$1.41 million
Full Disclosure (first novel) William Safire	1978	$1.35 million

These figures for advance paperback payments sound enormous, but in most cases the author shares the advance royalty half and half with the hardcover publisher. Also, there are usually special clauses in the agreement that make some of the total figure dependent on sales performance. For example, a certain amount will be paid for each week the book makes the paperback best-seller list, another amount for each week it is first on the list and so forth.

The actual figures for authors' and publishers' income on a book are only evident when all the figures for all types of sales are final. However these figures are often closely guarded secrets. Ten of the best-selling hardcovers and 10 of the best-selling paperbacks for 1978 are shown here with the most accurate figures available to give an estimate of the income received by publishing's fortunate few. Author's income alone is given for hardcover books, and combined royalty for both author and hardcover publisher is shown for paperbacks.

1978 Hardcover Fiction

Chesapeake by James Michener: sold over 1.1 million copies, earning the author an estimated $2.14 million in royalties.

Centennial (previous novel) by James Michener: sold 430,000 copies in hardcover, elicited a paperback advance of $1 million and earned more than $2.1 million for the author.

The Thorn Birds by Colleen McCullough: sold about 645,000 copies, earning the author an estimated $967,000 in royalties.

Fools Die by Mario Puzo: sold about 285,000 copies, earning the author royalties of $515,000 ($115,000 over the $400,000 he received as an advance for the book).

Illusions: The Adventures of a Reluctant Messiah by Richard Bach: sold 162,688 copies, earning the author an estimated $170,000 in royalties.

The Holcroft Covenant by Robert Ludlum: sold 153,820 copies, earning the author an estimated $252,500 in royalties.

1978 Hardcover Nonfiction

A Distant Mirror: The Calamitous Fourteenth Century by Barbara Tuchman: sold 259,954 copies, earning the author an estimated $621,290 in royalties.

Pulling Your Own Strings by Dr. Wayne W. Dyer: sold 317,105 copies, earning the author $424,920 in royalties.

If Life Is a Bowl of Cherries, What Am I Doing in the Pits? by Erma Bombeck: sold over 700,000 copies, earning the author approximately $840,000 in royalties.

The Complete Book of Running by James Fixx: sold over 620,000 copies, earning the author approximately $930,000 in royalties.

1978 Mass Paperback (Fiction and Nonfiction)

The Thorn Birds by Colleen McCullough: sold approximately 6.4 million, earning the author and the publisher about $2.1 million in royalties.

The Other Side of Midnight by Sidney Sheldon: sold 6.2 million in 1977-78, earning the author and the publisher about $2 million in royalties.

The Amityville Horror by Jay Anson: sold in 1978 and to date approximately 5.7 million copies, earning the author and the publisher about $1.9 million in royalties.

Your Erroneous Zones by Dr. Wayne W. Dyer: sold 4.2 million, earning the author and the publisher $924,000 in royalties.

The Crowd Pleasers by Rosemary Rogers: (original publication) sold 2.1 million copies, earning the author and the publisher about $820,000 in royalties.

Jaws 2 by Hank Searls: sold a reported 3,815,000, earning the author and the publisher about $840,000 in royalties.

The Lawless by John Jakes: sold 3,300,000 copies, earning the author and the publisher about $760,000 in royalties.

The Promise by Danielle Steel: sold 1,938,000 copies, earning the author and the publisher about $349,000 in royalties.

Holocaust by Gerald Green: sold 1,775,000 copies, earning the author and the publisher about $455,000 in royalties.

Twins by Bari Wood and Jack Geasland: sold 1,580,000 copies, earning the author and the publisher about $474,000 in royalties.

Historical Hardcover Best-Sellers

Listed below are the number of copies sold for the five best-selling hardcover books from 1895 to 1975.

Better Homes and Gardens Cookbook, 1930 and later editions (Meredith), 18,684,000.

The Prophet, Kahlil Gibran, 1923 (Knopf), 6,000,000.

Hop on Pop, Dr. Seuss, 1963 (Random House), 5,650,000.

Gone with the Wind, Margaret Mitchell, 1936 (Macmillan), 5,190,000.

The Robe, L. C. Douglas, 1942 (Houghton Mifflin), 3,132,000.

Historical Paperback Best-Sellers

Listed below are the number of copies sold for the five best-selling paperbacks from 1895 to 1975.

Pocket Book of Baby and Child Care, Dr. Benjamin Spock, 23,210,000.

Webster's New World Dictionary of the English Language, 18,500,000.

The Guinness Book of World Records, Norris McWhirter, 14,015,000.

The Godfather, Mario Puzo, 11,750,000.

The Exorcist, Peter Blatty, 11,500,000.

Of course, this list of all time best-sellers will soon be invaded by newcomers.

Beside income from book sales, authors and publishers garner substantial additional income from the sale of subsidiary rights, such as movie and TV rights. It is also possible for a movie to spawn a novel, reversing the traditional pattern. Either way, each media can increase the exposure and commercial value of the other.

Large numbers of books have been sold on option or outright for movie and TV production. Recently, *Fools Die* by Mario Puzo was sold to the movies for $1 million, which is considerably better than the $12,500 he got for film rights to *The Godfather*. The actual amount of money earned on movie and TV sales is usually tied to the degree of success achieved at the box office or in the ratings, and a surprisingly large number are unsuccessful. The rights to quite a few are purchased, yet the movie or TV series are often never made, because this can be a risky form of investment. However, many ventures have been tried and many have succeeded, including TV productions based on *Roots, The Holocaust, The Bastard, Captains and Kings, Blind Ambition, The Last Convertible, Backstairs at the White House, Scruples* and many others.

Selected sections of books are occasionally published in magazines or newspapers either as a one-time effort or as a serial. The two highest sums for magazine rights to book excerpts were $200,000 paid by *Ladies Home Journal* in 1974 for excerpts from *Times to Remember* by Rose Kennedy and $100,000 paid by *Playboy* magazine in 1979 for parts of Norman Mailer's book *The Executioner's Song*. Many other books are serialized for far less money, and publishers often look upon this outlet as a good means of advertising a forthcoming book.

Despite the impressive amounts of money discussed here, two out of every three of the approximately 35,000 titles published in 1979 actually lost money. For this reason it is important to put the publishing industry into a realistic perspective. The glamour, publicity and popular interest in the book business is far from justified by the relatively trivial amount of money involved.

The total domestic price paid for *Princess Daisy* was $3.6 million dollars (hardcover and paperback) and more is certain to come with movie, TV and serial rights. Nevertheless, this figure—the highest amount of money ever paid for a book to date—is slightly less than one-fifth the cost of a 727 airliner, of which Boeing has sold 1,701 around the world. The total sales of all types of books in the United States for 1978 was estimated at $5.77 billion, or $1.5 billion less than the 1978 sales of the Caterpillar Tractor Company, or about one-quarter of the 1978 sales made by Sears Roebuck.

Book sales can be broken down into a number of categories of different types of books, each requiring its own specialized approach. Some, but not all of the categories are shown here:

DOLLAR SALES OF BOOKS BY CATEGORY (1978)

Category	Millions of Dollars
Trade (adult and juvenile hardbound and adult and juvenile paperback, sold in bookstores at a price higher than mass paperback.)	$940.5
Mass Paperback (lower-priced paperback only, sold at newstands, variety stores, supermarkets etc., as well as in bookstores.)	$608.1
Religion (bibles, testaments, hymnals, prayerbooks and other books about religion and religious figures.)	$273.8
Professional and Medical (technical, scientific, business and other.)	$807.9
Textbooks (elementary, secondary, college and standardized texts.)	$1,624.7
University Press	$62.2

The three categories of trade, mass paperback and textbooks accounted for over half of all book sales in 1978.

Textbooks are not glamorous, as everyone remembers from his school and college days, and yet they have certain distinct advantages that explain the enormous financial success of many of them.

Textbooks are assigned to students who in most cases must buy them. Therefore the text market is a captive one; no one has to read *Princess Daisy*, but a lot of people who want to graduate from college had better read *Economics* by Paul Samuelson, or some similar assigned text. For this reason, when a major textbook becomes established, it can have a long and continuous market, with numerous revised editions at prices that rise to keep up with the cost of living. Bookstores may make less profit per copy from textbooks than from trade books, and publishers may have to spend more to produce a textbook than a novel, but the steadiness of the buying audience brings in relatively high incomes for both parties. In fact, it is often said that for some houses the textbook division with all its mundane regularity pays for the glamour and frothiness of trade publishing.

In 1978 there were over 150 college textbook authors (not counting secondary and high school textbook writers) who made $150,000 or better. Here are five of the all-time best-selling textbooks, the length of time they have been on the market and a rough estimate of the author's income.

College Textbooks

Accounting Principles by C. Rollin Niswonger and Philip C. Ness has been in its 11th edition since 1973 ($13.30 per copy). The book has been on the college market for over 45 years and to date has sold about two million copies. It tells all about how to make numbers work for you as a student or a breadwinner. The authors have earned roughly $2.6 million.

Economics by Paul Samuelson has been in its 10th edition since 1976 ($16.95 per copy). Two generations of Americans have learned their economics the Keynesian way with this unpretentious and at times humorous book. Since its first publication in 1948, it has sold at least 3.7 million copies and earned for its author and his various assistant editors over $6 million.

History of Art by H. W. Jansen has been in its second edition since 1977 ($17.95 per copy). A magnificent collection of color plates and a text that gracefully explains the appeals of art has impressed the experts as well as students. The first edition in 1962 sold for $11.95. Total sales at all prices have been over two million, and the author has earned approximately $3 million.

Harbrace College Handbook by John Hodges, revised by Mary Whitten, has been in its eighth edition since 1977 ($7.95 per copy). It has introduced writing, reading and appreciating the English language to generations of freshmen. The book has been on the market for 40 years, the second longest period of time for any major college text, and has earned the authors more than $2.5 million.

PUBLISHING, PROFITS AND PAYCHECKS

Publishing houses and their sales have never been large when compared to other American commercial enterprises. However, publishing houses have become attractive acquisition targets for large conglomerates. Communications groups and sometimes large holding companies may wish to acquire a prestigious publishing house to further diversify their activities and make a modest profit while enhancing their public image. Bantam Books, paperback publishers of *Princess Daisy*, is one example. In fact, all of the nine leading mass paperback publishers who were invited to bid for the book are owned by much larger corporations, ranging from CBS and RCA to Gulf and Western and Hearst.

An interesting illustration of the dynamics of such mergers occurred in late 1979 when both Mattel Toys, Inc. and ABC sought to acquire Macmillan, Inc. Previously American Express had considered Macmillan but decided to go after McGraw-Hill in a celebrated battle in which the publishing firm persevered and retained its independence. ABC continued its quest and Macmillan was about to become another major independent publishing house absorbed by a conglomerate. Because of the growing importance of the merger trend in the business of book publishing, it is worthwhile to look at some of the considerations that lead to a merger, using the proposed Macmillan acquisition by ABC as an example.

For the potential acquirer (ABC), Macmillan had the following advantages:

- a prestigious and historical name, combined with a reputation for excellent quality;
- a leading position in several textbook areas (religion, education, music), further enhancing an already strong textbook division;
- a standing as the fourth largest book club publisher, with a concentration in high-margin, specialized audience markets (for example, the Lawyer's Literary Club);
- two high-profit subsidiaries (Berlitz and Katherine Gibbs), adding diversification and growth;
- other money-making subsidiaries that could be sold off with relative ease if desired;
- a good international position; and
- one of the few publishers selling at less than "book value" (net asset value).

On the other hand, Macmillan had several unattractive subsidiaries that would be difficult to unload. In the past, management had shown reluctance to divest unprofitable operations. This was reflected in low book value and signaled possible difficulty in future relations with an incumbent management. Some divestitures would have involved write-offs. As with all publishers, Macmillan's growth rate was less than that of most of the perspective purchasers. Finally, for ABC a merger would have resulted in a temporary depression of the firm's overall earnings growth at an inopportune time.

At the last minute ABC reneged for both these and internal reasons. Macmillan was not merged at that time, but still may join the ranks of other major well-known houses: e.g., Random House/Knopf; Holt Rinehart & Winston; Little, Brown; and E. P. Dutton. None of these publishers declare their balance sheets or the salaries of their top officers separately, but rather their figures appear lumped into the total financial picture of the parent conglomerate.

Below are listed the 1978 executive salaries, total sales and net income figures for many of the major publicly owned, independent publishing houses whose principal source of income is books.

EXECUTIVE SALARIES, TOTAL SALES AND NET INCOME, SOME MAJOR HOUSES (1978)

Company and Officers	Executive Salaries	Total Sales (millions)	Net Income (millions)
Grolier		$242.8	$2.5
Robert Clarke, President	$298,970		
Harcourt Brace Jovanovich		$413.2	$7.3
William Jovanovich, President	$295,625		
Robert R. Hillebrecht, Vice President	$130,625		
Harper & Row		$129.06	$3.09
Winthrop Knowlton, Chairman	$163,038		
Brooks Thomas, President	$137,625		
Houghton Mifflin		$126.3	$9.9
Harold T. Miller, President	$162,850		
Richard B. Gladstone, Senior Vice President	$104,264		

McGraw-Hill	$761.2	$63.6
Harold McGraw, Jr., Chairman, President $302,980		
Alexander J. Burke, Jr., President (Books) $193,000		
Macmillan	$553.5	$21.9
Raymond C. Hagel, Chairman $225,206		
Robert A. Barton, President $142,592		
Prentice-Hall	$254.9	$26.7
Frank J. Dunnigan, President $211,200		
Howard M. Warrington, Chairman $132,000		
Scott Foresman	$189.9	$23.1
Gordon R. Hjalmarson, Chairman $198,327		
Larry Hughes, President of William Morrow $110,636		
Edward Wanous, President of South-Western $123,067		
John H. Williamson, President of Silver Burdett $99,743		
John Wiley	$90.36	$5.9
W. Bradford Wiley, Chairman $175,000		
Andrew Neilly, Jr., President $150,007		
Charles Stoll, Vice President $88,654		
Michael Harris, Vice President $96,954		
Robert Douglas, Vice President $79,185		
Zondervan	$41.4	$2.1
Peter Kladder, Jr., President $112,170		
P. J. Zondervan, Chairman $89,505		

Note: Doubleday is not included because, as a privately owned, independent publishing house, it does not make its figures public. However, in 1978, total sales were $336.7 million and net income was $18.4 million.

The top money earners in book publishing may not be on the verge of poverty, but their paychecks can't compare with those of sports stars, superlawyers or even some of their own best-selling authors. Numerous athletes, for example, make more than twice as much as Harold McGraw, who is president and chairman of the board of a multimillion dollar business, publishing books of all sorts and many well-known magazines including *Business Week*. Of course, Mr. McGraw also receives quite a large sum in dividends each year.

The levels below top management are no different. Book publishing is a low-paying industry and outsiders are often surprised by how little people earn who are frequently responsible for making available such influential and highly visible products. Listed below are many of the major jobs in publishing with average salaries for positions with companies under and over $20 million in annual sales in 1977-78.

SALARY SCALES IN PUBLISHING JOBS (1977-78)

Job	Companies up to $20 million	Companies over $20 million
Head of House	$83,896	$122,178
Executive Vice President	$47,896	$87,500
Publisher, Trade (all industry)	$78,500	$78,500
Publisher, El-Hi (texts)	$53,700	$61,550
Publisher, College (texts)	$78,870	$56,750
Publisher, Paperback (all industry)	$45,505	$45,505
Publisher, Professional, Technical etc.	$51,100	$51,750
Treasurer, Financial Officer	$45,000	$57,000
Personnel Director	$29,000	$51,000
Editor in Chief, Trade (Editorial Director)	$45,400	$51,000
Editor in Chief, El-Hi (texts)	$34,000	$50,000
Editor in Chief, College (texts)	$23,450	$29,400
Senior Editor, Mass Market Paperback (all industry)	$26,500	$26,500

2116254

Editor, Trade		
(all industry)	$23,500	$23,500
Editor, College		
(all industry)	$24,700	$24,700
Associate Editor		
(all industry)	$15,500	$15,500
Assistant Editor		
(all industry)	$12,000	$12,000
Vice President		
for Marketing	$38,300	$55,381
Sales Manager, Trade	$27,400	$32,000
Sales Manager, College	$25,751	$37,825
Regional Sales Manager		
(all industry)	$29,425	$29,425
Salesperson, Trade		
(all industry)	$21,500	$21,500
College Traveler		
(all industry)	$16,750	$16,750
Sales Advertising		
Manager	$20,500	$24,500
Senior Copywriter	$12,750	$15,500
Direct Mail Manager	$18,500	$19,500
Publicity Manager	$16,500	$19,750
Senior Book Designer	$15,900	$20,350
Art Director	$22,000	$27,500
Artist (jackets, pro-		
motion pieces, etc.)	$11,750	$14,250
Director, University		
Press (all industry)	$38,500	$38,500
Editor in Chief,		
University Press		
(all industry)	$24,750	$24,750
Senior Editor,		
University Press		
(all industry)	$16,750	$16,750
Director, Marketing		
and Sales, University		
Press (all industry)	$22,250	$22,250

These are the average in-house salaries. Certain editors make considerably more than the average, some by making their own imprint with a publishing house. Richard Marek with G. P. Putnam has brought out a number of best-sellers, and Henry Robbins did extremely well in conjunction with E. P. Dutton before his death. This is a new style of publishing in which the editor/publisher finds and develops his books and then markets, advertises, sells and distributes them in a profit-sharing arrangement with an established publishing house. This system is increasingly popular among all the parties and a successful editor/publisher can make well over $100,000 a year.

FREE-LANCERS

Publishing companies often pay for specific jobs to be done on a "free-lance" basis, which keeps overhead costs down. These jobs range from straight copyediting to rewriting, jacket writing and designing, photographing subjects and authors for jackets, book designing and publicizing books and authors. Below are some of the fees that free-lancers get for various jobs. Obviously the exact fee in every case depends on the difficulty of the work required as well as the skill and time involved.

Editing

Line editing for consistency, grammar, sense and general readability in a manuscript pays from $6.00 to $8.50 an hour, but for technical texts it can go up to $12.00 and $14.00 an hour.

Major editing of the theme, organization and treatment of a subject is normally paid by the job; $1,500 for a 300-page manuscript would be high average, but of course the fee can be more or less according to the requirements of a particular manuscript.

Book Designing

Designing a 280-page straight-text book earns from $275 to $425. For a book of the same length with tables and charts, the fee is about $300 for the basic design plus about $3.50 a page for mechanicals.

Jacket Designing

Jackets can be designed for a flat fee of $450 to $600 a jacket or the same fee plus expenses (materials, research etc.) incurred in the work. Expenses can run from $100 to $500 or more. Three of the top jacket designers are Paul Bacon, Larry Ratzskin and Bob Anthony.

Jacket Photos and Illustrations

The average fee for photo rights is about $300. Famous photographers have their own rates. Jill Krementz, one of the best when it comes to portraits of authors, charges a minimum fee of $500 for a photo and retains certain rights to its publication. Photo assignments involving models and props or for books such as cookbooks with schematic or complex jacket photos can cost up to $1,500 for the photo and expenses.

Full-color illustrations for covers or paintings for Gothic novels and the like can cost $1,000 or more. Paintings have proven to be more popular than ever for jackets.

Publicizing

Free-lance publicists who specialize in books charge $600 per day plus expenses for New York, Chicago and Los Angeles and $400 plus expenses for other areas. The expenses include such items as telephone calls, posters, brochures and renting space for author press conferences and the like. Tours are arranged and interviews and appearances booked. The latter include autograph sessions at department and book stores, as well as other promotional events. Betsy Knowland, Eileen Prescott and Alice Allen are three of the leading book publicists. Ms. Allen also arranges "events," i.e., thematic parties for authors, critics and friends to publicize a book in dramatic fashion.

Ghostwriting

Some people make a very nice living writing books for others, although frequently their names are not cited at all, or only quietly acknowledged: "By So and So and (Ghostwriter)" or "As told to (Ghostwriter)." Chris Chase wrote Betty Ford's "autobiography" for a fee of $100,000. Yvonne Dunleavy received a $100,000 advance fee for writing Xaviera Hollander's *The Happy Hooker*, plus 15% of the book's profit, which has gone over a million dollars. Joseph DiMona received a $75,000 advance and 50% of the royalties for writing H. R. Haldeman's *The Ends of Power*.

OTHER FORMS OF INCOME

Agents

There are several hundred literary agents who head or work in large agencies or represent authors on their own. Some of the most active agencies are the Richard Curtis Agency, Brandt and Brandt, International Creative Management, Scott Meredith Agency and Writer's House Inc. Other agents work alone, or with one or two assistants, including Georges Borchardt, Candida Donadio, Gerard McCauley, Knox Burger and many others.

The incomes of these agents vary according to their skill in selecting and selling talented authors. Morton Janklow makes over a million dollars a year representing Judith Krantz, William Safire, John Ehrlichman and others. The Scott Meredith Agency handles a great number of successful authors and Scott Meredith himself makes about $350,000 a year. Some of the individual agents mentioned here make from $60,000 to $100,000 or in some cases even more.

Literary Awards

There are more than 75 literary awards for all types of writing. The conditions for the award and the subject matter vary. Below are listed a few of the more significant awards:

- Academy of American Poets (annual), $10,000;
- Bancroft Prize, History (annual), $4,000;
- Bennet Award (biennial), to a writer whose work has not received recognition, $12,500;
- Neustadt International Prize for Literature (biennial), for outstanding literary achievement, $10,000;
- Nobel Prize for Literature (annual), $160,000.

CHAPTER 3
Journalism

I N 1942 NEWSPAPER columnists Drew Pearson and Robert Allen, who wrote the popular "Washington Merry-Go-Round" column, were lured from the *Washington Times Herald*, where they were making $35 a week, to go to the *Washington Post* for $100 a week. This was during the days when news coverage, commentary and analysis were being expanded and improved to deal with the global events of World War II.

Drew Pearson was at the top of his profession when he was making $5,200 a year. His paycheck, however, was small in comparison to his influence then, as is the approximately $85,000 a year that *New York Times* columnist Tom Wicker earns for presenting his widely read opinions on important domestic and international issues today. In 1979 A.M. Rosenthal earned $150,000 as executive editor of the *New York Times*, making him probably both the highest paid and most powerful editor in the United States. His newspaper is read by politicians and power brokers the world over, and the influence of his editorial direction, usually invisible, subtly molds their attitudes and actions. Yet he makes less than legions of athletes and actors.

Television journalists and anchormen fare better with their paychecks than print media colleagues, principally because they must manifest the poise, charm and charisma of an entertainer to capture and hold huge audiences. As early as 1959 David Brinkley was making $75,000 and Chet Huntley $100,000 a year for their news program on NBC. Soon after, their rival at CBS, Walter Cronkite, rose in the viewer's esteem and became identified in the public mind with the great events he reported over two decades. He was rated as America's "most trustworthy man" and made over $700,000 in 1979. Only once, when Barbara Walters was given a contract for $1 million a year in 1976 to coanchor ABC's evening news, was Cronkite's pay surpassed by another TV journalist. In order to placate Harry Reasoner, who was already the show's anchorman, ABC raised his salary to $500,000, creating an expensive combination that still failed to beat Cronkite or NBC in the ratings. After the dust settled, Cronkite once again emerged the top paid journalist on television, but not for very long. In early 1980 CBS announced that it had signed network correspondent Dan Rather to succeed Cronkite, who is expected to step down from his evening news spot sometime in 1981. Rather's contract gives him $8 million spread over five years, putting him on the same level as Cronkite and in the range of entertainment superstars like Johnny Carson.

These salaries are among the very highest in contemporary journalism, a profession that has expanded significantly in complexity and technical skills, breadth of coverage, range of treatment and sophistication in approaching and appealing to audiences and, most of all, its impact on our lives. In fact, the prevalence of news reporting and analysis in everyday American life has dramatically affected the way citizens think, feel and act about a myriad of events that their ancestors never even would have been aware of.

Journalism has made events in the distant corners of the globe immediately relevant to Americans to a degree that gives journalists an extraordinary influence on how things are perceived, and in some cases even how things happen. (Critics say that the reporting of the crisis in Iran that began in late 1979 determined much of what occurred then. The mobs of demonstrators reportedly timed the climaxes of their

chanting protests to coincide with the film deadlines of American TV
networks.)

NEWSPAPERS, MAGAZINES AND SYNDICATES

In 1978 there were 1,753 daily newspapers published in the United
States. Their cumulative circulation equaled 287 copies per 1,000
people. The United States has many more papers, although generally
with smaller circulations, than the other leading industrialized nations.
For example, the United Kingdom had 111 dailies in 1975, with 388
copies per 1,000 people; Germany had 320 dailies in 1974, with 289 per
1,000 and Japan had 180 dailies in 1974, with 526 copies per 1,000.

For the United States this represents a slight decline from 1,772
dailies published in 1959, and an increase in circulation that is roughly
equivalent to only one-half of the increase in population. This overall
drop can be attributed to the expansion of television viewing, particularly of evening news programs, which has had a devastating effect on
the circulation of afternoon papers around the country.

Nevertheless, the health of the newspaper business is sound; for
example, 29% of all the advertising money spent in the United States
in 1976 went to buy newspaper space and this was 50% more than
television, its nearest competitor, received.

The general financial well-being of publishing groups, syndicates
and individual newspapers and magazines is reflected in the rather
generous salaries their executives receive, especially when compared
with executive salaries in other businesses of comparable size.

KEY EXECUTIVE SALARIES IN PUBLISHING GROUPS, NEWSPAPERS, SYNDICATES AND MAGAZINES (1978)

Chairmen	Company	Total Remuneration
Andrew Heiskell	Time Inc.	$490,969
Franklin D. Murphy	Times Mirror Co.	$487,744
Harrington Drake	Dun and Bradstreet Co.	$450,000
Thomas S. Murphy	Capital Cities Communi- cations	$379,542
Katharine Graham	Washington Post Co.	$375,000
Paul Miller	Gannett Co.	$349,716
Arthur Ochs Sulzberger	New York Times Co.	$307,065

book publishing employees. Moreover, opportunities for promotion for those with the right skills are better than in most industries. Most of the major editors, columnists and even executives in the newspaper business began at the bottom of their trade, as copy or office boys, copy editors, editorial assistants and in other entry-level jobs.

Let's look at the salaries paid by a major city newspaper in the East, which are marginally higher than the national averages with the exceptions noted.

For editors, domestic correspondents, editorial writers, desk heads domestic bureau chiefs and some others, the minimum wage after six months on the job is $538 per week. At a lower grade, copy editors, editorial assistants, reportorial rewrite and news makeup people must be on the job for one year before they qualify for permanent employment and earn $485 a week minimum. Still lower on the scale are reporters and news photographers who must wait two years before becoming eligible for the same minimum wage of $485 a week.

The weekly salary of an office clerk and a mail clerk after one year is $250 and the weekly salary of a copy clerk or a messenger after one year is $265. A photo-cropping clerk and a proofpress operator make $280 after one year. A large city newspaper is big business, and provisions must be made for all sorts of functions and jobs. For example, a dishwasher in the employees' cafeteria makes $225 a week after two years and a salad maker earns $262 after three years, which is about as much as an associate editor in book publishing makes after the same period of time. A chef makes $395 a week after four years, or almost $20,000 a year, which is good money for a full editor in many publishing houses, but less than newspaper index and copy editors, who make $470 a week after one year.

Nationally, the average salary for a beginning reporter is $12,000 a year and $18,000 after four years. Paychecks for reporters range from $11,000 on a small daily to $26,000 on a large urban daily. Desk editors can earn $30,000 or more on some papers. Managing editors on the larger papers make around $50,000; on the largest papers, managing or executive editors can go above $100,000 (A.M. Rosenthal, for example).

Publishers make a comparable amount, unless they happen to own their own papers, in which case they pay themselves as little or as much as they choose, or as the books will bear. Reporters on the largest papers can also make in the range of $50,000 or better in exceptional cases, but at that level they frequently become top editors or columnists.

A senior reporter for one of the large news services, the Associated Press or United Press International, earns a high of about $19,000, and an editor/writer makes between $22,000 and $25,000 a year.

COLUMNISTS AND SYNDICATION

Well-known columnists earn salaries that are in the $100,000-a-year range. For example, both James Reston and William Safire of the *New York Times* make about that sum. Mike Royko of the *Chicago Sun-Times* is one of the highest paid columnists in the country earning $140,000 a year under a five-year contract.

However, straight salary is only one part of a successful columnist's income. Most also have agreements with one of the 300 syndicates in the United States to sell their columns to papers around the country. These syndicates registered a combined sale of over $100 million in 1978, and they are a major source of earnings for journalists, cartoonists and commentators of all sorts.

Mike Royko's column is distributed by the Field Newspaper syndicate as part of his columnist's salary arrangement. Jack Anderson is the most widely syndicated columnist in America; he makes more than $250,000 a year through United Features, which sells his column to 600 newspapers. James Reston syndicates his column through the New York Times Syndicate as part of his approximately $100,000 salary as a columnist and vice president of the *Times*. The same syndicate handles Tom Wicker's column under his $85,000 a year salary arrangement with the paper.

Other famous journalists with syndicated columns include James Wechsler, Evans and Novak, George Will, David Broder and Jimmy Breslin. In fact, there are hundreds of syndicated columnists, commentators, journalists and cartoonists. Of the last, the most successful is probably Garry Trudeau, who nets about $200,000 a year from *Doonesbury*.

Humorist Art Buchwald is also in the $200,000-a-year range. His former partner, Robert Yoakum, successfully syndicates and sells his own column, doing twice as well as he once did with the Los Angeles Times Syndicate.

MAGAZINES

There are about 9,500 magazines published in the United States. Each year about 350 are started and almost the same number fail. The major news and business news magazines exert enormous influence on public opinion. *Time, Newsweek, U.S. News and World Report, Business Week, Forbes* and *Fortune*, to name some of the most important, are read by over 10 million people on a regular basis. A presidential endorsement by *Time* or *Newsweek* is considered far more important than one by a major newspaper since each one of these magazines reach more people across a broader political spectrum.

Magazine salaries, except for the managerial ones, are somewhat lower than those paid by major newspapers. This is because magazine journalism is frequently "group journalism," with stories put together by reporters, writers and editors working together. The individual writer does not have the same prominence as his counterpart on a newspaper with its bold bylines.

Of course, this is not true of literary magazines or those which emphasize individual style, such as *The New Yorker*. There, Calvin Trillin and other regular contributors can make at least $100,000 a year from magazine articles and from writing books that are often, but not always, offshoots of magazine pieces. The regular writers also have drawing accounts with the magazine, which permit them to take advances against future writing projects and provide them with an ongoing security while working on lengthy or difficult pieces.

A senior editor at *Newsweek* or *Time* generally makes about $55,000 to $60,000 a year, and a senior writer like William Roeder, who writes the "Periscope" section of *Newsweek*, makes $50,000 a year. Assistant writers and editors are in the $25,000 to $30,000-a-year range. A *Newsweek* column with bylines by well-known people and experts such as Paul Samuelson, Milton Friedman, Shana Alexander and George Will earns $1,000 per column; contributors to the brief "My Turn" section are paid at the rate of $500 per contribution.

One of the key staff jobs at both *Time* and *Newsweek* is that of researcher or assistant to the editors. They start at about $14,000 a year and can earn up to $30,000 after several years.

Staff photographers earn salaries in the same range as their colleagues on newspapers, but a sizable proportion of magazine photographs are bought on a free-lance basis. *Life* magazine pays $400 for a full-page photo, and occasional shots of news and popular interest can earn from $50 up, depending on their importance to the magazine. For example, Michael Laughlin was in the right place with a camera to take photographs of the DC-10 disaster in Chicago in 1979. He sold the photos to the *Chicago Tribune* for $5,000. The newspaper in turn, through its photo agency, Sygma, sold and distributed the pictures worldwide, and both the paper and the agency made about $50,000 for them.

FREE-LANCE MAGAZINE WRITING

Writers who are paid by individual assignments rather than by a salary are called free-lancers, a popular term originally used to describe a roving knight who could be hired to use his lance in battle. The term is often considered synonymous with "being unemployed," for it is estimated that of the at least 28,000 people who call themselves free-lance magazine writers, only about 300 make a decent living at it. Free-lancing, though one of the most alluring of all occupations, is unfortunately one in which the list of successful writers keeps shrinking.

A few free-lance markets have become more lucrative, principally the "skin" magazines and regional publications such as *New West* and *Texas Monthly*, but generally free-lance rates have not kept up with inflation. There are naturally exceptions or so many people would not try to live in a world where the average stated income has dropped from $10,000 in 1973 to a current $7,500. Political writer Richard Reeves earns over $200,000 a year, including income for a regular column, and sports writer Bil Gilbert brings in about $50,000. Tad Szulc makes about $80,000 a year from magazine work and published books.

Below is a list of the going rates for a major article at some of the leading magazines using free-lancers.

FREE-LANCE RATES FOR SELECTED
MAGAZINES PER ARTICLE (1978)*

National Geographic	$4,500
Reader's Digest	$3,000
Woman's Day	$2,500
Family Circle	$2,500

McCall's	$2,500
Playboy	$2,250
TV Guide	$875

*These figures vary, of course, according to the reputation of the writer and the length of the piece, but they are accurate averages. A free-lance writing job can require widely varying amounts of time, and this can make the task either profitable or a financial disaster.

TV AND RADIO

Ninety-four percent of all American households are now able to receive four or more television stations, and the competition among news and commentary shows is fierce. Basically the same events are reported on all the stations, the difference is how the news is presented and by whom. The personality and appeal of the newscaster or anchorperson has become crucial in the battle for audiences; it is estimated that a single rating point up or down can mean the difference of $500,000 in annual income for a station in a large city.

Anchorperson salaries range from $10,000 to well over $225,000, with $34,000 being the national average. For the larger stations, with an income of $8 million or better, the average salary for an anchorperson is $67,300, and their careers can take off as rapdily as a movie star's. Jessica Savitch went from relative obscurity to reporting and anchoring TV news programs in a short time. She now earns $200,000 a year. The people who anchor the news are growing in numbers, and their salaries are rising at network affiliates all around the country. The list is impressive.

SALARIES OF SOME LEADING ANCHORPEOPLE
(1978)

Anchorperson	Station (owner)	Estimated Salary
Roger Grimsby	WABC New York (ABC)	$250,000
Paul Moyer	KNBC Los Angeles (NBC)	$250,000
Bill Kurtis	WBBM Chicago (CBS)	$250,000
Jim Jensen	WCBS New York (CBS)	$250,000
Jerry Dunphy	KABC Los Angeles (ABC)	$250,000
Larry Kane	WABC New York (ABC)	$250,000
David Horowitz	KNBC Los Angeles (NBC)	$250,000
Jim Vance	WRC Washington (NBC)	$210,000
John Schubeck	KNBC Los Angeles (NBC)	$200,000
Kelly Lange	KNBC Los Angeles (NBC)	$200,000

SALARIES OF SOME LEADING ANCHORPEOPLE
(1978)

Anchorperson	Station (owner)	Estimated Salary
Christine Lund	KNBC Los Angeles (NBC)	$200,000
Jess Marlow	KNBC Los Angeles (NBC)	$200,000
Mort Crim	WBBM Chicago (CBS)	$200,000
Chuck Scarborough	WNBC New York (NBC)	$200,000
Rolland Smith	WCBS New York (CBS)	$200,000
Ron Hunter	WMAQ Chicago (NBC)	$190,000
Fahey Flynn	WLS Chicago (ABC)	$180,000
Joe Benti	KNXT Los Angeles (CBS)	$170,000
Bill Bonds	WXYZ Detroit (ABC)	$160,000
Joe Daley	WLS Chicago (ABC)	$150,000

TV investigative reporting shows and morning news and features programs have hosts that make more than most anchorpeople. For example, Mike Wallace makes about $500,000 for doing "Sixty Minutes" and Tom Snyder about $400,000 for "Prime Time Saturday," while David Hartman of "Good Morning America" gets $750,000 a year and Tom Brokaw of "Today" about $450,000. These programs are not strictly journalistic in content, but the news is essential to the structure and many of the interviews are with people who are at the time prominent in the news. In sports journalism, Howard Cosell is at the top, making more than $1 million a year.

Although these salaries seem large in relation to those of columnists, reporters and editors at newspapers and magazines, the earnings of television executives are even larger. In fact, they are the highest paid managerial group in all of the media. The radio and television industries employ over 160,000 people, and revenue from television in 1978 amounted to nearly $8 billion, while that from radio was over $2 billion.

Many of the huge conglomerates such as CBS, ABC, RCA (NBC), Metromedia, Warner and others own numerous media companies other than their television stations and networks. In fact, most began as radio broadcasting companies but have expanded into television, then publishing and all other forms of entertainment. For example, Metromedia has major television stations in six cities around the country, reaching 20% of America's potential audience. The corporation also owns radio stations, advertising groups, direct mail operations and entertainment companies, including the Ice Capades and the Harlem Globe Trotters.

INCOMES OF TOP MEDIA EXECUTIVES (1978)

Chairmen	Company	1978 Income
John W. Kluge	Metromedia Inc.	$1,762,000
Steven J. Ross	Warner Communications	$990,000
Leonard H. Goldenson	ABC	$953,500
William S. Paley	CBS Inc.	$762,321
J. Kelly Sisk	Multimedia Inc.	$214,120
Presidents		
Elton H. Rule	ABC	$1,107,000
John D. Backe	CBS Inc.	$701,465
Frederick S. Pierce	ABC Television	$625,688
Edgar H. Griffiths	RCA (NBC)	$390,834 (plus contingency benefits)
Jay Emmett	Warner Communications	$363,000
Emanuel Gerard	Warner Communications	$363,000
Peter Storer	Storer Broadcasting Corp.	$201,118
Vice Presidents And Others		
Clemens M. Weber	Metromedia Inc.	$1,385,005
Walter R. Yetnikoff	CBS Inc.	$807,489
Alfred L. Schwartz	Metromedia Inc.	$674,774
Everett H. Erlich	ABC	$391,781
John Phillips	CBS Inc.	$370,578
Ross Barrett	Metromedia Inc.	$338,252
John R. Purcell	CBS Inc.	$330,772
Gene F. Jankowski	CBS Inc.	$297,953

People at the top of the communications industry have often negotiated income packages totaling far more than their salaries. Jane
Cahill Pfeiffer, NBC's vice chairman, has a three-year contract that will
earn her well over $1 million. She gets $225,000 per year in salary, with
guaranteed bonuses totaling a minimum of $400,000. She can also
exercise options to buy 10,000 shares of RCA stock. Fred Silverman, as
chairman of NBC, has a three-year contract worth $3 million, with
similar stock options.

Compared to these stratospheric salaries, the minimum and average
ranges for the people who perform the routine jobs involved in putting
out the news programs seem paltry indeed. The beginning salary for a
radio or TV announcer is about $14,000 and with experience the figure
goes to $21,000 for radio and $25,000 for TV. (Generally, TV is higher
at all levels.) In 1979 there were almost 30,000 announcing for one

media or the other. However a recent study for news directors at 900 TV and radio stations found the average salary at both was $19,250. The salary of an established TV reporter can reach $30,000 to $35,000 per year. Some go higher at major stations in large cities, reaching $50,000 to $75,000. Such reporters as Richard Valeriani are in this range. Sander Vanocur, a nationally known reporter, made $100,000 in 1979.

Journalism has grown enormously in scope since the first days of World War II when Drew Pearson was writing his famous column. The ordinary citizen is aware of news events in places in this world that were previously known only to a few. Riots, political upheavals, assassinations and elections are casually reported from localities barely on the map 30 years ago. The average person, almost without being aware of it, has become the repository of more facts and opinions on more subjects than the busiest student in the Renaissance. This is surely not to say he is more intelligent or wiser, just more aware of what's going on. Whether it serves to divert, amuse, terrify, inform, or only preoccupy us, journalism is an unceasing, expanding, and often financially lucrative profession.

CHAPTER 4
Entertainment and the Arts

BOOM OR BUST, America is the mother lode for entertainment superstars. In 1923, when things were good, Tom Mix was making $17,000 a week. In 1927, when things were even better and the dollar was worth four times what it is today, movie writer Emil Jannings was making $3,000 a week.

In the early 1930s, when Babe Ruth was making $80,000 a year, it was bust and things were very bad. The Babe's salary and those of many Hollywood stars were being compared with that of the president of the United States. Entertainers were at the top then as now. A column in the *New York Herald Tribune* on Oct. 12, 1933 remarked, "Although authentic figures of the earnings of motion picture stars are seldom available, estimates popularly accepted fully bear out the belief that many of the leading screen players receive salaries far in excess of that paid to the president of the United States."

Then came a long list of stars and their salaries; five of them are shown below. Weekly salaries in this calculation were based on a 40-week year, and sometimes less.

WEEKLY SALARIES OF FILM STARS
(EARLY 1930s)

Name	Weekly Salary
William Powell	$4,000
Marion Davies	$3,000
Edward G. Robinson	$1,975
Joan Crawford	$1,950
James Cagney	$1,000

In 1933 Kate Smith was also making $3,000 a week, and 12 million families owned radios on which to hear her.

In 1979, when things were comparatively good again, a number of movie stars were making $3 million a film plus percentages of the gross income. Thus regardless of the state of the economy, film superstars were and are among the top money earners in the nation and will undoubtedly continue to be as long as there are audiences seeking diversion from the daily grind.

But entertainment earnings neither were nor are democratically distributed. In 1933, for example, an extra on a Hollywood set was making between $5.00 and $7.50 a day. Nor is success common. Today it is estimated that less than one-half of the members of the Writers Guild of America make their living by writing, and more than one-half of the aspiring actors and actresses in the country at any one time are unemployed or working in a job that has nothing to do with their craft. The same is true for dancers, sculptors, painters, musicians, magicians, acrobats and others who seek to make their livelihood from the arts, both high and lowbrow.

Entertainment is a business whose great purpose is to bring in the largest possible paying audiences in as many ways and forms as it can. Those who are successful at attracting crowds use as many attributes and skills as they can—talent, expertise, sex appeal, sentiment, guile, deceit, whatever is possible and necessary—and the rewards to the entertainer are lavish when the turnstiles are clicking. Tom Mix and William Powell made stunning salaries by bringing in the money paid by a public always ready to spend, in both good times and bad, and respond, in humor and sorrow, to the magic of a good performance.

The zest for entertainment covers a wide spectrum: movies, TV, radio, theater, music and dance, and spectacles of all sorts in endless variations and outlets. The few at the top of this hurly-burly make millions, a middle range draws smaller crowds or holds supporting jobs at unspectacular but comfortable incomes and a vast group at the bottom struggle to earn anything at all.

MOVIES AND TV

In 1916 Charlie Chaplin signed a contract for $670,000 to make comedies for one year. When Mary Pickford heard of this, she walked out of the studio and did not return until she had a contract for $1.04 million plus a $300,000 bonus for the same year. (The dollar then was worth approximately six times what it is now in purchasing power.) In 1917 Chaplin received a $1 million contract for directing and starring in eight two-reel comedies, plus $15,000 for each reel over two and 50% of the profits on all pictures of five reels or more. The amount of money he made over the years on *A Dog's Life, Shoulder Arms* and *The Kid* under this contract is staggering as well as incalculable.

In 1979 Steve McQueen, an actor whose talents hardly match Chaplin's, completed a movie entitled *The Hunter* for $3 million plus approximately 10% of the gross profits. He has announced that he will make no more films for less than $5 million and 15% of all domestic and foreign gross profits. (He has even rejected one movie on these terms.) Burt Reynolds, another star not on the same level with Chaplin, received $3 million per film plus 10% of profits before taxes. Clint Eastwood was paid a $3 million advance for starring in *Escape from Alcatraz* plus escalating bonuses of $500,000 that could bring his total earnings to about $10.5 million, if the film grosses $60 million, which is a realistic goal.

Marlon Brando was paid $3.7 million for his brief and uninspired appearance in *Superman* plus 11.3% of the box-office gross receipts. (By contrast, Christopher Reeve, who played the title role, made only $250,000 for his effort.) For the superstars, a $3 million advance plus a percentage of gross receipts is becoming common for a major part in a full-length movie. Jane Fonda received nearly that much for agreeing to do a film which at the time had no script but only the bare skeleton of an idea around which to create a vehicle for her talents and immense box-office appeal.

However, all stars negotiate each contract as it comes, in both movies and TV, and there is no real going rate for any job. Marlon Brando received $250,000 payable per day for 11 days work on a movie entitled *The Formula*. Another example, Audrey Hepburn, once at the very top and still a powerful name at the box office, though less so, received $1.25 million plus 10% of the gross for her role in *Bloodline*. James Mason got $500,000 for his smaller role and Romy Schneider, Maurice Ronet and Omar Sharif received from $150,000 to $250,000 in the same movie.

For shorter roles, the superstars demand and make sums that are in keeping with the generally grandiose scales. In 1978 Elizabeth Taylor made $100,000 for a nonspeaking cameo role, one day's work, in the film *Winter Kills*. She was also to receive a mink coat but that became the subject of a dispute which will probably never be settled. In 1979 Fred Astaire received $200,000 for a few days work starring in a movie built around a Christmas theme that NBC hopes to establish as a holiday classic and put on the screen every year. Whatever the type or length of the role, the paychecks of these personalties reflect the fact that superstars are "bankable," that they draw vast audiences and make staggering sums for both themselves and the industry.

The incomes of TV stars have skyrocketed along with the growth of the industry. In 1949 there were one million TV sets in America. Six years later 67% of all households had sets and in 1979, 98% of all households had one or more sets (the average being over one and one-half sets per household).

Today's star of stars is Johnny Carson, the master of ceremonies and guiding force behind the "Tonight" show. His program brings in about 10% of all the gross profits for NBC, and he is reputed to make a salary of $2.5 million plus another $2.5 million from a percentage of the commercial earnings. Carson is truly the Muhammad Ali of the television world, and his statements concerning his future have as much news impact as the pronouncements of the great boxing oracle on his retirement once had.

The TV mini-series and the movie made for TV are two art forms that may have reached their peak in 1979. Peter Strauss now commands a fee of between $450,000 and $600,000 for starring in a TV movie. He earned $35,000 per segment for Book II of "Rich Man, Poor Man." Costar Susan Blakely earned $60,000 for her role in Book I of the same series and now receives $100,000 per film. Carol Burnett has a contract to do five TV movies for $2 million, of which two, "Friendly Fire" and "The Tenth Month," have already been shown. The fact that their ratings were not as high as expected is one reason for anticipating a decline in the number of these ventures.

One of the most successful series over recent years has been "Columbo," for which Peter Falk earned $333,000 per episode. Carroll O'Connor made $110,000 per episode in "All in the Family." Mary Tyler Moore earned over $2 million for the final season of the series named after her. "Bewitched" was another series with a great following; in its eight years of existence it earned over $6 million for star Elizabeth Montgomery, who also gets 20% of the proceeds from future syndicated showings. "Charlie's Angels" has been one of the most successful of recent TV series, and both Jaclyn Smith and Cheryl Ladd make $50,000 per episode. In "Dallas" Linda Grey and Victoria Principal make $10,000 an episode and Charlene Tilton makes somewhat less. Robin Williams has been earning $30,000 an episode for "Mork and Mindy," but his success has been so phenomenal that his price is going up all the time. For a series entitled "House Calls," Wayne Rogers receives $50,000 per episode, far more than the $1,600 Gary Coleman reportedly had been making a week on "Different Strokes." (A recent court action, however, indicated that Coleman's annual income is now about $600,000.)

While the numbers are impressive, paychecks for roles in prime time TV series may be here today and gone tomorrow. In the period from 1978 to 1980, approximately seven out of 10 new series were canceled. A more durable TV form has been the soap opera, many of which have been running through one convoluted plot after another for years. A one-time or an occasional appearance on a soap opera can earn a high of $500. Stars who appear every day make as much as and sometimes more than $3,000 a week; several of the highest paid soap opera stars earn $150,000 to $200,000 a year. Many have contracts that pay them for every show in their series whether they appear or not.

Soap operas are one of the most profitable areas of television. A soap opera episode can be rehearsed and produced in one day, whereas a weekly show done in Hollywood generally requires five days of preparation, which costs the studio significantly more for the same length of commercial product. This is one of the reasons why soap operas have tended to lengthen the episodes, thereby increasing the highly priced advertising space.

Another lucrative form of work for TV performers is in commercials. They can usually be depended on to offer some of the best entertainment on TV, regardless of their essential purpose. More time, directorial care and money goes into the production of one commercial than numerous regular programs many times its length. The actors are paid for the original commercial and receive residual income for each series of reruns that is shown. Name actors can make truly enormous sums through contracts for appearing in commercials, and this has become a very common source of income for them.

Not everyone involved in movies and television is an on-camera star. There are supporting players, writers, producers, directors and others who labor to create the movie, series or program to entertain the public. Work is not always available for actors, but when it is, the minimum wage is $189.50 per day and $785 per week. The earnings of movie extras have gone up significantly since 1933; they now earn a minimum of $57.60 a day. These figures are based on union contracts and they are constantly subject to negotiation and change.

It is estimated that 75% of all actors and actresses in all areas of the art who are members of relevant unions (Actors Equity, Screen Actors Guild, AFTA) earn less than $2,500 a year, and only about 3% make $25,000 or more a year. Frequently the union scale is considerably lower than money made through free-lance work. For example, a stunt man earns $250 a day minimum, but a top stuntman such as Bob Anthony makes over $150,000 a year by working more hours and signing contracts far above union scale.

A staff, or company, cameraman works approximately 100 days of the year and earns about $38,000. A free-lance cameraman, filming documentaries, features and commercials for independent producers, can work 150 days or more in a year and earn $70,000.

Writers for movies and TV normally make individual deals. An example is the flat fee of $75,000 that Oliver Stone negotiated for doing the screenplay of *Midnight Express*. Fees can go much higher than that. The pilot scripts for the television serial "Hart to Hart" brought the writers an average of $20,000 for a 30-minute show and $40,000 for an hour show. Thirty segments were made providing a number of writers with some lucrative work. (Only seven of the shows

actually made the Fall 1979 schedule.) Some writers, especially nove-
lists who write the screenplays of their work, receive a percentage of
the box-office proceeds.

The minimum for writing one complete TV screenplay plus a
treatment (a working outline that precedes the script) is from $12,220
to $22,695 depending on length. The minimum for rewriting a screen-
play is $4,582 and for polishing a screenplay into final form after it has
been written by someone else is from $2,291 to $3,491. The minimum
for writing one week of a soap opera, five 30-minute segments, is
$4,582. Most soap opera writers make more than this, particularly if
the segments are an hour long, and frequently the head writer farms
out parts of the script to other writers in a literary cottage industry. On
the other hand, writers working full time on an ongoing show can
make about $2,000 a week.

Producers often take a fee, sometimes a salary and normally a
percentage of the gross earnings of whatever they are producing. For
example, the movie *Bloodline* based on Sidney Sheldon's novel is
produced by Sidney Beckerman and David Picker. They each set a fee of
$250,000 plus 25% of what is left of the gross after the author and
principal actress (Audrey Hepburn) get their shares. Thus the producer's earnings are more dependent on the success of a movie than the
earnings of any other person connected with it. The producers of *Jaws*,
Richard Zanuck and David Brown, earned about $25 million from the
movie, which is an all-time high. Of course, if a movie fails financially,
the actors still have a guarantee, but the producer goes down with the
production.

In television, producers make far more than writers. A person who
produces a prime time, half-hour situation comedy earns between
$7,000 and $10,000 a week. If a producer is doing an hour-long
adventure show, his or her income can double. Finally, if a show goes
into reruns or foreign sales, the producer's income can multiply many
times.

A director is generally paid a salary or fee and less commonly a
percentage of the gross or net receipts, unless his or her name or
reputation is a great boost at the box office. The Directors Guild
minimum for directing a feature film is $53,066, which Robert Red-
ford is accepting to direct his first movie, *Ordinary People*. Alan
Parker directed *Midnight Express* for a straight payment of between

$250,000 and $300,000, plus 7.5% of the net profits. TV directors who work on staff for a network can make about $50,000 a year, but the average runs lower.

The salaries of movie and TV stars are so enormous that they overshadow everyone in the business; the incomes of even executives and management seem almost small in comparison, including the earnings of the exceptional Alan Ladd, Jr., who made over $2 million in 1978-79 in salary and bonuses. However, executive salaries in the entertainment industry are far above those in other American businesses. But when Christopher Reeve, a relative unknown, makes $250,000 for his first major film, *Superman*, or James Coburn earns $500,000 for his role in the movie *Golden Girl*, the executive pay structure somehow becomes irrelevant. Below are the estimated salaries and total incomes in 1979 plus bonuses for key executives of one of the major independent movie companies. The names of the company and the individuals have been withheld, but the figures indicate the very high level of compensation involved.

EXECUTIVE SALARY STRUCTURE, INDEPENDENT MOVIE COMPANY (1979 ESTIMATED)

Position	Salary	Bonus	Total Compensation
President	$260,000	$254,800	$514,800
Executive Vice President	$225,000	$214,200	$439,200
Chairman, Executive Committee	$250,000	$238,000	$488,000
Movie Division			
President, International Foreign Distribution	$104,000	$102,000	$206,000
Vice President, Business Affairs	$119,600	$68,000	$187,600
Vice President Marketing	$153,400	$187,000	$340,400
President, Product	$275,000	$224,000	$499,000
TV Division			
President	$140,000	$57,800	$197,800

Movies and TV, along with the record business, are the biggest money makers in the entertainment industry. In 1978 nearly twice as many people in New York City went to the movies as to theater performances, all musical events, dance concerts and professional sports combined. Almost twice as much money ($200 million) was spent on the movies than on all the others, except theater, combined. As for TV, it is in almost every American home, and in the years 1978-79 alone, there were five programs seen at the same time by an estimated one-third or more of the nation's population. It is not surprising, therefore, that the paychecks of the chosen few in these mass audience industries are so large, and that the high priority assigned to being entertained by the American consumer will keep them there regardless of what happens to the economy.

RADIO

There are also superstars and vast audiences in the world of radio, where over 7,000 commercial stations cover the nation. Experienced announcers, disc jockeys and commentators, normally earn between $18,000 and $27,000 a year on stations with substantial listening audiences. However, Larry King, who has the only coast-to-coast network radio talk show, earns $90,000 a year. Other radio personalities build devoted regional followings and earn sizable incomes; one example is Barry Farber, who makes a reputed $100,000 a year.

THEATER

In 1978 live theater in the United States had total box-office receipts of over $600 million. This is a bit more than one-tenth of the book sales for the same year and somewhat less than one-hundreth of the sales recorded by the Caterpillar Tractor Company. By itself one movie, *Star Wars*, has grossed upwards of $350 million. These figures together might depress a lover of the stage. Yet, theater is thriving on its own terms in a fiercely competitive industry where two out of every three Broadway musicals fail to make money and three out of every four commercial plays are financial flops.

The successes and failures in dollars and cents terms are peanuts compared to most other segments of American business, but the impact of the stage reaches far beyond its financial importance. Nearly 10 million people paid to attend theatrical performances in New York City alone last year, and the box-office receipts from them totaled $136 million. Here are nine of the top money-making plays (musical and straight theater) for 1978 in New York. The figures include profits for Broadway and prior performances out of town.

NINE TOP THEATRICAL MONEY MAKERS
ON BROADWAY (1978)

Play	Profit
Annie	$1,500,000
Dracula	$1,500,000
Beatlemania	$682,000
Ain't Misbehavin'	$592,533
Deathtrap	$487,222
Tribute	$465,959
Da	$441,725
Dancin'	$155,079
They're Playing Our Song	$92,032

Many of the plays produced now have multiple investors; *I Remember Mama* had a record of 322, with one, Universal Pictures, putting up $626,000 and the rest putting up $600,000 more. *Tribute* was well financed by multiple investors and was sold as a movie before the play was performed. Thus the investors were in the black on opening night. But Universal also invested $525,000 in *Alice*, a musical that closed in Philadelphia, and the returns on *I Remember Mama* were disappointing for both the film company and the other investors. On the positive side, Universal was the sole investor and producer for *The Best Little Whorehouse in Texas*, which paid back its $800,000 investment in six months.

Relatively big money passes hands among the investors and at the box offices, and the salaries of the actors and actresses can be high for the name stars, but the financial rewards for the rest are low indeed. Top earnings for theater stars are paid by a weekly guarantee that can range from $1,000 a week to $15,000 or more for someone like Yul Brynner plus a percentage of the gate negotiated in each case.

Among the lesser lights, the paychecks for working actors are strictly regulated by unions in every phase of the production. The New York local is the largest and one of the most affluent components of Actor's Equity, which has 28,000 members. Yet the average annual income of New York actors was only $8,000 in 1978.

MINIMUM ACTING RATES FOR URBAN
THEATERS (1978)

Type of Theater	Weekly Rate
Broadway	$400.00
Off-Broadway (250 seats)	$170.56
Off-Broadway (150 seats)	$138.58
Regional Theaters	$202.30 to $257.00

The $400 weekly minimum for Broadway and the other minimums include both musicals and nonmusicals and apply to straight acting roles, chorus roles and whatever else. Naturally the minimum is exceeded when the role is larger, and it can go to $600 a week or even higher, depending on what is negotiated.

Understudies for leading roles can earn somewhat more than the acting minimum: about $460 a week plus $75 for every performance when they take over the role they are understudying. This is still not very much money, since acting jobs rarely last more than six months or so, but being an understudy is considered a step up on the ladder of recognition.

Ironically, in the theater, union rates for nonactors are generally higher than those for performers. Stagehands earn a minimum of $11.29 an hour, plus $42.48 a performance; the minimum weekly salary for a stagehand is $364 and $475 for his supervisor. Musicians earn a minimum of $425 a week, and some theaters require a minimum number of musicians, or in any case pay them, regardless of the particular needs of the production.

Besides stagehands, there are other jobs both behind and in front of the curtain. Directors, musical composers, choreographers and set designers negotiate their incomes for each individual production. Famous ones, such as Joshua Logan or Jerome Robbins, are sometimes coproducers and receive a large percentage of the receipts. Less well-known personalities are paid a fee or salary and sometimes a percentage of the receipts. Successful off-Broadway playwrites such as Lamar Wilson (author of *The Hot l Baltimore*) earn up to $30,000 a year. Famous ones, such as Neil Simon, earn an advance of $100,000 or more and get a large percentage of the receipts and of movie and TV sales as coproducers and/or screenwriters.

The cost of putting on a straight Broadway play, including rental fees, various overheads and advertising, comes to about $375,000, going somewhat higher or lower depending on the production. The cost of a musical is around $2 million and the operating costs are proportionally higher. Broadway theaters vary in size, but the range is between 1,040 and over 1,700 seats. The optimum gross also ranges from $160,000 to over $280,000 per performance, depending on the day of the week and the price of tickets. Thus a fine line must be walked at first to pay back the investment and cover the ongoing overhead, and it is during the early days that a show is most vulnerable. Once success is established, the run can go on for an indeterminate period. In early 1980, after nearly 2,000 performances, *Chorus Line* was still filling between 85% and 90% of the seats and grossing over $150,000 a day.

The longest run for a Broadway show has been achieved by *Grease*, which in seven years has made about $70 million dollars and has had over 3,300 performances. *Fiddler on the Roof* had the second longest run with 3,242 Broadway performances between 1964 and 1972. It earned $64 million from that and from other worldwide performances, which added significantly to the total revenue.

POPULAR MUSIC, DISCO AND NIGHTCLUBS

In 1978, $4.2 billion was spent on records and tapes. The great boom in the record business started with the Beatles over 15 years ago. Since that time, both several million singles and albums of their music have been sold. In 1979 three of the Beatles gathered informally to play and it was estimated at that time that if all four could reunite for just one performance, it would earn $50 million. As it is, former Beatle Paul McCartney has a three-album contract guaranteeing him $2 million for each album and 22% of the royalties thereafter. Paul Simon has a contract with CBS extending over several years for a guaranteed $13 million. The Bee Gees made over $1 million from their album *Saturday Night Fever*. In 1979 the Bee Gees made a 10-week tour of the United States that netted them about $16 million. Two nights performing at Dodger Stadium in Los Angeles alone earned them $2 million.

Since 1977 Kenny Rogers' records, led by the hit *Lucille*, have grossed over $100 million and Rogers himself has been earning about

$13 million a year. Four years ago he was $65,000 in debt and living in a rundown apartment in the San Fernando Valley. But rags to riches stories are as rare in the record business as in any other industry. Only one out of 10 individuals or groups who make records succeed, and of them a miniscule number make great sums of money. Furthermore, it is common for a star today to fade away completely in practically no time; only rarities such as the Beatles and Elvis Presley go on indefinitely. The latter made an incredible 80 Gold records before his death and his records are still big sellers.

The record business is brutal, melodramatic and loaded with hard luck stories. Billy Joel's first album sold a million copies but due to the terms of the contract netted him only $7,763. Under the astute business guidance of his wife Elizabeth, the singer now has seven companies, which were expected to gross a total of about $10 million in 1979. Talking about the change in his fortunes and life in general, Joel said: "People never expected me to be as smart as I was, and they wouldn't be totally frank because they didn't realize that I was building my empire. They taught me that money is the bottom line of everything. It's an actual, factual scale of how to see things."

Despite the enormous success of individual recording stars, there is now a crisis in the business. The cost of producing records is high. Contracts provide vast sums and percentage incentives to the star artists, and promotion and production costs have skyrocketed. The big companies are cutting back; many of the smaller ones have gone under. Some think that a contributing cause of the hard times is disco, which encourages people to get out and spend money dancing at clubs rather than staying home listening to their albums.

There are now well over 10,000 discos in the country and more are opening all the time. Perhaps the best known—for reasons that include its elegant clientele, flamboyant public relations, and tax irregularities and alleged use of cocaine on the premises—is Studio 54 in New York. In 1978 the profits were almost $1 million after expenses, which were very high. About 2,000 customers attended Studio 54 nightly and the annual gross business was about $8 million. The owners, Steve Rubell and Ian Schrager, were found guilty of tax evasion in early 1980, but the club remained open.

Chains of discos are now being franchised on a national basis and are spawning new specialty products in their wake: disco clothing, disco lighting, and disco skates for "roller discos," among others.

More traditional nightclubs continue to flourish in America's entertainment world. After her triumphant performance in the 1933 Chicago World's Fair, Sally Rand could draw $5,000 a week for her fan
dancing act. In 1980-82 Diana Ross has a contract guaranteeing her
$2.52 million for 72 singing performances in Atlantic City, which
works out to $35,000 per performance. At jazz nightclubs, such as
Jimmy Ryan's or Eddie Condon's in New York, the musicians are paid
according to their drawing power and kind of performance. A top jazz
player can make $500 a night.

Other nightclubs specialize in famous singers, comedians and
dancers. Las Vegas is the center of the world for this type of entertainment, and stars can make staggering sums. For example, Steve Martin,
Johnny Carson and a number of other entertainers earn over $225,000
plus expenses for a one-week appearance.

BALLET, OPERA, SYMPHONIES AND CONCERTS

There is a pecking order among ballet dancers, especially emigres,
that is precisely reflected in their paychecks. After Mikhail Baryshnikov left the Soviet Union to dance in America, he earned $200,000 a
year from 1975 to 1978 at the American Ballet Theater. Then, weary-
ing of the world of highly commercial ballet, he took a cut to $50,000 a
year to join the New York City Ballet Company. For an individual
performance abroad, or anywhere not connected with the New York
City Ballet, he can ask for and get $5,000 without trouble; he some-
times takes more and often accepts less, for artistic or other reasons.

The newest Soviet emigre, defector Aleksandr Godunov, was to
have started with the American Ballet Theater at $150,000 a year when
his proposed salary became known publicly. Even though this amount,
given the effect of inflation, was considerably less than his confrere
Baryshnikov made, it was enough to contribute to a strike at the
American Ballet Theater that revealed exactly how little dancers in the
corps de ballet make. The starting salary until mid-1979 had been $235
a week plus $30 a day when traveling. (In 1965 it was $1.50 an hour.) In
1980 and for several years after, the dancers will receive a minimum of
$400 a week after three years with the company. Soloists will receive
$540 a week and principals $650 per week, all based on a 40-week
season. While traveling the company will pay all hotel bills plus $24 a
day for meals after three years' employment.

Stars such as Gelsey Kirkland and Natalia Makarova make well over $150,000 a year and considerably more for individual performances outside of the American Ballet Theater.

Musicians who play for the ballet, opera, symphonies and concerts all fall roughly into the same salary level. The base salary ranges from $415 a week, with an increase of about $120 over three years, in New York to $500 a week for playing with the Chicago Symphony. These figures, as well as per diem arrangements, are subject to negotiation between the management of various performing groups and the American Federation of Musicians.

Soloists, as in all artistic, talent-oriented enterprises, must negotiate for their paychecks. Some make around $30,000 to $35,000 a year, and very well-known soloists, such as Jascha Heifetz, Isaac Stern and Vladimir Horowitz and many others in the various artistic fields, command guarantees and percentages of the gross that can reach between $5,000 and $10,000 per performance. For example, Joan Sutherland and Luciano Pavarotti made $5,000 each when they appeared on public television together singing various opera pieces and lieder. Opera singers work under contracts that vary from star to star. For example, Pavarotti has reportedly received as much as $20,000 for a single recital concert.

Entertainment, whether highbrow or lowbrow, is considered a basic human need, and therefore money is always found to pay for it and, in the case of the very talented or opportunistic, to pay very well for it.

LECTURES AND MISCELLANEOUS

Celebrity lectures have achieved a new popularity in recent years. The reason for this is uncertain, but many feel that face-to-face personal contact with famous and successful people is especially desirable and worth paying for in an age of technological isolation and distant contact. Some of the top lecture fees—plus expenses, of course—go to Henry Kissinger ($15,000); and Joseph Califano, Gerald Ford, James Schlesinger, Mike Wallace, Michael Blumenthal and Alexander Haig (all $10,000). Other celebrity lecturers are Milton Friedman ($12,000); Bob Hope ($35,000 plus major expenses, if you can get him) and Johnny Carson ($40,000, but seldom available). John Dean will tell all for $6,000; Chubby Checker will reminisce for $5,000; and David Frost will tell you and your friends about his interviews for $6,000.

Many lecturers are former government employees who capitalize on their experience gained, in part, courtesy of the taxpayers. Gen. Haig reportedly made well over $500,000 in the first six months after his retirement from the Army. Other popular lecturers are authors, entertainers and glamour queens. For example, Marilyn Van Derbur, a former Miss America, will speak for $2,500.

In other fields of entertainment, some poets will read for $50; circus clowns in New York City will perform for fees varying from $55 to the $100 that George Koury gets; and magicians will do their tricks for $65 a session. Seances can be held for $100 and up, while good jugglers, very much in fashion recently, command up to $150 for a performance.

Entertainment is what happens when one or more people do something to amuse, exhilarate, sadden, outrage or just generally divert one or many other people. Some do this constantly as an occupation and can make remarkable amounts of money often, but not always, because they have a unique knack or talent for captivating and directing an audience in ways that will give pleasure or enlightment. Some do it out of compulsion and make no money, but their talent may be great whether recognized or not.

Entertainment, passing the time in some enjoyable or at least memorable way, seems to be as important to most of us as the basic necessities of life, including food, shelter and medical care. Certainly, if we measure its importance by what we are willing to pay to support those who provide it, its value is priceless.

Part Two
TAXPAID JOBS

CHAPTER 5
The U.S. Government

THE TOP PEOPLE in the federal government and its many agencies often wield enormous power. Many have intriguing or even glamorous jobs; for better or worse their names become household words as the public watches their actions and responds to the impact of their efforts and decisions.

Government employees frequently get less in their pay envelopes than those who hold positions of similar or less responsibility in industry and the professions. Their taxpaid salaries, however, are often substantial and sometimes more than generous. Yet, except for those who make government service their career, people who hold either high elective or appointed office usually earned more before they came to government, and most will parlay their years of public service into far higher incomes after they reenter the private sector.

The presidency itself provides the most vivid example of this principle of deferred compensation for high government officials. While no amount of salary could be really commensurate to the wear and tear, the power and the responsibility of the office of the president of the United States, the office provides extravagant official and unofficial retirement benefits.

President Jimmy Carter earns $200,000 a year (taxable), receives $50,000 a year for official expenses (taxable) and another $40,000 (nontaxable) as a travel allowance. He lives in the White House with an ample domestic staff and, in addition, has the use of Camp David in the hills of Maryland with another staff for work or relaxation. Moreover, he's provided with instant transportation between these two locations, to his home in Plains, Ga. or around the world. For this purpose he has two jet aircraft, helicopters and limousines. Several hundred agents of the Secret Service protect him and his family at all times and places. He inherited a yacht with the job, which he had sold, but as commander in chief he can commandeer any seaworthy craft of the United States Navy that he chooses.

There are nice psychic perks that go with the job as well. For instance, the President can persuade the great artists and entertainers of the world to appear before him because of the power of his office; go on television virtually any time that he feels the need; and have a band announce his arrival and departure when he travels.

Such is the current compensation package—to borrow a term from private business—of the President, who fills the most powerful job in the world and yet makes less than countless industrialists, financiers, sports figures, artists, entertainers, physicians, lawyers and just plain criminals. It is, however, more than most other heads of state make: President Giscard d'Estaing of France, for one, makes $80,000 a year.

It is much less than the current income of his two only living predecessors, who are well cared for in their retirement years by the taxpayer. Both have made considerable sums of money from activities that are lucrative only because they have been presidents. This was also true of other former presidents before they died.

In 1978-79 Gerald Ford received a $100,000 government pension and Richard Nixon got $78,000. In addition to this sum, Ford will receive in 1979-80 $309,000 for office expenses, rentals, staff salaries and travel, as well as an undisclosed amount that will be spent to provide him with Secret Service protection. Nixon will receive $240,000 for the same purposes, plus the cost of his Secret Service security. In the first six months of his retirement, Lyndon Johnson received $375,000 in expense money and pension payments.

All this money was appropriated under the Former Presidents' Act and is official public funding. Beyond this, all three men and other retired presidents have merchandised their previous occupancy of the Oval Office to make or multiply their fortunes.

Richard Nixon has been undoubtedly the most successful at this activity. He has made over a million dollars on domestic hardcover sales of *The Memoirs of Richard Nixon*, which was on the best-seller list, selling over 300,000 copies (and 2,500 autographed leather-bound copies at $250 each). A paperback, two-volume edition of this book was published in 1979 and sold at $5.90 a copy, adding to his literary income. Also, *Six Crises*, his first book, was reissued in paperback at $2.95 around the same time, and his new book, *The Real War*, is being published in 1980 with major foreign rights and syndication sales. Nixon also earned over $500,000 for his TV interview series with David Frost.

Aside from being well compensated out of the public purse, Gerald Ford receives additional income from the publication of his memoirs, *A Time to Heal* (1979), and from a consultancy with NBC and other television deals. He also gets $10,000 to $12,000 each time he goes to the podium for one of his frequent lectures. Lyndon Johnson earned less money from his book, *The Vantage Point*, published in 1971, but he made $25,000 a lecture before his death and had a large income from real estate and other investments.

Writing books after leaving office has appealed to many presidents. Back in 1884 Ulysses Grant was offered the then astounding sum of a $25,000 advance per volume and a 20% royalty by Mark Twain to publish his memoirs with Webster and Co. He completed the second volume on his deathbed. The books sold over 300,000 copies and in the late 1880s his widow received $440,000 in royalties, the equivalent of approximately $3 million today.

It is notable that these four ex-presidents had entered public life with modest means, yet all attained wealth, even though in Grant's case posthumously. This is not to imply that their fortunes were accumulated illegally, rather that the financial rewards of having been a president can far surpass the "book value" of the job itself. As we shall see, this is also true for many lower ranking government officials.

The president, vice president and other major government positions have a history of slow salary increases enacted by law from time to time throughout the history of the Republic.

ANNUAL SALARIES OF FEDERAL POSITIONS
SINCE 1789
(with approximate dollar equivalents in buying power)

1789 ($1.00 equaled approximately $4.00 now.)

President	$25,000
Vice President	$5,000
Cabinet Secretaries	$3,000
Supreme Court Justices	$3,500

1873* ($1.00 equaled approximately $8.30 now.)

President	$50,000
Vice President	$8,000
Members of Congress	$7,500

1903 ($1.00 equaled approximately $8.00 now)

| Chief Justice of the Supreme Court | $13,000 |
| Associate Justices of the Supreme Court | $12,500 |

1912 ($1.00 equaled approximately $7.30 now.)

President	$75,000	salary
	$25,000	for official expenses
Vice President	$12,000	
Cabinet Secretaries	$12,000	

1949** ($1.00 equaled approximately $3.10 now.)

President	$100,000	salary (taxable)
	$40,000	for travel (nontaxable)
	$50,000	for official expenses (nontaxable)
Vice President	$30,000	
Speaker of the House	$30,000	
Cabinet Secretaries	$22,500	

1969 ($1.00 equaled approximately $2.00 now.)

President	$200,000	salary (taxable)
	$40,000	for travel (nontaxable)
	$50,000	for official expenses (taxable)
Vice President	$62,500	
Speaker of the House	$62,500	
Members of Congress	$42,500	

Today

President	$200,000	salary (taxable)
	$40,000	for travel (nontaxable)
	$50,000	for official expenses (taxable)

Vice President	$79,125	salary
	$10,000	for expenses (taxable)
Majority Leader of the Senate	$68,575	salary
	$10,000	for expenses (taxable)
Minority Leader of the Senate	$68,575	salary
	$10,000	for expenses (taxable)
Members of Congress	$60,663	salary
	$6,500	for expenses (taxable)

(Members of Congress receive additional expense funds for being committee chairmen or members.)

*This salary increase was stipulated under the "Salary-Grab Act" of 1873, so called by its opponents because the raise in congressional salaries was to be retroactive for two years. That provision was repealed under pressure from an outraged public and it was several years before congressmen got the annual increase they were seeking. Nevertheless, President Grant was the first to benefit from the new salary scale and was the highest paid president to date in terms of real income, making the modern equivalent of about $415,000 per year. At the time there was no official expense account, but President Lincoln was reimbursed $10,000 one year for expenses during his tenure.

**The president's salary and official expense allotment were nontaxable until passage of the 16th Amendment in 1913. After that his salary, and everybody else's, was taxed but his official expense allotment continued to be tax free up to Jan. 3, 1953, when Congress lifted the exemption. However the president's travel allotment remained nontaxable.

These salaries have risen over a long period of time and clearly have neither kept up with the cost of living nor achieved parity with those of the private sector. For President Carter to make as much in real buying and spending power as President Woodrow Wilson did in 1913, he would have to earn about $547,000 a year. He would have to make slightly over five times as much as he does now to equal the 1978 salary of Henry Ford, chairman of the Ford Motor Company ($1,056,000).

The president of the United States is immediately responsible for the executive branch of the government, which is divided into three main areas:

- the Office of the President;
- the executive departments; and
- the independent agencies.

The three together employ approximately 2,750,000 civilians in the federal civil service, within which salaries range according to type of job, experience and other factors and are established by a universal grade and pay schedule covering most U.S. government employees.

Higher ranking officials, both elected and appointed, can be paid according to a higher executive scale or, in some cases, at salaries set at the discretion of the president, but always within limitations imposed by Congress.

Below are the main components of the federal government, with many of the more important jobs, the people who hold them and their salaries. Included where relevant are various career service posts within executive departments and some of the more interesting independent agencies.

KEY SALARIES IN THE OFFICE OF THE PRESIDENT (1,715 employees)

Chief of Staff	Hamilton Jordan (cabinet rank)	$56,000
Counsel to the President	Lloyd Cutler (cabinet rank)	$56,000
White House Staff Director	Alonzo McDonald	$56,000
Special Representative	Sol M. Linowitz (cabinet rank)	$56,000
Press Secretary to the President	Jody Powell	$56,000
Assistant to the President for Domestic Affairs	Stuart Eizenstat	$56,000
Assistant to the President for Communications	Gerald R. Rafshoon	$60,663
Adviser to the President on Inflation	Alfred E. Kahn	$60,663
Staff Director for the East Wing of the White House	Edith J. Dobelle	$56,000
Chief Speechwriter	Hendrik Herztberg	$50,100
Assistant to the President for National Security	Zbigniew Brzezinski	$60,663
Director, Office of Management and Budget	James T. McIntyre (cabinet rank)	$69,630
Director, Central Intelligence Agency	Stansfield Turner	$60,663
Chairman, Council of Economic Advisors	Charles L. Schultze	$60,663

EXECUTIVE DEPARTMENTS

There are presently 13 executive departments: Agriculture, Commerce, Defense, Education, Energy, Health and Welfare, Housing and

Urban Development, Interior, Justice, Labor, State, Transportation and the Treasury. This number changes from time to time; for many years the Post Office Department was included, but no longer. New departments are also added from time to time; the Department of Education is the latest, being established in 1979. The secretaries receive the highest salaries for nonelected officials in the government. There are five other positions with the rank and salary of cabinet officer, four included in the previous list under the Office of the President plus the ambassador to the United Nations, now held by Donald McHenry ($69,630).

KEY SALARIES IN EXECUTIVE DEPARTMENTS

Agriculture (114,427 employees)

Secretary .... Bob Bergland $69,630

(Income year before becoming secretary $76,000; net worth $423,000.)

Assistant Secretary, Mar-
   keting and Transporta-
   tion Service .... P.R. (Bobby) Smith $52,750
Administrator, Animal and
   Plant Inspection Service .... F. J. Mulhern $50,100
Administrator, Federal
   Grain Inspection Service............Leland E. Bartlett $50,100

(Inspectors' starting salary for both services is $9,391 to $11,712.)

Assistant Secretary, Food
   and Consumer Service...........Carol Tucker Foreman $52,750
Administrator, Food Safety
   and Quality Service ....Donald Houston $50,100
                                    (acting)

(Inspectors for meat, poultry, dairy products, fresh and processed fruit and vegetables with some experience can earn $14,414 and go to $20,000-$23,000.)

Assistant Secretary, Con-
   servation, Research and
   Education .... M. Rupert Cutler $52,750
Chief, U.S. Forest Service .... John R. McGuire $50,100

(Forest Rangers can start at $9,391. However, because of stiff competition, most foresters have either an M.A. and start at $11,712 or a Ph.D. and start at $14,414 to $17,532. The Forest Service has 10 regional offices and 10 experimental stations. The median salary for foresters exceeds $20,000 and salaries can go to $25,000 and higher for management positions.)

Commerce (38,925 employees)

Secretary .... Phillip Klutznick	$69,630
Assistant Secretary for Policy .... Jerry J. Jasinowski	$52,750
Administrator, National Oceanic and Atmospheric Administration .... Richard A. Frank	$55,388
Assistant Administrator for Fisheries .... Terry L. Leitzell	$50,100
Assistant Administrator for Coastal Zone Management .... Robert W. Knecht	$50,100
Assistant Secretary for Maritime Affairs .... Samuel B. Nemirow (acting Head of Maritime Administration)	$52,750
Assistant Secretary for Tourism .... Jeanne R. Westphal (Head of United States Travel Service)	$52,750
Assistant Secretary for Communications and Information .... Henry Geller	$52,750
Director, Bureau of the Census .... Vincent P. Barabba	$50,100

(Census takers or interviewers work on a "permanent part-time basis." This means that they can hold no other full-time job. They are paid an hourly rate of $4.02 and can get as much as 80 hours of work a month depending on the size or number of the surveys.)

Assistant Secretary for Science and Technology .... Jordan Baruch	$52,750
Director, National Bureau of Standards .... Ernest Ambler	$50,100

(Starting salary for engineering and science technicians with a B.A. is $9,391. Annual average salary is $18,700.)

Commissioner of Patents and Trademarks .... Donald W. Banner	$50,100

Defense (982,000 civilian employees)

Secretary .... Harold Brown	$69,630

(Income year before becoming secretary $150,000; net worth between $50,000 and $100,000.)

Deputy Secretary of Defense	W. Graham Claytor	$60,663
Adviser to the Secretary and Deputy Secretary	Robert W. Komer	$60,663
Undersecretary of Defense for Policy.........................	(vacant)	$55,388
Director for Intelligence Policy	James L. Vance	$50,100
Director for Counterintelligence and Investigative Programs	Rowland A. Morrow	$50,100
Principal Deputy Assistant Secretary and Director, SALT Task Force............................	Walter Slocombe	$50,100
Undersecretary of Defense for Research and Engineering	William J. Perry	$55,388
Assistant Secretary of Defense for Public Affairs	Thomas B. Ross	$52,750

Joint Chiefs of Staff

Chairman	Gen. David C. Jones, USAF	$58,176
Chief of Staff, Army	Gen. Bernard Rogers	$58,176
Chief of Staff, Air Force............................	Gen. Lew Allen	$58,176
Chief of Naval Operations	Adm. Thomas B. Hayward	$58,176
Commandant, Marine Corps	Gen. Louis Wilson	$58,176

Armed Forces (2,059,000 men and women)

SELECTED PAY GRADES AND SALARIES OF COMMISSIONED OFFICERS (20 years service)

Rank	Grade	Salary
General (USA, USAF, USMC); Admiral (USN)	0-10	$49,633.20 plus $5,088.00 housing allowance with family

Rank	Grade	Salary
Brigadier General (USA, USAF, USMC); Rear Admiral (USN) (lower half)	0-7	$36,468.00 plus $5,088.00 housing allowance with family
Major (USA, USAF, USMC); Lieutenant Commander (USN)	0-4	$21,862.80 plus $3,261.60 housing allowance with family
Second Lieutenant (USA, USAF, USMC); Ensign (USN)	0-1	$11,064.00 plus $2,325.20 housing allowance with family

(Many high-ranking officers have gone on to lucrative jobs after their retirement from the military. Some go into defense industries because of their intimate knowledge of the people and policies that determine defense expenditures. Others go into jobs related to their military careers. One of the most successful examples is Frank Borman, the former Air Force general and astronaut who is now chairman of the board and president of Eastern Air Lines. His salary in 1977-78 was $216,000, and he received 30,360 in stock options with the stock valued at $9.26.)

SELECTED PAY GRADES AND SALARIES OF ENLISTED PERSONNEL (20 years service)

Rank	Grade	Salary
Command and Staff Sergeant Major (USA); Chief Master Sergeant (USAF); Sergeant Major (USMC); Master Chief Petty Officer (USN)	E-9	$20,048.00 plus $3,067.20 housing allowance with family
Sergeant (USA, USMC); Staff Sergeant (USAF); Petty Officer 1st Class (USN)	E-5	$8,661.60 plus $2,228.40 housing allowance with family
Private 1st Class (USA); Airman 1st Class (USAF); Lance Corporal (USMC); Seaman (USN)	E-3	$6,300.00 plus $1,710.00 housing allowance with family

Special Pay

Incentive pay for hazardous duty with 20 years of service is $110 a month for all commissioned grades and $55 a month for all enlisted grades. Hostile fire pay is $65.00 a month for all grades. (During the Civil War it was $2.00 a month.)

For duty as a crew member of an aircraft or a submarine with 20 years of service, the rates of incentive are as follows:

0-6	$245 a month
0-4	$240 a month
0-2	$185 a month
E-9	$105 a month
E-5	$95 a month
E-3	$60 a month

Education

Because this new department of the executive branch was established in late 1979, as of this writing it is just getting organized. Most of its key positions were formerly under the Department of Health, Education and Welfare, from which the new department in large measure has been carved.

Energy (19,600 employees)

Secretary	Charles W. Duncan	$69,630
Deputy Secretary	John C. Sawhill	$60,663
Undersecretary	Dale D. Myers	$55,388
Deputy Undersecretary for Strategic Petroleum Reserves	Jay Brill	$52,750
Chairman, Federal Energy Regulatory Commission	Charles B. Curtis	$55,388
Assistant Secretary for Policy and Evaluation	Alvin L. Alm	$52,750
Assistant Secretary for International Affairs	Harry E. Bergold	$52,750
Assistant Secretary for Conservation and Solar Applications	Thomas E. Stelson	$52,750
Office of Energy Research, Director	John M. Deutch	$50,100

Health, Education and Welfare (158,600 employees)

Secretary	Patricia R. Harris	$69,630

(Declared joint income of $130,000 a year before entering government service; net worth: small real estate holdings valued at less than $100,000.)

Undersecretary........................ Hale Champion		$60,663
Director, Office for Civil Rights ....David Tatel		$55,388

Administrator, Office
  of Human Develop-
  ment Services.................... Arabella Martinez
		$52,750

Commissioner, Admin- istration on Aging ....Robert C. Benedict		$50,100

Commissioner, Admin-
  istration for Native
  Americans .... A. David Lester
		$50,100

Assistant Secretary (Education) ....Mary F. Berry		$52,750
Commissioner of Education .... Ernest L. Boyer		$50,100

Assistant Secretary
  for Health and
  Surgeon General .... Julius B. Richmond
		$52,750

Administrator, Alcohol,
  Drug Abuse and Mental
  Health Administration .... Gerald D. Klerman
		$55,388

Director, National
  Institute of
  Mental Health ....Herbert Pardes
		$55,388

Director, National
  Institute of Alcohol
  Abuse and
  Alcoholism ....John R. DeLuca
		$55,388

Commissioner, Food and Drug Administration ....Dr. Jere E. Goyan		$52,750
Director, Bureau of Food .... Sanford A. Miller		$50,100
Director, Bureau of Drugs .... J. Richard Crout		$50,100
Commissioner, Social Security Administration .... Sanford G. Ross		$52,750

Housing and Urban Development (17,896 employees)

Secretary............................Moon Landrieu		$69,630
Undersecretary............................ Jay Janis		$60,663

Assistant Secretary
  for Community Planning
  and Development .... Robert C. Embray
		$52,750

Administrator, Federal
  Disaster Assistance
  Administration .... William H. Wilcox
		$50,100

(The Federal Disaster Assistance Administration has 10 regional offices: Boston, New York, Philadelphia, Atlanta, Chicago, Dallas, Kansas

City, Denver, San Francisco and Seattle. The regional officers are political appointees whose salaries range from $44,756 to $47,500. The appointees are often between elective offices or are aspiring to one.)

Interior (85,007 employees)

Secretary .... Cecil B. Andrus $69,630

(Declared income of $42,000 year before becoming secretary; net worth $100,000)

Undersecretary .... James A. Joseph $60,663
Assistant Secretary—
  Indian Affairs .... Forrest Gerard $52,700
Commissioner, Bureau
  of Indian Affairs .... William Hallett $50,100
Assistant Secretary—
Fish and Wildlife
  and Parks .... Robert L. Herbst $52,750
Director, U.S. Fish
  and Wildlife Service .... Lynn A. Greenwalt $50,100
Director, National
  Park Service .... William J. Whalen $50,100

(For both the Fish and Wildlife Service and the Park Service, the starting salary with a B.A. is $10,507. With a Ph.D. and/or a B.A. and three years experience or an M.A. and two years experience, it can be $17,532. The higher-salaried jobs in the services proper, such as park manager or superintendent, range from $27,000 to $34,000.

The Fish and Wildlife Service has six regional offices and is responsible for 391 wildlife refuges comprising more than 34 million acres, 13 major fish and wildlife centers, 45 research units, and 91 national fish hatcheries. The National Park Service has nine regional offices and is responsible for 300 units in the National Park System, including national parks and numerous riverways, seashores, lakeshores, reservoirs and historic sites.)

Assistant Secretary—
  Land and Water Resources .... Guy R. Martin $52,750
Assistant Secretary—
  Energy and Minerals .... Joan M. Davenport $52,750
Director, Bureau of
  Mines .... Lindsay D. Norman $50,100

(Average salary for experienced mine inspectors in 1979 was $21,750.)

Justice (53,199 employees)

Attorney General .... Benjamin R. Civiletti $69,630
Deputy Attorney General .... Charles F.C. Ruff $60,663
Solicitor General .... Wade H. McCree $55,388

Assistant Attorney General, Anti-Trust Division	Kevin D. Rooney	$52,750
Assistant Attorney General, Civil Division	Barbara Allen Babcock	$52,750
Assistant Attorney General, Criminal Division	Phillip B. Heymann	$52,750
Assistant Attorney General, Tax Division	M. Carr Ferguson	$52,750
U.S. Attorney, California, Southern	Michael H. Walsh	$52,750
U.S. Attorney, New York, Southern	Robert B. Fiske, Jr.	$52,750
U.S. Attorney, Georgia, Middle	Denver L. Rampey, Jr.	$50,100
U.S. Attorney, Nevada	B. Mahlon Brown	$38,160

(It is interesting to compare the salaries of these top U.S. attorneys with their counterparts in private practice. Salaries of the latter are considered at length in a subsequent chapter.)

Administrator, Drug Enforcement Administration	Peter B. Bensinger	$55,388
Commissioner, Immigration and Naturalization Service	Leonel J. Castillo	$50,100
Director, U.S. Marshals Service	William E. Hall	$50,100
Director, Bureau of Prisons	Norman A. Carlson	$50,100
Chairman, U.S. Parole Commission	Cecil B. McCall	$50,100
Administrator, Law Enforcement Assistance Administration	Henry S. Dogin	$55,388
Director, Federal Bureau of Investigation	William H. Webster	$60,663

(Under a new reorganization scheme there are three assistant directors of the FBI each making $47,500. The bureau has approximately 8,600 special agents, whose starting salary with B.A. and appropriate experience is $17,532 and can go as high in grade as $35,688. Supervisors generally start at $32,442, going to a grade high of $42,171. Assistant special agents in charge start at $38,160 and special agents in charge can make up to the current limit of $47,500.)

Labor (17,320 employees)

Secretary	Ray Marshall	$69,630

(Income year before becoming secretary was $76,000.)

Undersecretary....................... Robert J. Brown		$55,388
Deputy Undersecretary for International Affairs .... Howard D. Samuel		$52,750
Assistant Secretary for Policy, Evaluation and Research........................ Arnold H. Packer		$52,750
Assistant Secretary for Labor-Management Relations .... Rocco de Marco (acting)		$52,750
Assistant Secretary for Employment Standards .... Donald E. Elisburg		$52,750
Commissioner of Labor Statistics .... Janet L. Norwood		$50,100
Assistant Secretary for Mine Safety and Health .... Robert B. Lagather		$52,750

State (30,090 employees)

Secretary............................... Cyrus Vance		$69,630

(Income of $280,000 a year in lawyer's and company director's fees before becoming secretary.)

Deputy Secretary .... Warren M. Christopher		$60,663
Ambassador at Large .... Alfred L. Atherton		$60,663
Ambassador at Large .... W. Beverly Carter		$60,663
Ambassador at Large .... Henry D. Owen		$60,663
Ambassador at Large .... Elliot L. Richardson		$60,663
Undersecretary for Political Affairs .... David D. Newsom		$55,388
Undersecretary for Economic Affairs .... Richard N. Cooper		$55,388
Undersecretary for Security Assistance, Science and Technology .... Lucy Benson Wilson		$55,388
Policy Planning Staff Director .... W. Anthony Lake		$50,100
Director, Foreign Service Institute .... George S. Springsteen		$50,100

The Foreign Service consists of about 13,700 officers, most of whom are employed on a career basis. The lowest starting grade is FS08 at a salary $13,014 and the highest grade is FS01 at $47,500. Above these are the grades of minister and career ambassador, which is essentially an honorific position.

American representatives serve in 140 embassies, 111 missions, 66 consulates general, 48 consulates, three branch offices and 12 consular agencies throughout the world. Ambassadors of the United States are appointed by the president and are paid on an executive schedule that ranges from grade V, $50,100, to grade II, $60,663. In two cases, those of special representative and ambassador to the United Nations, the position is of cabinet rank and rated executive grade I, paying $69,630. Most ambassadors are drawn from the ranks of the career Foreign Service officers, but a number of them, often in the larger and more important countries, are "political appointees," selected outside of the Foreign Service by the president for political or other considerations.

Foreign countries are given one of four classifications by the Department of State, mainly according to their importance to U.S. foreign policy, size and difficulty of assignment. Ambassadors are paid according to classification of country. A few class one, class two and class three and four posts are listed below:

SALARIES OF SOME AMBASSADORIAL POSTS

Class One

Ambassador to
  Brazil .... Robert Marion Sayre $60,663
Ambassador to
  West Germany.................. Walter J. Stoessel, Jr. $60,663
Ambassador to
  Italy.......................... Richard N. Gardner $60,663
Ambassador to
  the USSR .... Thomas Watson $60,663

Class Two

Ambassador to
  Argentina......................... Raul H. Castro $55,388
Ambassador to
  Liberia .... Robert P. Smith $55,388
Ambassador to
  Poland .... William E. Schaufele $55,388

Class Three and Four

Ambassador to
  Austria .... Milton A. Wolff $52,750
Ambassador to
  Morocco .... Angier Biddle Duke $52,750
Ambassador to
  Trinidad and Tobago .... Irving Cheslaw $50,100

The classifications of the posts change continually due to world events or political crises, realignments and other considerations.

There is also an expense allowance given to ambassadors, which varies by classification of post and the amount of representational expenditure that is required. In previous times certain very large posts, such as London and Paris, that required expensive representation were given to wealthy political supporters of the president who could afford to hold them. This practice, while not ended, has diminished in recent years.

American diplomatic representatives abroad receive both housing and cost-of-living allowances, and the ambassador always has an official residence owned and provided by the U.S. government. Finally, some posts qualify as "hardship" assignments, and this can increase the salary as high as 25% in the most extreme cases. "Hardship" can mean unfavorable climate, low local standards of living, inaccessibility or political tension. For many years, for example, Moscow has been a hardship post, partly because of the tension and isolation caused by Soviet surveillance and general attitudes toward foreigners, especially Americans.

The office of secretary of state is a good example of a public position that can lead to considerable wealth after retirement. Secretary Vance was financially successful before he took office, but his predecessor, Henry Kissinger, was not a wealthy man before he became secretary of state in 1972. However, his years after retirement from the job have been almost as good to him as they have been to his former employer, Richard Nixon. His present income stems mostly from lecturing ($15,000 per lecture, one of the highest fees in the country), teaching at two institutions and consultancies with NBC and Goldman Sachs and Co. He is receiving $1 million over five years as an expert on international affairs from NBC plus approximately $250,000 a year from Goldman Sachs. With other consulting jobs that crop up from time to time, Kissinger presently earns more than $500,000 a year.

The former secretary will earn additional income from his writing. The hardcover edition of his book based on his years as head of the State Department will earn him about $1.5 million. Adding foreign sales ($1 million in West Germany already) and paperback sales, he could make as much as $5 million. All this illustrates that the commercial vistas of life after retirement can broaden not only for presidents but also for their appointed subordinates. There is no reason to think that this trend, more evident now than ever before, will not increase in the future.

Transportation (74,354 employees)

Secretary	Neil Goldschmidt	$69,630
Deputy Secretary	Alan Butchman	$60,663
Assistant Secretary for International Affairs	(vacant)	$52,750
Commandant, U.S. Coast Guard	John B. Hayes	$48,633
Administrator, Federal Aviation Administration	Langhorne M. Bond	$60,633

(Aviation inspectors are among the highest paid of all federal inspectors. They start at $14,414 and their average pay is over $25,500.)

Administrator, Federal Highway Administration	Karl S. Bowers	$60,633
Administrator, Federal Railroad Administration	John M. Sullivan	$55,388
Administrator, Urban Mass Transportation Administration	(vacant)	$55,388
Administrator, St. Lawrence Seaway Development Corporation	David W. Oberlin	$52,750

Treasury (136,675 employees)

Secretary	G. William Miller	$69,630

(Miller was previously chairman of the Federal Reserve Board. For his last private job his income in 1977 was $400,000—$200,000 in salary and a $200,000 bonus.)

Deputy Secretary	Robert Carswell	$60,663
Director, Bureau of Alcohol, Tobacco and Firearms	G. R. Dickerson	$50,100
Comptroller of the Currency	John G. Heinmann	$55,388
Commissioner, U.S. Customs Service	Robert B. Chasen	$52,750
Director, Bureau of Engraving and Printing	Harry R. Clements	$50,100

(Engravers and printers of U.S. currency, bonds, notes, stamps, some security documents and other jobs form a unique group in federal employment. The bureau has 20 engravers and apprentices (10-year apprenticeship) who each make over $40,000. There are approximately

*220 printers who make about $15 per hour normally and much more
with overtime. Almost 100 employees of the bureau make over $45,000
a year.)*

Director, Bureau of
the Mint .... Stella B. Hackel $50,100
Commissioner Internal
Revenue Service .... Jerome Kurtz $55,388
*(IRS agents, who audit and examine the books and records of
individuals, corporations etc. to see if their declarations are accurate and
in proper order, start at between $10,507 and $13,014 according to
experience. Special agents, whose job it is to examine records for
possible criminal activity, start at the same salary. Those in management positions can earn up to $50,100.)*

Director, U.S.
Secret Service .... H. Stuart Knight $55,338
*(The Secret Service has 5,100 employees, of which only 1,600 are agents.
The service was established in 1865 to deal with a flood of counterfeit
money that made up a third of all the currency in circulation. Pay for
agents on protective detail today ranges from $10,500 to $23,087 and
goes higher for managerial positions.)*

Treasurer of
the United States .... Azie T. Morton $50,100

The salary histories of men who have served as secretaries of the
treasury lend strong support to the rule that people who go into high
government service have usually been making more money before they
entered and will earn still more after they leave. The first treasury
secretary, Alexander Hamilton, founded the Bank of New York among
other ventures. Another secretary, Andrew Mellon, inherited a great
fortune and went on to make it greater.

The present secretary, G. William Miller, was chairman of the board
of Textron, Inc., a conglomerate with over $2 billion in annual sales,
before he joined the government. His predecessor, Michael Blumenthal, was board chairman of Bendix Corporation before joining the
government. His income in the year before becoming secretary of the
treasury was $401,000 plus $192,000 in capital gains. In 1980 he
became vice chairman of the Burroughs Corp with an annual salary of
$215,000 plus the same amount in bonus.

Blumenthal's predecessor, William Simon, was in office during both
the Nixon and Ford Administrations. Before that he had amassed a
fortune in the bond market. After leaving office he wrote the seem-
ingly obligatory book about his experiences with the government, the

Treasury Department and Watergate. Called *A Time for Truth*, it has sold over 250,000 copies in hardcover; Simon has given the proceeds to his alma mater, Lafayette College. But income from his job as a consultant with Blyth, Eastman Dillon and Co., as well as other firms, plus directorships on boards and extensive real estate and capital holdings worldwide garner him an income of over $500,000 per year. Just like Kissinger, it is Simon's contacts and prestige—largely obtained from his government service—that has now made him so valuable to private business. Also like Kissinger, former Secretary of the Treasury Douglas Dillon and former Undersecretary of State George Ball, Simon is known in financial circles as a "heavy hitter." This is a person whose reputation and influence easily open doors around the world. While in no way illegal and in fact considered by some to be admirable and a further proof of ability, the use of such influence is, nevertheless, a form of merchandising government experience for personal gain.

THE INDEPENDENT AGENCIES

In Washington independent agencies come and, less frequently, go depending on what issues become important, pressing or merely popular. Sometimes they are set up to deal with new technological developments that require federal supervision; sometimes they fit new needs such as ACTION. Sometimes they die long after they have outlived whatever usefulness they once had, if any, such as the Subversive Activities Control Board. Others are absorbed into executive departments when the latter are created or reorganized.

At present there are over 70 independent agencies. The ones listed below have been selected either because they are powerful and important or just because they are not. Washington is a jungle of these agencies, each of them a tree ripe with desirable jobs. Some of these jobs are simply political plums and some require a great deal of work and involve very significant responsibilities.

KEY SALARIES IN INDEPENDENT AGENCIES

Architect of
  the Capital . . . . George W. White $52,750
Acting Director,
  U.S. Botanic
  Garden . . . . George M. White   none

Public Printer,
Government Printing
Office . . . . John J. Boyle $52,750
Librarian, Library
of Congress . . . . Daniel J. Boorstin $52,750
Federal Co-Chairman,
Appalachian Regional
Commission . . . . Robert W. Scott $55,388
Director, ACTION
(2,074 employees) . . . . Sam Brown $55,388
Chairman, American   without
Battle Monument   compen-
Commission . . . . Gen. Mark W. Clark (retired)   sation
Director, Community
Services Commission . . . . Graciela Olivarez $60,663
Deputy Director,
Community Services
Commission . . . . William B. Allison $55,388
Chairman, Consumer Product
Safety Commission . . . . Susan B. King $55,388
Commissioner,
Delaware River
Basin Commission . . . . Sherman Tribbitt $50,100
Administrator,
Environmental
Protection Agency
(12,520 employees) . . . . Douglas M. Costle $60,663
Chairman, Federal
Communications
Commission
(2,130 employees) . . . . Charles D. Ferris $55,388
Chairman, Federal
Election Commission . . . . Robert O. Tiernan $52,750
Chairman, Federal
Maritime Commission . . . . Richard J. Daschbach $55,388
Chairman, Federal
Trade Commission
(1,791 employees) . . . . Michael Pertschuk $55,388
Chairman, Board of
Governors, Federal
Reserve System . . . . Paul A. Volcker $60,663
Director, International
Communications
Agency (8,348 employees) . . . . John E. Reinhardt $60,663
Executive Director,
Marine Mammal
Commission . . . . John R. Twiss, Jr. $50,100

Administrator, National
Aeronautics and Space
Administration
(24,182 employees) .... Robert A. Fresch $60,663
Chairman, National
Foundation on the
Arts and Humanities ....Livingston L. Biddle, Jr. $55,338
Secretary, Panama Canal
Company-Canal Zone
Government (3,317
employees) .... Thomas M. Constant $50,100
Chairman, Securities
Exchange Commission ....Harold M. Williams $55,388

(Securities investigators require five to six years of experience in examination of books and analysis of securities. They start at between $16,000 and $20,000.)

Chairman, Tennessee
Valley Authority
(40,932 employees) .... S. David Freeman $55,388
Postmaster General*
U.S. Postal
Service (649,642
employees) .... William F. Bolger $69,630
*Formerly a cabinet position.

(There are nearly 30 deputy, assistant or regional postmasters general, all making over $40,000. In addition there are over 150 managerial positions in the Postal Service with a salary of $34,000 per year or more. The lowest Postal Service grade (grade 1) begins at $7,175 and the highest grade (grade 30) is $47,500. All salaries above that are excepted from civil service rules and statutes. Postal clerks and mail carriers account for some 540,000 of the jobs in the Postal Service, and their salaries range from $12,000 to approximately $20,000 according to time in service.)

Secretary, Smithsonian
Institution (3,996
employees) .... S. Dillon Ripley $52,750
Administrator, Veterans
Administration
(228,450 employees) .... Max Cleland $60,663

CONGRESS

Members of Congress reinforce the notion that most people are relatively well off before being elected to government posts and need not worry about entering the poorhouse when they leave. Members of both Houses receive a salary of $60,663 plus $6,500 for expenses. They receive additional money from funds established for travel and other expenses related to the various committees on which they serve. General funds are also available; for example, $70,881,000 was voted for "administrative, clerical and legislative assistance to senators" for fiscal year 1979. A sum of $411,000 was voted for "offices of the secretary for the majority and the minority." It was estimated recently that the average House member gets $75,000 a year and the average Senate member $143,000 a year in expense money.

But these are only the official funds. In 1978 only two senators and 16 representatives reported no income from outside businesses, honoria or investments. Generally, House members are more likely than Senate members to have earned income from outside jobs. Senators take home more money from honoria (speeches, appearances or magazine articles, etc.), although there is now a limit of $25,000 on the amount of such income that may be kept, while any amount over that must be donated to other causes and activities. Practically all members of both houses declared at least a few thousand dollars in unearned income from stocks, savings and other investments.

TEN TOP MONEY EARNERS IN CONGRESS—
SENATORS (1978)

Senator	Earned Income	Honoria	Broad Categories of Unearned Income
John Heinz (R-Pa.)	None	None	$437,101 to $836,000
Edward M. Kennedy (D-Mass.)	None	$3,050	$288,401 to $581,500
John Glenn (D-Ohio)	None	None	$288,001 to $412,000
Claiborne Pell (D-R.I.)	None	$3,200	$267,401 to $524,000
Sam Nunn (D-Ga.)	None	$4,400	$274,501 to $371,000
Mark O. Hatfield (R-Ore.)	None	$22,466	$299,001 to $387,500
Charles H. Percy (R-Ill.)	None	$7,550	$235,101 to $663,500
John C. Danforth (R-Mo.)	None	$6,500	$230,801 to $385,000
Lloyd M. Bentsen (D-Tex.)	None	None	$162,601 to $441,000
Bill Bradley (D-N.J.)	$166,534	$1,800	$31,901 to $89,000

TEN TOP MONEY EARNERS IN CONGRESS—
REPRESENTATIVES (1978)

Representative	Earned Income	Honoria	Broad Categories of Unearned Income
Cecil Heftel (D-Hawaii)	$928,967	$1,000	$189,800 to $505,000
Frank J. Guarini (D-N.J.)	$624,129	None	$15,900 to $54,000
Harold S. Sawyer (R-Mich.)	$29,657	None	$525,149
S. William Green (R-N.Y.)	$16,317	$1,500	$435,900 to $725,500
James M. Collins (R-Tex)	None	None	$304,600 to $601,000
Fred Richmond (D-N.Y.)	$175,000	None	over $100,000
Bill Nelson (D-Fla.)	$10,233	None	$194,600 to $326,000
Jack Brooks (D-Tex.)	$55,685	$1,000	$167,100 to $251,000
Gene Snyder (R-Ky.)	$177,491	None	$15,800 to $58,000
Claude Pepper (D-Fla.)	$146,944	$550	$16,700 to $54,500

Twelve members of the Senate earned $25,000 or more in honoria; they included Sen. Howard Baker (R-Tenn.), Sen. Daniel Moynihan (D-N.Y.), Sen. Jacob Javits (R-N.Y.) and Sen. Henry Jackson (D-Wash.). All of these men gave their earnings away to charity. Seven representatives earned the statutory limit of $25,000 in honoria. These included John Murphy (D-N.Y.), Al Ullman (D-Ore.), Ken Holland (D-S.C.) and Thomas Ashley (D-Ohio). None of these men gave any of their honoria earnings to charity.

Besides elected officials there are many people working in the Congress, some in official capacity as employees of the government and others as employees of the various members.

SALARIES OF OFFICIAL POSITIONS IN SENATE (1979)

Chaplain . . . . Edward Elson $24,948.00
Secretary of the Senate. . . . . Joseph Kimmitt $52,500.00
Administrative
 Director . . . . Marilyn E. Courtot $42,147.00

Sergeant at Arms .... Frank N. Hoffman $52,500.00
Superintendent of
  Press Gallery .... Donald C. Womack $44,415.00
Chief Barber .... Mario Dangelo $20,317.50
Driver/Messenger .... Robert Collins $17,369.96
Postmaster .... Jay A. Woodall $44,604.00
Chief Clerk of a
  Committee or Chief
  Staff Member .... N.A. $50,432.00
                                                      (average)

SALARIES OF OFFICIAL POSITIONS IN HOUSE OF REPRESENTATIVES (1979)

Chaplain .... James D. Ford $42,222.24
Parliamentarian .... William H. Brown, Jr. $54,000.00
Sergeant at Arms .... Kenneth R. Harding $52,500.00
Doorkeeper .... James T. Molloy $52,500.00
Chief Clerk of a
  Committee or Chief $47,792.00
  Staff Member .... N.A.   (low average)
Clerk of the House .... Edmund L. Henshaw, Jr. $52,500.00
Postmaster of the
  House .... Robert Rota $46,038.96
Chauffeur/Messenger .... Roger C. Brooks $22,548.00
Barber, House
  Barber Shop .... John Merle Allen $4,165.40
                                                      plus tips
Beautician, House
  Beauty Shop .... Kutley Hancock $7,858.80
                                                      plus tips
Chef, House
  Kitchen .... Pasquale Bonnani $28,123.20

SALARIES OF EMPLOYEES OF ELECTED SENATORS (1979)

George V. Cunningham, Administrative
  Ass't. to Sen. George McGovern (D-S.D.) $49,941.00
Allan M. Fox, Legislative Ass't.
  to Sen. Jacob Javits (R-N.Y.) $47,500.00
Franklin Gannon, Administrative Ass't.
  to Sen. John Heinz (R-Pa.) $49,932.96
William R. White, Administrative Ass't.
  to Sen. John Glenn (D-Ohio) $49,940.00
Kim B. Wells, Administrative Ass't.
  to Sen. Robert Dole (R-Kan.) $34,587.00

SALARIES OF EMPLOYEES OF ELECTED REPRESENTATIVES
(1979)

Margaret Anne Allen, Legislative Ass't. to Rep. Millicent Fenwick (R-N.J.)	$19,566.95
John D. Barry, Administrative Ass't. to Rep. Hamilton Fish (R-N.Y.)	$45,475.32
Sidney S. Ellerton, News Secretary to Rep. Barry Goldwater, Jr. (R-Calif.)	$24,320.14
Patricia E. Richter, Executive Ass't. to Rep. S. William Green (R-N.Y.)	$41,618.36
Amber E. Scholtz, Administrative Ass't. to Rep. Paul McCloskey (R-Calif.)	$33,672.00

There is a large group of individuals who earn money by advising elected officials, consulting with them, running their campaigns, polling for them and doing numerous odd tasks. These are the nonelected professionals in the democratic process, and their services become more and more essential as incumbents and candidates gain wider coverage in the media and seek to gauge public reaction to their actions and views in order to weigh the possible success or failure of their campaigns. The salaries for some of these individuals are shown below, as well as the incomes that are made in various types of professional political jobs.

An incumbent senator running for the presidency, Sen. Kennedy for example, often uses members of his staff to help him direct his campaign. Carl Wagner at $47,000, Carey Parker at $49,500, Jan Kalicki at $47,500 and Kenneth Feinberg at $47,500 have all served on both the senator's office and campaign staffs. Mark Siegal was a political consultant for Kennedy at about $55,000 a year; Tim Kraft is a campaign manager and consultant for President Carter at approximately the same salary. (Campaign assistants and consultants are often paid by the month since they are not employed on a year-long basis in many cases, particularly when the candidate is unsuccessful.)

In a survey done recently, the following salary highs and lows were found for six major campaign jobs in House races.

HOUSE CAMPAIGN STAFF JOBS AND
HIGH AND LOW MONTHLY SALARIES

Job	High Salary	Low Salary
Campaign Manager	$2,150	$750

Press Secretary	$1,250	$525
Secretary	$1,000	$300
Field Coordinator	$1,675	$250
Scheduler	$850	$250
Researcher	$750	$200

The pay for a House campaign is naturally lower than for a Senate or a presidential campaign unless the aspirant can afford higher salaries. The low range of the salaries shown above indicates that many campaign workers supply their time for little and often for no compensation; these people are frequently lawyers or businessmen whose voluntary support is crucial to the success of a campaign.

Often campaign staffers who have worked for a candidate or his group on a regular basis are rewarded with full-time jobs in Washington after the election. Good examples of this are Richard Goodwin, John Kennedy's main speech writer, who was made an assistant secretary of state in 1961, and Tim Kraft and Gerald Rafshoon, who were made assistants to President Carter after working on his 1976 campaign.

Also prominent in political campaigns are public opinion organizations such as the Gallup or Roper polls, which analyze trends, or Pat Caddell's organization, which acts as a paid adviser to one candidate. Caddell's Boston-based firm grosses over $1 million a year, and he and his organization have worked principally for President Carter. Public relations and advertising companies often take candidates as clients. Their fees are negotiated for the individual job, whether it be a TV ad series or a special public appearance by the candidate or his backers.

Many entertainment stars support their favorite politician with public appearances, benefits, rallies and other events where they can back their candidate, receive personal publicity and gain tax benefits. Prominent among these are Frank Sinatra, Dean Martin, Jane Fonda, Robert Redford, Peter Lawford, Bob Hope and many, many others. Another group of people who have great influence on the governmental process are former holders of elective office or appointed officials. Some of the more spectacular cases of very successful men of this type were discussed earlier in this section after their appropriate executive departments.

Many lawyers or consultants based in Washington have held government jobs or have influence and seek to affect the shape or outcome of legislation in ways favorable to the special interests of their clients, be they corporations, organizations (profit and nonprofit), political groups, governments or even individuals. As such, these people are known as lobbyists and they perform a very powerful and often valuable function in a democratic society. In fact, with the gradual decline of party discipline in Congress, special interest groups are more influential now than ever before. Lobbyists must register with Congress stating for whom they are working and for what purpose or legislation.

Disclosure requirements concerning the amount of money they make in performing such activities have been left vague by Congress. This is done intentionally. While some groups such as Common Cause seek greater disclosure of lobby spending and income, others feel that this would be an invasion of privacy. In any case, the earnings of lobbyists remain one of the mysteries of political Washington. Informed sources assert that successful and active individual lobbyists often make as much as $100,000 or more a year, while the salaries of people employed by large corporations for the same purpose range between $40,000 and $80,000 a year.

CHAPTER 6
State and Local Government

THE FEDERAL GOVERNMENT employs approximately 2.8 million civilians with an aggregate monthly payroll of nearly $3.8 billion. The states employ approximately 3.46 million people with a monthly payroll of $3.2 billion. City and local governments, taken together, are by far the largest segment of government in the United States, employing approximately nine million people with an aggregate monthly payroll of $8.08 billion.

These figures help put the immense size of state, city and local governments into perspective. They employ almost five times as many people as the federal government and their payroll is more than three times as much; their growth in size, complexity and expenditures since 1940 is impressive. In that year the federal government employed 1,128,000 people, while state, local and city governments employed a combined total of 3,345,000. In other words, state and local government as a unit has grown almost twice as much as the federal government in the intervening years.

STATE GOVERNMENT

The highest paid governor in the Union today is New York's Hugh Carey at $85,000 a year; the lowest is Forrest James of Alabama at $29,955 a year (plus some expense account funds).

The highest paying legislature is California's, where members of both houses receive $25,555 per year plus $46 per diem, and the lowest is New Hampshire, where the members receive $200 for each two-year term they serve. (In New Hampshire the upper house has 24 members, the lower between 375 and 400.)

The highest paid justices are those of the California Supreme Court—they make $62,935 per year (the chief justice makes an additional $3,934). The lowest paid are in Maine, where the justices of the Supreme Judicial Court make $29,000 a year (and the chief justice makes an additional $1,500 a year).

For sake of comparison here are the salary figures (where available) for most of the same offices in 1919.

SALARIES OF SELECTED STATE OFFICE HOLDERS (1919)

Governor of New York: .... Alfred E. Smith $10,000
Governor of Alabama: .... T. E. Kilby $7,500
Legislature of California: $1,000 for one regular session lasting two years and $10 per day for each day of extra sessions.
Legislature of New Hampshire: $200 for two-year term (the same pay as today).
Justice, Court of Appeals, New York: $14,200
Justice, Supreme Court, Maine: $5,000

The list that follows includes selected offices and the names of incumbents (where available) for eight states to indicate a geographical and financial cross-section of the country. Also given are the salaries for governors and the legislature in 1919 for comparative purposes.

SALARIES OF STATE OFFICER HOLDERS (1979 & 1919)

California

1979

Governor .... Edmund G. Brown, Jr. $49,100
Secretary of State .... March Fong Eu $42,500
Attorney General .... George Deukmejian $47,500

Chief Justice,
    Supreme Court .... Rose Elizabeth Bird $66,869
Members of Legislature ........................N.A. $25,555
                                             annually

Police and Highway
    Patrol............................. C. B. Craig $37,920
Higher Education ....Glenn S. Dumke $65,625
1919
Governor......................... W. D. Stephens $10,000
Members of
    Legislature............................. N. A. $1,000
                                           biennially

Chief Justice .... N A. $8,000

Florida
1979
Governor........................... Bob Graham $50,000
Secretary of State .... George Firestone $40,000
Attorney General .... Jim Smith $40,000
Justice, Supreme Court............ Arthur J. England $43,200
Members of Legislature...................... N. A. $28,200
                                         biennially

Police and
    Highway Patrol.......................J. E. Beach $27,500
Higher Education ....E. T. York $54,000
1919
Governor.......................... Sidney J. Catts $6,000
Members of Legislature .... N. A. $6 per day
                                      (60-day limit
                                      per two-year
                                      session)

Chief Justice.............................. N. A. $4,500

Illinois
1979
Governor..................... James R. Thompson $58,000
Secretary of State..................... Alan J. Dixon $50,500
Attorney General ....William J. Scott $50,500
Chief Justice
    Supreme Court ....Joseph J. Goldenhersch $50,000
Members of Legislature .... N. A. $28.000
Police and
    Highway Patrol...................... Lynn Baird $38,000
Higher Education ....James M. Furman   N. A.
1919
Governor.......................... F. O. Lowden $12,000
                                        (highest

SALARIES OF STATE OFFICER HOLDERS
(1979 & 1919)

in U.S. at
that time)

Members of Legislature .... N. A. $3,500
biennially

Chief Justice ..............................N.A. $10,000

Pennsylvania

1979

Governor .... Dick Thornburgh $66,000
Secretary of
   Commonwealth...................... Ethel Allan $38,500
Attorney General .... Edward G. Biester $44,500
Chief Justice,
   Supreme Court .... Michael J. Eagen $57,500
Members of Legislature .... N. A. $37,440
biennially

Police and
   Highway Patrol.................... Paul J. Chylak $41,250
Higher Education .... Edward C. McGuire $39,981
1919
Governor .... W. C. Sproul $10,000
Members of Legislature .... N. A. $1,500 per year
Chief Justice .... N. A. $13,500

New York

1979

Governor .... Hugh Carey $85,000
Secretary of State .... Basil Paterson $47,800
Attorney General .... Robert Abrams $60,000
Chief Justice,
   Court of Appeals .... Lawrence H. Cooke $63,143
Members of Legislature .... N. A. $47,000
biennially

Police and
   Highway Patrol.............. William G. Connelie $47,800
Higher Education .... T. Edward Hollander $57,650
1919
Governor .... Alfred E. Smith $10,000
Members of Legislature .... N. A. $1,500 per year
Chief Judge .... N. A. $14,200

Oregon

1979

Governor .... Victor G. Atiyeh $50,372 plus
$12,000

		per year expenses
Secretary of State	Norma Paulas	$41,461
Attorney General	James A. Redden	$41,461
Chief Justice, Supreme Court	Arne H. Denecke	$45,707
Members of Legislature	N.A.	$24,657 biennially
Police and Highway Patrol	Robert Fisher	$35,304
Higher Education	R. E. Lieuallen	$53,000
1919		
Governor	B. W. Olcott	$5,000
Members of Legislature	N. A.	$3 per day (40-day limit per year for two years)
Chief Justice	N. A.	$4,500

Texas
1979

Governor	William P. Clements	$71,400
Secretary of State	George W. Stroke, Jr.	$42,700
Attorney General	Mark W. White, Jr.	$45,200
Chief Justice, Supreme Court	Joe R. Greenhill	$50,300
Members of Legislature	N. A.	$18,640
Police and Highway Patrol	William E. Speir	$43,700
Higher Education	Kenneth H. Ashworth	$41,400
1919		
Governor	W. P. Hobby	$4,000
Members of Legislature	N. A.	N.A.
Chief Justice	N. A.	$6,500

Utah
1979

Governor	Scott M. Matheson	$40,000
Lieutenant Governor/ Secretary of State	David S. Monson	$26,500
Attorney General	Robert B. Hansen	$30,000
Chief Justice, Supreme Court	J. Allan Crockett	$35,000
Members of Legislature	N. A.	$3,200 biennially
Police and Highway Patrol	Robert Reid	$31,224

SALARIES OF STATE OFFICER HOLDERS
(1979 & 1919)

Higher Education .... T. H. Bell $53,292
1919
Governor .... S. Bamberger $6,000
Members of Legislature .... N. A. $4 per day
                                                                (60-day limit
                                                                per year)
Chief Justice .... N. A. $5,000

There are striking variations in the salaries paid for state administrative positions. Alaska always fares well, but the argument there is
that the cost of living is much higher than the national average. The
administrative functionaries in the District of Columbia are also highly
paid, and this is often the subject of considerable political controversy.
California pays well, while certain Southern and New England states
pay less, perhaps reflecting the comparative wealth of the states. All in
all, the following table is a very partial but revealing economic profile
of one aspect of income distribution in America.

COMPARISON OF SELECTED STATE
ADMINISTRATIVE POSITIONS (1978)
(highest salary within job range given)

High	*Middle*	*Low*
Director of Personnel		
Alaska	Florida	Arkansas
$52,152	$34,882	$27,196

Correctional Superintendent (warden for state or municipal prison)

District of Columbia	Iowa	North Carolina
$47,025	$30,004	$22,392

Correctional Officer

Alaska	Arizona	West Virginia
$24,796	$13,929	$11,892
	New York	
	$13,109	

Director of Social Services

Alaska	Minnesota	New Hampshire
$52,152	$33,178	$20,572
New Jersey		
$49,492		

Library Services Director

District of Columbia	Massachusetts	Georgia
$47,500	$25,219	$19,218
Washington		
$37,960		

Librarian

Alaska	New York	Kentucky
$24,096	$14,324	$10,872

Director of State Planning

Alaska	Mississippi	New Hampshire
$52,152	$27,000	$21,260
District of Columbia		
$47,500		
North Carolina		
$39,674		

Chief Conservation Officer (Fish and Game)

Alaska	Connecticut	Mississippi
$52,152	$23,172	$19,680
Wyoming		
$38,436		

Conservation Officer

Alaska	Ohio	Nevada
$29,112	$13,146	$11,672
California		Louisiana
$20,016		$13,020
Oregon		
$19,296		

Principal State Civil Engineer

Alaska	Georgia	New Hampshire
$52,152	$25,098	$19,333
District of Columbia		
$47,025		

Civil Engineer

Alaska	District of Columbia	Connecticut
$22,392	$15,935	$13,815
North Carolina		
$21,348		

Director of Forestry

California	Indiana	Connecticut
$37,358	$28,872	$21,836
South Carolina	Montana	
$34,320	$26,084	

COMPARISON OF SELECTED STATE
ADMINISTRATIVE POSITIONS (1978)
(highest salary within job range given)

High	*Middle*	*Low*
Director of Probation and Parole Services		
District of Columbia $47,025	Rhode Island $24,264	Kansas $20,316
Wisconsin $40,582		
Alaska $40,320		
Probation and Parole Officers		
California $21,480	Nebraska $15,400	Kentucky $11,976
Alaska $20,796		
Manager of Data Processing		
Alaska $52,152	California $27,180	Arkansas $19,266
District of Columbia $47,025		
Arizona $38,833		
Computer Programmer		
Alaska $20,796	Illinois $15,744	South Dakota $11,710
Texas $17,832		Connecticut $10,884

CITY GOVERNMENT

The salaries for mayors and other officials of the larger cities is surprisingly high in relation to those for elected and appointed positions in the federal and state governments. In fact, mayors sometimes make as much or more than the governors of their states, more than members of the presidential cabinet, more than undersecretaries of federal departments and more than representatives and senators. And often mayors and lesser urban officials make equal or better salaries than holders of offices with national or statewide responsibility. For example, the deputy mayor of New York City, Nathan Levanthal at $57,500 (there can be as many as five others), makes almost as much as

William Webster, director of the Federal Bureau of Investigation ($60,663). Even more impressive, the police chief of Los Angeles, Daryl F. Gates, at $73,686, made more than any U.S. cabinet officer and nearly as much as an associate justice of the Supreme Court. The city manager of Phoenix, Marvin A. Andrews, who makes $54,294, and Augustus Beekman, fire commissioner of New York City, who makes $54,000, both surpass the $52,750 salary of Dr. Jere Edwin Goyan, commissioner of the Food and Drug Administration, who guards the purity of the products the whole nation consumes.

There are many other examples of the relatively high pay of urban officials, which is an indication of the size of the cities, their complexity, their influence, the enormity of their needs and the varying levels of their resources.

The list that follows compares some incomes of mayors and governors of their states to illustrate the point made above. The list after that shows the historical change in urban office salaries.

SALARIES OF GOVERNORS AND MAYORS IN SELECTED STATES (1978)

*California**
Governor Edmund G. Brown, Jr.
$49,100

Los Angeles
Mayor Tom Bradley
$57,750

Colorado
Governor Richard D. Lamm
$40,000

Denver
Mayor William H. McNichols
$40,000

Illinois
Governor James R. Thompson
$50,000

Chicago
Mayor Jane Byrne
$60,000

Michigan
Governor William Milliken
$58,000

Detroit
Mayor Coleman Young
$61,950

New York
Governor Hugh Carey
$85,000

*New York City***
Mayor Edward Koch
$80,000

North Carolina
Governor James B. Hunt
$45,000

Charlotte
City Manager David Burkhalter
$52,000

SALARIES OF GOVERNORS AND MAYORS IN
SELECTED STATES (1978)

Ohio
Governor James A. Rhodes
$50,000

Cleveland
Mayor George V. Voinovich
$50,000

Texas
Governor William P. Clements
$71,400

Houston
Mayor Jim McConn
$72,000

Washington
Governor Dixy Lee Ray
$50,000

Seattle
Mayor Charles Royer
$56,652

*In California the mayors or city managers of three other cities have higher salaries than the governor:
Oakland City Manager David Self (Acting)—$52,680;
San Francisco Mayor Dianne Feinstein—$55,496; and
San Jose City Manager James Alloway—$50,820.

**In 1950 the mayor of New York made $40,000 a year, one-half of the present amount in dollars, but approximately one-half again as much in buying power. This is the identical ratio of increase in those 30 years for President Carter's salary compared to President Truman's in 1950.

MEDIAN SALARIES OF SELECTED ADMINISTRATIVE
AND MANAGERIAL POSITIONS
(1969 & 1979)
(cities of over 500,000 but not over one million)

	1969	1979
Mayor	$26,000	$40,000
City Manager (where applicable)	$22,500	$54,294
Controller	$20,000	$27,397
City Clerk	$16,224	$27,267
Treasurer	$16,500	$25,000
Fire Chief	$21,850	$35,000
Police Chief	$22,170	$37,200
Superintendent of Streets	$17,680	$29,049
Superintendent of Schools	$32,500	$48,000
Director of Parks and Recreation	$19,750	$30,000
Health Officer	$28,500	$40,029
Planning Director	$22,500	$37,769

Attorney	$25,958	$48,244
Librarian	$22,000	$40,111
Chief Building Inspector	N. A.	$31,375
Director of Data Processing	N. A.	$37,860

A comparison of pay for patrolmen (police officers) and fire fighters in selected cities is interesting. Figures are taken for January 1978 since subsequent increases are not generally available. Pay is for maximum level of the scale for the lowest ranking career position in the respective departments. After that, the salaries for the chiefs of these departments in six large cities are shown.

SALARIES OF POLICE OFFICERS AND FIRE FIGHTERS (1978)

City	Police Officer	Fire Fighter
Baltimore	$14,537	$13,905
Boston	$13,900	$14,266
Chicago	$18,312	$18,312
Cleveland	$15,569	$15,569
Detroit	$19,063	$19,271
Houston	$15,632	$15,665
Los Angeles	$20,045	$20,358
New Orleans	$13,848	$13,848
New York	$17,548	$17,548
Philadelphia	$15,769	$15,769
San Francisco	$19,056	$19,056
Washington, D.C.	$16,629	$16,629

In 1959 the highest median entry salary for policemen in major cities was $4,800. For firemen, it was $4,509. In 1969 the highest median entry salary for policemen in major cities was $8,819. For firemen, it was $8,760.

Pay scales for sanitation men (sometimes called refuse collectors) are less available since many cities have contracts with private organizations for this work. However, in 1978-79 the median entry salary for sanitation men in cities with public sanitation departments and populations between 500,000 and one million was $10,368.

PAY FOR FIRE AND POLICE CHIEFS IN SIX OF
THE LARGEST CITIES: (1979)

	Fire Chief	Police Chief
Chicago	Richard Albrecht $48,600	Joseph di Leonardi $48,600
Detroit	Melvin Jefferson $48,500	William L. Hart $51,500
Houston	W. E. Rogers $50,826	H. P. Caldwell $50,572
Los Angeles*	John C. Gerard $66,406	Daryl F. Gates $73,686
New York	Augustus Beekman $54,000	Robert McGuire $50,000
San Francisco	Andrew C. Casper $51,139	(vacant) $51,139

*Los Angeles pays the highest salaries in the nation for both positions by a considerable amount.

These figures show New York City officials to be in the high middle income range, except for the mayor, whose income is the highest of any mayor in the nation. The uniform services and other positions, however, give a good indication of the general pay scales throughout the country for large cities and more are shown for New York to give a broader picture in a range of city jobs and salaries. (All figures are as of 1978.)

NEW YORK CITY SALARY SCALES (1978)

Police Department (3,741 employees)

Patrolman	$17,458
Sergeant	$23,175
Detective Sergeant, First Grade	$26,725
Lieutenant	$26,725
Captain	$35,122
Inspector	$39,049
Chief	$43,083
Chief of Operations	$44,266

Fire Department (11,002 employees)

Fireman, First Grade	$17,458
Fire Marshal	$19,270

Fire officers salaries range from $21,600 to $38,299 according to grade.

Sanitation Department (9,700 employees)

Sanitation Worker	$15,731

Sanitation Foreman		$20,904
Sanitation Senior Superintendent		$28,096
Commissioner, Department of Sanitation	Norman Streisel	$54,000

Correction Department (prisons) (3,343 employees)

Correction Officer, First Grade (guard)		$18,156
Captain (men's or women's prison)		$22,675
Assistant Deputy (warden)		$26,175
Chairman, Department of Correction	William Ciures	$54,000*

*This is $3,900 a year more than the director of the U.S. Bureau of Prisons earns.

Cultural Institutions (1,006 employees)
Salary range: $7,200 to $17,425

Motor Vehicle Operators (1,450 employees)
(Citywide, civilians driving and maintaining vehicles for most agencies.)
Salary range: $10,500 to $13,750

Seasonal Lifeguards, Parkhelpers etc. (5,239 employees)
Salary range: $26.50 to $47.50 per diem

Parks and Pubic Works (1,139 employees)
Salary range: $9,200 to $23,925
Commissioner of Parks   Gordon Davis $50,000

Librarians (1,025 employees)
Salary range: $10,000 to $21,525

Library Custodians (159 employees)
Salary range: $8,450 to $15,765

Book Repairers (15 employees)
Salary range: $8,150 to $13,110

Attorneys (425 employees)
Salary range: $14,500 to $28,150
District Attorney for each county (5) $48,998

Parking Enforcement Agents and Supervisors (metermaids and metermen) (635 employees)
Salary range: $8,960 to $10,460
114 Supervisors, Salary range: 10,900 to $18,200

Aqueduct (Water) Police (33 employees)
Salary range: $9,450 to $16,330

NEW YORK CITY SALARY SCALES (1978)

Highway and Sewer Inspectors (90 employees)
Salary range: $11,800 to $16,570

Mortuary and Laboratory (119 employees)
Salary range: $8,350 to $15,260

Chief Medical Examiner   Dr. Elliot Gross $50,000

Public Relations Units (77 employees)
Salary range: $8,700 to $16,325

Part Three
ELITE JOBS

CHAPTER 7
The Law

CLARENCE DARROW, FAMOUS during his lifetime and later immortalized on stage, and Perry Mason, among the best-known and admired characters in American literature and on television, personify the dramatic role of the lawyer in the American psyche. Few things capture the imagination of Americans more than a good courtroom battle or a young lawyer's crusade for equality and justice, nothing except possibly a young surgeon's fight against some dreaded disease.

The law is sometimes viewed as the arena of high drama, and lawyers are depicted as heroes in this country, a nation that, in theory at least, lives sublimely under and by the rule of law. And this rule of law is far more than an abstract principle in America, it is a way of life, making the practice of law a very busy occupation. Litigation is rampant and lawyers are multiplying at a prodigious rate; some 35,000 graduate from law school each year. The services of lawyers are expensive and their incomes high. Indeed, justice is rarely available at bargain rates.

Since 1950 the number of lawyers has grown nearly twice as fast as the population. In that year there were about 175,000 members of the bar, or one for every 900 Americans. The median income for lawyers in 1950 was about $8,500. In 1979 there were 495,000 lawyers, or one for approximately every 440 citizens, higher than the ratio for doctors. (For sake of comparison, West Germany had roughly 41,000 lawyers for 61 million people in 1979, or about one lawyer for every 1,500 people; Japan had 11,000 lawyers for 115 million people, or about one lawyer for every 10,000 people.)

Logically enough, litigation has increased to keep pace with the number of lawyers. For example, the number of cases in the federal district courts went from 38,477 civil and 31,823 criminal cases commenced in 1941 to 130,567 civil and 39,786 criminal cases commenced in 1977. Civil cases increased by more than three times, while criminal cases rose by somewhat less than one-quarter. In the federal appeals courts, the total number of cases commenced went from 3,093 in 1943 (including 1,531 civil and 363 criminal cases) to 19,118 in 1977 (including 11,020 civil and 4,738 criminal cases).

Does more legal business create the need for more lawyers or do more lawyers create more legal business? This question has been asked from time to time ever since the law first emerged as a profession, sometimes plaintively, sometimes angrily. Regardless of the answer, the fact is that litigation of all sorts is increasing and along with it costly legal negotiations, bargaining, arbitration, court trials, backlogs in the courts etc. Along with this trend comes a greater need for legal advice, competition among lawyers and an increased value placed on their services; in other words, more opportunities for increasing legal incomes. Moreover, to the great satisfaction of the legal fraternity, Americans are renowned for their litigiousness temperament, an insight about us made almost 150 years ago by de Tocqueville. Given this situation, the number of lawyers is bound to increase until the time when there are too many, which some say will be soon.

Of the 495,000 lawyers in 1979, approximately 360,000 were in private practice; 40% of these worked alone, while the rest were employed by law firms. Of the remaining 135,000 lawyers, about 45,000 worked as counsels for business firms and another 30,000 worked for the federal government. Most of the rest were employed in state and local governments, while some 9,000 taught full or part time in law schools.

A significant number of people who have legal training do not work as lawyers. Indeed, legal education and experience often prove to be invaluable assets in numerous other careers, politics and business being the two outstanding examples. A few prominent lawyer/businessmen are listed elsewhere in this chapter, and the proportion of politicians who got their start as lawyers is enormous at every level of government in this country. More than half of the presidents of the United States were lawyers before entering politics; Thomas Jefferson, Abraham Lincoln, William Taft and Richard Nixon are just a few of the more famous.

Lawyers have provided much of the zeal and expertise that have fueled our political movements in or out of government. Lawyers have been in the forefront of social and governmental reform, consumer protection, civil rights and the related struggles for minority equality that continue today.

The average income for lawyers practicing in the United States in 1979 was $32,500. This is three times as much as the median lawyer's income in 1955 and about twice as much as the average income for someone pursuing education as a career, but it is less than half of the median income for a physician in this country.

The law has the well-deserved reputation of being a most lucrative as well as glamorous profession, and there are a substantial number of lawyers who make very substantial incomes. Many of them work at the large law firms around the country, of which there are over 80 with 100 or more lawyers, counting partners and associates (the largest, Baker and McKenzie of Chicago, had 512 lawyers in 1979). Of these largest firms, 56 had 50 or more partners, and most of those firms had one or more partners making well over $300,000. Such lawyers are sometimes referred to as "rainmakers" (those who bring in business) or "heavy hitters."

One New York-based firm, Skadden, Arps, Slate, Meagher, and Flom, had 49 partners in 1979. About six of them made between $600,000 and $800,000 in 1978; as many as nine others exceeded $450,000 in earnings for the same year. The firm's most successful lawyer, Joseph H. Flom, received more than $1.1 million for the year, which is surely one of the highest legal salaries on record. The success of Skadden, Arps is exceptional, based in large measure on the firm's reputation for successfully engineering—or fighting off—"unfriendly" corporate takeover attempts.

Price Waterhouse reported that the median salary of a partner at the top 50 or so firms was $193,310 in 1978. The median salary of an associate lawyer at one of these firms was reported to be $36,835. The average salary for secretaries was $14,768 and that of paralegals (lawyers' assistants without law degrees) was $16,611.

The biggest earners among lawyers vary greatly from year to year, depending on the amount of time spent on the practice, exceptional cases handled, the type and number of cases handled etc. The billing rates or fees of leading lawyers offer a fair indication of their income potential. (But this is not always so. Some "rainmakers" are paid for representational services far beyond the sums they bill, if any.) Clients are generally billed by the hour, and pay fees largely based on this total for the services and advice of a lawyer and the resources of his firm. There is a legend among lawyers that Thomas E. Dewey kept an hourglass on his desk at the firm of Dewey, Ballantine, Bushby, Palmer and Wood. When a client walked into his office, Dewey would turn over the hourglass and each grain of sand would register a few cents of his $500-an-hour fee. The client was left in no doubt about how much money his time with Mr. Dewey was worth.

On the other side of the coin, former Sen. Sam Ervin of North Carolina tells the story about an old lady who came to the country lawyer's office for advice. The lawyer leafed through a few tomes and finally gave her an answer to her legal problem. The woman listened, and got up to leave; whereupon the lawyer mentioned that she owed him $5. "For what?" she asked. "For my advice," the lawyer answered. "But I'm not going to take it," she said and marched out the door.

Those days are over, and fees now range anywhere from $40 an hour for small, relatively unheralded law firms to $300 and even more for big names at large, prestigious firms, whether you accept their advice or not. Many of the larger firms have computers or secretaries keeping very accurate ledgers of attorney's office and court appearance time, phone calls, secretarial and paralegal services, travel time and expenses and whatever else that can and will go into a client's bill. It adds up. For example, if a high-priced lawyer must go from New York to California to advise a client or make an appearance in court, all hours including travel time to California and back again are often billed at the attorney's rate. As one high-placed lawyer said, "Nothing pays like an appearance in Nome, Alaska." (He also suggested that this is one of the reasons why famous lawyers are usually visited at their offices.)

Listed below are some of the billing rates of top money-earning lawyers.

BILLING RATES AND/OR FEE ARRANGEMENTS
OF 10 SUCCESSFUL LAWYERS (1978-1979)

Lawyers	Firm or Location	Billing Rate or Fee
Melvin Belli	San Francisco	$250 per hour, but usually works on a negotiated contingency fee basis
Charles Ballon	Phillips, Nizer, Benjamin, Krim & Ballon	$250 per hour
Louis Nizer	Phillips, Nizer, Benjamin, Krim & Ballon	$350 per hour
Arthur Fleischer	Fried, Frank, Harris, Shriver & Jacobson	$225 per hour
Sargent Shriver	Fried, Frank, Harris, Shriver & Jacobson	$225 per hour
Franklin Bass	Fried, Frank, Harris, Shriver & Jacobson	$200 per hour
James St. Clair	Hale & Dorr	$175 per hour
Marvin Mitchelson	Los Angeles	$10,000 retainer fee plus $125 per hour
Ramsey Clark and Melvin I. Wulf	Clark, Wulf, Levine and Peratis	Charge three-tiered system of fees, based on client's ability to pay and "compelling importance of case": 1) no fee 2) $25 to $50 per hour 3) $75 to $150 per hour

To see just how these billing rates affect annual earnings, here is one specific example. From March to September of 1978 Arthur Fleischer billed 1,300 hours for a total of $264,000. This does not mean that he received all of that as personal income; rather, partners receive a share of the firm's total income based on many factors, including cases handled, work brought in, amount of overhead, contracts made, reputation in the field and so forth. Salaries are handled quite differently at the firm of Clark, Wulf, Levine and Peratis. Mr. Clark is an internationally famous figure and former attorney general, and Melvin Wulf was formerly legal director of the American Civil Liberties Union with a worldwide reputation in law and civil rights activities. Regardless of the considerable money-making potential of the firm, the partners have agreed to limit their own incomes to a range of $50,000 to $75,000 per year. Money earned in excess of that is invested back into the firm to hire new associates and take on new cases.

It is common for some lawyers, sometimes referred to as Washington lawyers because so many of them practice and/or do most of their work in the capital, to alternate between private practice and government service at all levels. The experience of both worlds is beneficial in the opinion of many, pernicious in the minds of some. A good example is Lloyd Cutler, who was made counsel to the President in August 1979. Before this, Cutler had been a senior partner in the prestigious Washington firm of Wilmer, Cutler and Pickering, where he earned $318,277 in 1978. In that year he also made an additional $52,506 in director's fees, but he gave up all of this to earn $56,000 as the President's chief legal counsel. In his private practice Cutler has made a point of encouraging young associates in his firm to join the government for a while to gain experience that would later benefit them with the firm.

Other lawyers who straddle the gap between government and private practice are Secretary of State Cyrus Vance, who earned $280,000 as a lawyer in 1976 before taking office; former Secretary of Health, Education and Welfare Joseph Califano, who earned $505,000 in 1976 with his law firm before joining the cabinet and who has now returned to private practice; former Secretary of Defense Clark Clifford (an adviser to many presidents), who made considerably more than $500,000 in 1978 at his firm, Clifford, Glass, McIlwain and Finney; and former Watergate Special Prosecutor Leon Jaworski, who earns more than $500,000 per year at his Houston-based firm, Fulbright and Jaworski.

Public interest lawyers also abound in Washington, representing all ranges of political opinion. On the right there is Daniel Popeo, executive director of the Washington Legal Foundation, who earned $25,000 in 1978 for, among other things, winning a decision from a federal district court that the termination of the Taiwan defense treaty by the U.S. was unconstitutional, a decision that was reversed on appeal. Elsewhere on the political spectrum are environmental lawyers representing one-shot public action groups on specific litigation or established national groups such as the Sierra Club, Common Cause or Ralph Nader's Public Citizen. These lawyers rarely make more than $30,000 to $40,000 a year. For example, Melvin Wulf made $33,000 with the American Civil Liberties Union in 1977.

During the Nixon Administration, lawyers fared well. The chief himself had been a partner at the firm of Mudge, Rose, Guthrie and Alexander, where he earned in the range of $150,000 a year from 1963 to 1967. (This is approximately equivalent to $320,000 today. Although he was disbarred in New York and resigned from the bar in California, Nixon has done well in other fields, as described in the chapter on U.S. government.) Nixon appointed one of his partners, John Mitchell, as his attorney general in 1968; Mitchell had made about $2 million a year in bond counseling. His immediate postgovernment years were spent mostly in prison. He is out now, but still disbarred. John Dean made $44,600 as counsel to the president before he was dismissed by Nixon. Dean was later disbarred and sent to prison. Since his release he has made about $300,000 from the sale of his book *Blind Ambition* and the TV mini-series based on it.

Lawyers are also well represented in Congress. Fifty-eight members of the House and 17 members of the Senate reported income from law practices in 1978. The highest earner of these in 1978 was Rep. Frank J. Guarini (D-N.J.), who made $624,129 from his practice. He continues to act as a lawyer but restricts his outside income to the $8,625 established by a House rule. This rule became effective for the House in 1979 and will apply to the Senate in 1983. The ultimate effect will be to virtually eliminate the part-time practice of law by congressmen. Guarini was one of 23 representatives who had substantial earnings from law practices in 1978. Others were Jim Courter (R-N.J.), $39,750; Dan Lungren (R-Calif.), $44,000; Claude Leach (D-La.), $21,559; and Marc L. Marks (R-Pa.), $27,500. The biggest earners in the Senate were David F. Durenberger (R-Minn.), $48,500; Howell Heflin (D-Ala.), $65,434; and Alan K. Simpson (R-Wyo.), $30,999. Beyond those in the 96th Congress reporting income from the practice of law, 205 out of a total of 435 House members and 65 out of a total of 100 Senate members hold law degrees, and 20% of state legislators are lawyers, further underscoring the connection between law and politics and the pervasive importance of lawyers in American life.

People with law educations, whether they have ever practiced or not, are also becoming increasingly prominent in the upper ranks of big business. In fact, many of the best-paid graduates of law school are found not in the law firms but rather in the executive suites of major corporations, where they hold top jobs. Sixteen percent of the highest executive officers of the country's 500 largest companies are lawyers, and the number is rising every year. Some of the better known lawyer/ executives in 1978 are listed here.

SALARIES OF LAWYER/EXECUTIVES (1978)

Name	Firm	Salary
Leonard Goldenson	ABC	$953,500
Irving S. Shapiro	E. I. DuPont	$843,000
J. Paul Austin	Coca Cola	$718,000
Simon Sheib	Avnet	$551,575
John T. Connor	Allied Chemical	$440,000
Robert Dewar	K-Mart	$380,000
F. Ross Johnson	Standard Brands	$374,591
Darwin E. Smith	Kimberly-Clark	$341,678
Donald B. Smiley	Macy's	$270,000
George B. Monroe	Phelps Dodge	$264,200
Richard M. Furland	Squibb	$257,406
William S. Beinecke	Sperry and Hutchinson	$234,257
J. Hugh Roff	United Energy Resources	$211,959

Aside from this world of exalted lawyer/executives, it is the legal fees that are the lifeblood of the traditional law practice. As mentioned earlier, fees vary enormously according to a multitude of factors. To emphasize this point, a journalist made up a hypothetical but plausible situation involving the loss of a wedding ring at a jewelery shop where it was taken for adjustment. The journalist took the problem to nine different law firms and asked each one how to proceed in either retrieving or replacing the ring and what the fee would be for advice and assistance.

The firms suggested a variety of actions and quoted fees ranging from a high of $2,122 (by one branch of Jacoby and Meyers which advertised inexpensive legal work) to a low of $45. The lawyers recommended suing for the value of the ring in small claims court, settling out of court or suing in New York State Supreme Court. Fees cited varied in format from a retainer of $350 plus $40 an hour to a straight contingency arrangement. If the loss of a wedding ring can offer such latitude, imagine the possible variations in advice and size of fees that might be charged for the complex legal work involved in giant corporate mergers, murder trials, malpractice suits, negligence cases, antitrust actions, divorces, and other forms of litigation and settlement.

A recent example is that of the $1 million fee, one of the largest ever recorded, that was awarded to attorney Moses Lasky for his representation of the Telex Corporation in a number of related antitrust suits. Another is the $43 million settlement negotiated by attorney Arthur Crowley of Los Angeles in the divorce suit involving Barbara Jean Cooke and her husband, sports mogul Jack Kent Cooke. Mrs. Cooke got $39 million in cash besides other valuables including a house and works of art, while Crowley received $250,000 in advance fees and is expected to make $2 million upon final settlement.

The superstars of the profession in terms of publicity, and sometimes, but by no means always, in terms of fees, are the criminal lawyers, who create followings like great entertainers and whose courtroom exploits often make the biggest headlines of the day. Criminal lawyers are frequently successful because of their ability to deal with witnesses through an often devastating and manipulative knowledge of human character and a short-term mastery of the nuances of a particular case, rather than by an exceptional historical grasp of the law and the long tedious preparation associated with many major civil cases. Criminal lawyers are frequently colorful personalities, some having press agents to publicize their eccentricities, be they exotic art collections, a fascination with helicopters or whatever. (A prominent professor of criminal law observed that a surprising number of criminal defense lawyers are consistently in financial difficulty regardless of their incomes.)

F. Lee Bailey is one of the most famous criminal lawyers. A measure of his success is his claim that in 1978 he made about $600,000 from two practices, one in Boston and one at the firm of Bailey and Broder in New York. But Bailey occasionally runs into difficulties; his famous defense of Patty Hearst, after subsequent countersuits by the Hearsts, yielded him far less than was supposed (a fee of $100,000 was reported, but a firm figure has never been revealed.) Bailey and Broder's recent effort to represent the victims of the Three Mile Island accident has turned up contractual difficulties stirring controversy within the legal profession and will be a highly competitive and time-consuming effort. Bailey has hopes for future litigation of the 1979 DC-10 crash in Chicago, since air crash negligence cases have always been one of his specialties.

Criminal lawyer James LaRossa was reputed to be receiving a total fee of $250,000 for himself, his assistants and his expenses (including press agent) in the defense of Anthony Scotto, a well-known New York union leader charged with extorting payoffs from employers and later convicted. LaRossa's annual income has been estimated at approximately $225,000 to $300,000, which is very good even for a top practitioner. Some criminal lawyers specialize in handling cases for organized crime figures. Edward Bennett Williams made a considerable reputation defending Jimmy Hoffa and other union officials for a retainer fee of $100,000 per annum from the Teamsters Union plus fees and expenses for his work over the years. But in Williams' case, it is the man himself who is unique, for he has expanded now into the world of sports with great success. Generally, criminal law itself has more ups and downs, drama, bright lights and newsprint than steady income.

It is sobering to remember how much less the prosecuting attorneys earn than defense or criminal lawyers in virtually every type of case. In the Scotto trial, for example, the federal prosecutor was Robert B. Fiske, who as U.S. attorney for the Southern District of New York, makes $52,750. For that salary he oversees the handling and prosecution of all federal trials in his area. The average state and local prosecuting attorneys make about $32,000 to $38,000, while the salary range for a legal aide lawyer in New York State is $16,500 to $35,000.

Liability cases, particularly negligence and malpractice, are probably the most lucrative for litigating attorneys. The fees or settlements in such court cases are often paid on a contingency basis. This means that the lawyer receives a percentage of the financial award or agreement contingent upon his winning or negotiating the settlement for his client; both the lawyer and his client get nothing if he loses the case. (The percentage, which is agreed on by the parties in advance, can range from 10% of the total value of the award to a rare 50% or higher, depending on the case, the lawyer and the client.)

Critics of this system allege that it clearly can encourage unnecessary litigation, on the one hand, or can tempt lawyers to settle out of court to their own advantage rather than their clients', on the other hand. In any case, it is an increasingly common form of legal action that can garner counsel and client a great deal of money. Critics further charge that besides leading to more and more litigation, contingency arrangements between clients and lawyers increase insurance expenses and inhibit the actions of potentially liable people such as doctors, who must constantly be alert to the possibility of malpractice suits. This is a practical and ethical controversy not likely to be resolved very soon, especially when it is proving so lucrative for so many.

The highest damages ever awarded in a negligence case went to Robin Yocum, a girl who suffered brain damage during birth in 1972. The court found that the medical treatment for her was culpably negligent and awarded her $1.1 million outright, plus $40,000 per year with 4% interest compounded annually for the rest of her life. The total settlement counting interest and assuming a life span of at least 65 years could amount to nearly $17 million. San Francisco attorney David Baum received 25% of the $1.1 million cash settlement, or $275,000, on behalf of his firm. He waived a 25% cut of the annual payments.

Liability awards have recently been paid out in either lump sums and/or graduated amounts to take into account the cost of inflation. Indeed, one prominent tax lawyer points to inflation as a major cause of increased litigation, saying that since the real value of money in disputes can change radically, it could be to the advantage of one of the parties in a case to have sums of money tied up in the courts for long periods of time. In this sense, delay can be profitable.

In any case, liability settlements and awards in the past few years have reached levels where lawyers for plaintiffs are given sufficient incentive by the possibility of huge contingency fees to undertake weak cases despite a considerable risk of defeat. Some of the recent awards listed below make it clear that one such victory with a 25% contingency fee arrangement would be worth a great deal of legal work and time.

RECENT LARGE AWARDS BY JURIES IN LIABILITY CASES

Amount (millions)	Injury and Cause	Location and Date
$1.5	Unnecessary hysterectomy; medical malpractice	Maryland 1979
$6.5	Severe burns; crash of auto with defective gas tank design	California 1978
$4.7	Quadriplegia; diving board accident	Washington, D.C. 1977
$2.5	Rape; inadequate motel security	New York 1976

RECENT LARGE AWARDS BY JURIES IN LIABILITY CASES

Amount (millions)	Injury and Cause	Location and Date
$1.1	Traumatic neurosis; false arrest for shoplifting	New York 1976
$2.0	Wrongful death; crash of auto with faulty head restraint	New Jersey 1974
$2.1	Quadriplegia; defective polio vaccine	Pennsylvania 1973
$5.5	Wrongful death; crash of twin-engined aircraft	California 1971

The salaries of lawyers coming out of law school depend on the school they attended, on their academic record and on the field of law they are entering. A top ranking graduate of one of the most prestigious law schools (Harvard, Yale, Columbia, Chicago, and Stanford, to name a few) can begin as an associate in a large- or medium-size commercial firm for as much as $30,000 a year (and even up to $35,000 in some rare cases). Typical starting salaries at less prestigious firms begin at $18,000. If a recent graduate goes into government practice, he or she normally starts at about $17,800 a year, an amount only slightly more than what legal aid pays its new lawyers. If a lawyer starts professional life at a small law firm or in the legal department of a corporation, he or she will probably be hired at a salary between $17,000 and $21,000 a year.

The classical route for the bright young attorney—the kind who will someday become a "rainmaker," a corporation executive, a politician or perhaps the president of the United States—is a predictable and well-trodden path. Beginning as an associate at one of the nation's prestigious firms, he will receive salary raises of $4,000 to $7,000 a year for five or six years until he is selected for partnership, at a time when he is making about $60,000 a year. From then on he is paid a percentage of the firm's total income, and rises according to both his intellectual and technical skills as a lawyer and his ability to bring in new clients, whether due to his legal reputation, business or social connections, personality or a combination of all these.

Associates who are not chosen as partners often join another firm, become in-house corporate lawyers, often for the clients of their former firms, or enter some other law-related career. For those lawyers who join the legal departments of corporations either out of law school or later, the average pay scale is well below that of the better private firms. The following figures are based in part on studies done by the American Management Associations Executive Compensation Service.

CORPORATE LEGAL PAY SCALES (1978)

Top Legal Executive (averages)

Manufacturing, nondurable goods	$130,300
Manufacturing, durable goods	$99,800
Gas and electric utilities	$68,800
Life insurance companies	$45,600

General Attorney (medians)

Companies with sales over $1 billion	$45,800
Companies with sales under $200 million	$32,500

Patent Counsel (medians)

Companies with sales over $600 million	$38,000
Companies with sales under $200 million	$30,000

Patent Attorney (averages)

Senior patent attorney, experience over 8 years	$35,500
Patent attorney, experience 5-8 years	$29,900
Patent attorney, experience 2-4 years	$26,600
Junior patent attorney, experience 0-1 year	$24,400

Attorney (averages)

Senior attorney, experience over 8 years	$33,500
Attorney, experience 5-8 years	$27,000
Attorney, experience 2-4 years	$22,600
Junior attorney, experience 0-1 year	$19,700

Some law school graduates go directly into teaching, some make a career in practice and then join a faculty, and some teach and practice on the side. Obviously, some of the leading law professors also make successful consultants for day-to-day legal problems and activities. A top professor at a prestigious law school usually makes $50,000 to $55,000 a year for his teaching and work with students. He could probably be making four or five times this amount practicing full time, but can enjoy both careers if he is content with somewhat less money.

Constitutional lawyer Lawrence Tribe of Harvard bills his occasional commercial clients $250 an hour and charges other clients, such as the city of Boston, $175 an hour. He also helped to write a constitu-

tion for the Marshall Islands, earning a fee of $20,000 plus $10,000 in
travel expenses. Yale's criminal law expert Steven Duke estimates that
he has made about $100,000 in 18 years of moonlighting while teach-
ing. Some tax professors at New York University Law School are
reputed to gross an average of about $50,000 from outside work.
However, since they could be making so much more practicing full
time, one must conclude that the nonmonetary rewards of academe
make up for a smaller paycheck.

The legal profession obviously involves more than just lawyers.
First in importance are the judges. There are seven levels of federal
courts in America, the highest being the Supreme Court. The courts are
listed below with the annual salary and name of the chief justice or
chief judge (where applicable) and the annual salaries and numbers of
associate justices or judges.

FEDERAL COURTS WITH NAME AND SALARY OF CHIEF JUSTICE OR JUDGE, AND SALARIES OF JUDGES FOR EACH COURT (1980)

Supreme Court of the United States

Chief Justice Warren Burger	$84,700
8 Associate Justices	$81,300

U.S. Court of Appeals (11 circuits)

11 Chief Judges,	$65,000
97 Judges	

U.S. District Courts (94 courts)

516 Judges	$61,500

U.S. Court of Customs and Patent Appeals

Chief Judge Howard T. Markey,	$65,000
4 Judges	

U.S. Customs Court

Chief Judge Edward D. Re,	$61,500
8 Judges	

U.S. Court of Claims

Chief Judge Daniel M. Friedman,	$65,000
6 Judges	

U.S. Tax Court

Chief Judge C. Moxley Featherston,	$61,500
14 Judges	

In addition to the federal court systems, each state also has its judicial system. In 1977 there were 3,588 state courts of general jurisdiction, over 12,000 courts of special jurisdiction and 122 state appelate courts. The salaries in the state courts vary widely for judgeships, as can be seen in the chapter on state government.

The legal profession also includes a number of jobs that are needed for the smooth functioning of the courts but that do not require law degrees. With their special training, legal secretaries can earn as much as $19,500 to $23,000 a year. Legal assistants (paralegals) normally start at from $9,000 to $11,000 a year and sometimes can go as high as about $18,500. Legal stenographers, or court reporters, as employees of the court earn between $11,250 and $15,500 a year. When working for themselves in private practice, they can earn considerably more, up to $25,000 or even $28,000 a year.

The salary ranges for employees within the state court system vary from locality to locality and by level of court. The following salaries are applicable, with modifications, for several states—New York, California, Illinois and other large ones. A court officer, the lowest paid employee in the courtroom, begins at about $10,000 and can earn up to $17,500, depending on the area of the country. Uniformed court officers generally work in criminal courts, acting as guards, keeping order in the courtroom and insuring the safety of the jury, the attorneys and the magistrates. Nonuniformed court officers perform the same functions in civil courts and receive comparable pay.

In every state the system of clerks of the court is slightly different. In New York, for example, the chief clerks are paid according to experience, the size of the court's jurisdiction and the consequent problems stemming from possible judicial errors, and the type of court. The highest grade chief clerk in a jurisdiction is responsible for overall supervision and coordination of nonjudicial personnel and for the development of uniform procedures and policies for all the courts within his or her purview. Chief clerks hold great responsibility for the smooth and successful functioning of the courts, and at the top of their profession, they can earn $36,772, which is the highest nonjudicial salary payable.

Law is a complex and growing profession in the United States. It is estimated that by 1983 there will be nearly 600,000 lawyers, and one can assume a steady increase in the amount of litigation in this legally contentious land. This trend is expensive, time consuming and often counterproductive to the very concept of equal justice for all under the law, which is after all the stated goal.

As the courts are given more and more administrative and executive roles—overseeing school systems, regulating business and supervising environmental programs, ad infinitum—their complexity and resources in people and money required will multiply. And yet Americans believe that justice, like education and health, are obtainable for everyone and worth spending vast amounts to get. Those in the profession are the recipients of incomes stemming from a national propensity to litigate and a national optimism that believes every problem has a logical, reasonable and legal solution.

CHAPTER 8
Medicine

THE CONTROVERSIES OVER rising health care and physicians' costs have become major economic and political issues in the country and with good reason. Nevertheless, we look to the medical profession for help and even miracles, and doctors are common heroes in everything from novels to soap operas, from TV shows to best-selling books. The mystique of the hospital, the kindly, attentive figure in the white coat, the new wonder drug, the incredible new operation are powerful factors in a land where science and technology are so admired. It is not surprising then that the work force of the health care industry has grown enormously and that the size of its payroll has grown even faster, becoming the envy of other occupations.

Besides the nearly 410,000 physicians in the United States, there are about 125,000 dentists, almost 100,000 medical practitioners—chiropractors, osteopathic surgeons, optometrists etc.—over one million registered nurses, about 500,000 licensed practical nurses, approximately 110,000 therapists of different types and numerous other workers in health-related professions. Together, they add up to over 4.5 million people, and each year about 15,000 new medical doctors, 5,000 dentists and over 5,000 medical practitioners join the ranks upon completing their educations.

Americans believe that through medicine they can protect their health and prolong their lives, and they visit the doctor frequently and normally with a general optimism. Partly for this reason, and for many others, the costs for patients and the incomes of some practitioners have escalated at an extraordinary pace in the past three decades and have become a heavy burden on the entire economy.

The rate of inflation for medical goods and services has been nearly double that for other consumer goods and services in the economy. An apple that cost 11 cents in 1968 cost around 22 cents in 1978, or twice as much in 10 years. Shockingly, the average cost of one inpatient day at a hospital went from $56 in 1968 to $154 in 1978, almost three times the original. In 1950 total health expenditures were about $12 billion, in 1975 they were $122 billion and in 1978 they came to nearly $190 billion, or almost one-tenth of the gross national product. This has made the health care industry the third largest in America, behind only agriculture and construction in terms of expenditure.

But despite the importance of health care, the ratio of doctors to people in the United States has not been particularly outstanding. For instance, in 1975 the number of physicians per population was one per 583; both West Germany, with one doctor per 522 people, and Greece, with one doctor per 499 people, had more physicians per capita. (To give an example near the other end of the scale, India had one doctor for every 4,264 people.) Nevertheless, the portion of national wealth spent on health has been far greater in the United States than in any of these countries.

Why does health care cost so much more every year, and who is getting the money? These are questions that absorb the nation, aggravate the average citizen and inspire the politicians to dream up grander and more complex solutions all the time. Much of the cause lies in the growth of fee-for-service health insurance programs and the effect they have had so far on hospital costs and physicians' services. This insurance includes private, group and government (Medicare and Medicaid) programs. Between 1950 and 1978 physicians' fees increased at a rate of 5% per year, going from $2.7 billion in 1958 to $35 billion in 1978. General hospital costs have climbed almost as steeply.

Among the reasons for this whacking inflation is the lack of competition in pricing and increasing specialization and quantity of service. In connection with these, the enhanced sophistication and expense of hospital equipment (such as CAT scanners) have pushed up the cost of health care dramatically.

In 1940 there were 175,000 physicians in the United States, of whom 76% were general practitioners, and the remainder were specialists. The median income of doctors then was $3,265 per year. (The average wage for full-time employees was $1,280.) In 1955 there were 225,000 physicians in the United States, of whom 51% were general practitioners and the rest specialists; the median physician income at the time was $16,107. (The average wage for full-time employees was $3,923.) In 1978 there were approximately 395,000 physicians in the United States with a median income of $68,000. Of the total, 86.5% were specialists. (The average wage for full-time employees was approximately $12,800.) In short, since 1940 the median earnings of physicians have increased 20 times, while the rest of the population has seen its earnings rise only 10 times.

The number of physicians, their degree of specialization, the subsequent increase in fees and the extent of health care received by the public have increased in an economic environment where insurance will pay most "reasonable" costs and fees, and where what is "reasonable" is defined by upper limits of expenditure. Above the 90th percentile, an operation, procedure or hospital service is deemed too high; beneath that high plateau exists a wide range of costs for various treatments in different locales that are all reimbursable through insurance programs. Naturally, the highest price accepted for an insurance claim influences the future price of that particular treatment, until a new adjustment is authorized.

Thus the cost of a blood test, an x-ray, or an operation only varies within a pricing framework set by insurance payment schedules. And as direct payments by the patient have been replaced by insurance programs, the exact expense of an individual health treatment becomes of less importance to both the patient and the doctor. In 1950, 85% of all physicians' expenditures were paid directly by the patient, whereas in 1979 61.3% of the costs were paid by insurance and public health care funds and only 38.7% were paid directly by the patient.

The 1978 median income of $68,000 for all medical doctors represents a 2,100% increase in their earnings from 1939. Furthermore, it is about twice the median for dentists and lawyers and nearly four times as much as that for other professional (educators etc.) and technical workers. It is true that the amount of time and money spent on medical school and subsequent training is great, and the apprenticeship is long and hard. For example, some of the very best paid interns coming out of medical school earn $16,000 a year at New York Hospital, but they average 100 hours of work a week, which means they earn about $3.00 an hour. Nevertheless, the doctors make up for lost time rapidly, and the return on investment for each education dollar is considerably higher in medicine than in other professions.

It is the remarkably high median that makes the practice of medicine one of the most lucrative ways to earn a living in the United States. True, there are a small number of lawyers, businessmen, entertainers and others who, like certain doctors, make $500,000 or even a million dollars a year. But few, other than in the highly selective world of certain professional sports, can surpass the median income in medicine.

In 1979, 20% of all doctors made over $100,000 after expenses and half of these made over $125,000. Only 29% of all doctors made $50,000 or less. Seven percent of the nation's surgeons made $150,000 or more net and another 23% exceeded $100,000, while 15% of the nation's obstetrician-gynecologists earned $125,000 or more after expenses.

Pathologists and radiologists were the highest earners in the specialities. Although precise figures for them are lacking, the mean income for pathologists connected with nonteaching hospitals was about $140,000 a year and for radiologists $125,000 a year. Over half of all pathologists and radiologists are connected with hospitals. Others divide their time, earning salaries from hospitals and fees-for-service in private practice. Some have only private work and make somewhat smaller paychecks on the average.

These two fields, radiology and pathology, are the highest paying for particular reasons; the skills they offer are needed by all doctors to help them diagnose and treat various illnesses in their many manifestations, and thus both specialities are in constant and crucial demand. Furthermore, in community hospitals pathologists frequently are in charge of all laboratory testing and receive a fee for all work performed. The same is true for radiologists on all x-ray work.

Physicians' expenses are generally high, and the highest are in the area of general practice, pediatrics, surgery and radiology. The lowest are in psychiatry, where the basic equipment required is an office, chairs, perhaps a couch, notebooks and a supply of pencils. However, because of the nature of the work, psychiatrists see the fewest number of patients per work day and usually make the lowest income of any speciality.

A significant chunk of expenses is attributable to malpractice insurance, but less than often thought, amounting to about 5% of professional costs. However, when malpractice suits are settled in favor of the patient-plaintiff, it is often big news. In 1979 Ms. Virginia O'Hare was awarded $854,219.61 for an unsuccessful cosmetic operation (plastic surgery) performed on her abdomen by Dr. Howard Bellin of New York. Ms. O'Hare claimed extreme suffering and distress caused by the improper placement of her belly button. This case was one of thousands of malpractice suits brought in the United States every year.

To deal with their incomes, expenses, deductions and profits in the most favorable manner, physicians with ever increasing frequency have been incorporating themselves individually or with a group into so-called professional corporations (PCs). Incorporated MDs do better than their nonincorporated brethren; for example, the median gross income for an unincorporated general practitioner in 1978 was $82,930, compared to $138,330 for a GP who was incorporated.

OFFICE-BASED MEDICAL PRACTICE

About 250,000 doctors operate out of their own office. The rest are either full-time members of hospital staffs or do the majority of their work in some connection with hospitals.

Despite the sophistication and number of specialities, general practice (including family practice) still accounts for the largest single group of doctors; about 20% of the total number of physicians are GPs who use their offices as the center of their operation. There, they are second only to pediatricians in the number of patients they see.

As a patient sits in the doctor's office, whether it is a GP's or specialist's, and whiles away the time watching other patients and the clock, his or her mind often turns to questions such as: How many patients does this doctor see a week? How much is he charging everyone for a visit? Here are some answers to these questions, keeping in mind that cost figures vary considerably in different parts of the country and that these are nationwide medians.

MEDIAN NUMBER OF OFFICE AND HOSPITAL
VISITS TO DOCTOR BY SPECIALITY
AND MEDIAN COST FOR FIRST
VISITS AND REVISITS BY SPECIALITY (1978)

Doctor	No. of Visits/Week office	hospital	Median Cost first visit	Median Cost revisit
Psychiatrists*	33	6	$51.00	$61.00 (hospital)
Cardiologists	52	39	$57.00	$19.00
Ophthalmologists	113	10	$28.00	$19.00
Internists	77	38	$26.00	$18.00
Obstetric-Gynecological Specialists (OBGs)	102	22	$26.00	$18.00
Orthopedic Surgeons	84	38	$25.00	$16.00
Urologists	63	39	$25.00	$16.00
All Surgical Specialists	82	25	$25.00	$15.00
All Nonsurgical Specialists**	78	21	$24.00	$17.00
Otolaryngologists	102	16	$21.00	$15.00
Pediatricians	123	18	$19.00	$13.00
General Surgeons	58	39	$19.00	$12.00
General Practitioners	121	31	$16.00	$12.00

*Psychiatrists charge a median of $75 per session for family therapy and $21 per person for group psychotherapy.
**Pathologists and radiologists, the highest earners of all, are not included.
Note: It must be remembered that these are median fees. At the high end, for example, 21% of internists, 2% of surgeons and OBGs and 6% of orthopedists charge over $50 per visit.

On top of the base cost for an office visit, there are, of course, often numerous other charges relating to the speciality and the needs of the patient. A few common tests and treatments and their median costs are listed below.

MEDIAN COST OF SOME COMMON
TESTS AND TREATMENTS (1978)

History and Physical Exam: GPs $35; Internists $52
Electrocardiograms: CGP or technician $22
Newborn Care (Pediatricians): $45
Dilation and Curettage (OBGs): Diagnostic $175; Abortion $200
Appendectomy (Surgeons): $350

Cholecystectomy (Surgeons): $545
Total Hysterectomy: General Surgeons $587; OBGs $640
Eye Examination (Ophthalmologists): $31
Unilateral Cataract Extraction (Ophthalmologists): $750 to $1,500
Hip Arthroplasty (Orthopedists): $1,500
Cardiac Evaluation (Cardiologists): $105
Prostatectomy (Urologists): $743
Tonsillectomy (Otolaryngologists): $201
Laryngectomy (Otolaryngologists): $1,100
Neurosurgery: The fees vary enormously according to the type and complexity of the surgery.
Heart Surgery: Bypass $3,000-$6,000
Plastic Surgery: Average prices are subject to change according to surgeon and area.
  Face Lifts: $1,500 to $3,000
  Bust enlargements: $1,500 to $2,500 plus cost of silicon (approximately $200)
  Removal of fat from around eyes: $1,500 to $2,000

The variation in median income of office-based doctors is sizable, ranging from the lowest of $51,030 for general practitioners and $53,790 for psychiatrists to a high of $91,940 for orthopedic surgeons. Psychiatrists, once the symbol of opulence in popular song and story, have suffered from the limitations on the number of patients that can be seen in one day, a situation only partially alleviated by the growth of group and family therapy. It must be remembered that the medians for radiologists and pathologists are higher than the median for orthopedic surgeons by a considerable margin, but, due to the dispersion, complexities and characteristics of their practice, exact figures are not available for them.

Suffice it to say that none of the many different types of medical doctors are deprived, and while they work hard, their hours and the trials of their education and apprenticeship are amply rewarded. The table below testifies to this conclusion.

MEDIAN INCOMES OF OFFICE-BASED MDs (1977)

Types of Physician	Median Income	Percentage Earning Above $100,000	Percentage Earning Below $50,000
Orthopedic Surgeon	$91,940	41%	11%
Urologist	$80,770	27%	17%

MEDIAN INCOMES OF OFFICE-BASED MDs (1977)

Types of Physician	Median Income	Percentage Earning Above $100,000	Percentage Earning Below $50,000
Opthalmologist	$78,750	28%	18%
Obstetric-Gynecological Specialist	$78,420	32%	21%
Cardiologist	$77,620	30%	12%
Otolaryngologist	$71,720	24%	25%
General Surgeon	$68,720	20%	30%
Internist	$66,140	14%	27%
Pediatrician	$54,180	4%	42%
Psychiatrist	$53,790	5%	43%
General Practitioner	$51,030	7%	48%

Dentists

Dental colleges normally require from two to four years of predental education; in fact, over 85% of all students entering dental school in 1978 had a B. A. or M. A. Dental school lasts four years (in some cases, three), and the last portion is spent in a dental clinic treating patients. As with physicians, the education is expensive and long, and in many states the specialists (orthodontists, periodontists, oral pathologists etc.) are required to undergo an even lengthier instructional period.

Almost 90% of all dentists are in private practice, 78% working alone and the remainder in groups, either incorporated or unincorporated. But most are still unincorporated. Salaried dentists, other than those in incorporated groups, work either full time in hospitals or in some arrangement with nonmedical organizations such as the military, industry etc.

Below are some median income figures for dentists and dental assistants. They show that dentistry is less lucrative than general or specialized medicine. One of the reasons for this is that the overhead and expenses for dentists—equipment, space, tests and auxiliary personnel—are very high, even higher than for most specialists in medicine, where more of the elaborate procedures are performed in a hospital. The mean professional dental expenses in 1976-77 were $55,338 for general dental practitioners and $66,917 for specialists.

The main items in these expenses were salaries (31%), rent (7.5%) and commercial laboratory charges (31%).

The figures below are net incomes of independent dentists, and they help to underscore the impact of the operating costs just mentioned.

MEDIAN ANNUAL NET INCOMES OF ALL INDEPENDENT DENTISTS (1976-77)

Types of Practitioners	Median Net Income
Oral Surgeons	$59,921
Orthodontists	$58,000
All Specialists	$55,003
Endodontists	$52,000
Periodontists	$51,050
General Practitioners	$39,259

Once again, however, the range of income encompasses substantial paychecks for the majority, as it does with physicians, although the total scale is lower. Of the general practitioners, 11% earned more than $65,000, while only 30% made less than $25,000. For the specialists, 35% netted more than $65,000 and only about 10% earned less than $25,000.

In the field of dentistry, the assistants and technicians fared noticeably less well, for the most part.

MEDIAN ANNUAL SALARIES OF DENTAL ASSISTANTS AND TECHNICIANS (1976-77)

	Median Salary
Laboratory Technician (ceramics)	$12,000 to $25,000
Laboratory Technician	$12,000 to $18,000
Hygienist	$12,900
Chairside Assistant	$6,960

Finally, due to the nature of the work, dentists, like psychiatrists, are limited by the number of hours in the day and the number of patients that can be seen. In 1977 the average dentist saw 78 patients a week, the highest number visiting orthodontists (127) and the lowest number general practitioners (74). Of course, many dentists supplement their income by teaching in dental schools and teaching clinics. Nevertheless, although dentistry must be judged a very well-paying profession, with earnings somewhat higher than the average in law, it is considerably below the exalted world of physicians.

Medical Practitioners

The main categories of medical practitioners are chiropractors, osteopaths, podiatrists, optometrists and veterinarians. For each of these specialities, the licensing requirements are demanding and the regulations are strict. In most states both osteopaths and chiropractors must take four-year study programs after completing at least two years of college.

The average income for an experienced chiropractor is about $33,000 a year. For osteopaths the average is about $37,000 a year. One chiropractor, Flavian Santivicca, earns more money from his work than almost anyone else in the country. His personal practice in Florida yielded him over $1.2 million in 1978, and he is a consultant and teacher of nearly 200 students and professional chiropractors who pay a tuition of $30,000 per year each. Thus, Dr. Santivicca's annual earnings totaled over $7 million, placing him in the ethereal financial world of entertainment superstars.

Optometrists also have strict standards, as do veterinarians and podiatrists. The average salary ranges for all of them are between $34,000 and $37,000, although some make considerably more.

There are about 36,000 veterinarians practicing in the United States, about 9,000 podiatrists, about 21,000 chiropractors, roughly the same number of optometrists and nearly 19,000 osteopathic physicians.

HOSPITAL-BASED MEDICAL PRACTICE

About 110,000 physicians in the country are either working full time on hospital staffs or are in residence at hospitals for the majority of their practice. This includes both private and government (public) hospitals, and the range of income varies between the two. Besides physicians, hospitals employ administrative, nursing, therapeutic and technical staffs, which total over three million people. Other people engaged in the field of health care are employed in related industry, clinics, laboratories, pharmacies, nursing homes, mental health centers, private offices etc. Listed here are the salaries for many of the jobs at larger hospitals (500 beds or more), both government and private, throughout the country. The incomes differ according to location, in some cases very significantly, so the figures given are national medians.

The jobs are broken down into five major categories, beginning with hospital staff physicians. This group, except for the interns and the

residents, is the highest paid. Hospital physician incomes in this list
are stated either as salary alone or as salary plus outside fees earned
from private practice and/or share or compensation from departmental income. In teaching hospitals, doctors' incomes would be faculty
salary alone or faculty salary plus fees for outside practice and/or
departmental income, as discussed in the chapter on education. Some
of the figures given below are based in part on studies done by the
American Management Associations Executive Compensation Service.

AVERAGE ANNUAL INCOMES OF HOSPITAL STAFF DOCTORS
(1978-79)

Position	Income
Director of Pathology	$132,300 salary plus fees
Director of Radiology	$125,000 salary plus fees
Radiologist	$105,000 salary plus fees
Internist	$102,600 salary plus fees
Pathologist	$98,700 salary plus fees
Pediatrician	$98,000 salary plus fees
Anesthesiologist	$97,000 salary plus fees
Cardiologist	$90,000 salary plus fees
Chief of Surgery	$86,000 salary only
Psychiatrist	$84,000 salary plus fees
Emergency Room Physician	$80,000 salary plus fees
Director of Obstetrics/Gynecology	$68,200 salary only
Medical Director	$63,400 salary only
Surgeon	$52,700 salary only
General Practitioner	$43,000 salary only
Dentist	$31,000 salary only
Resident	$14,800 to $20,5000 salary only
Intern	$13,600 to $16,000 salary only

The second category is administrative staff, and here, as with the
remaining categories of hospital employees, the incomes are subdi-
vided according to private and government hospitals. It is interesting
that, for the most part, government hospitals pay better than private
ones, just as public educational institutions frequently pay better than
private schools. Here, private hospitals are those profit and nonprofit
institutions owned by individuals or private corporations, religious
organizations etc. Government hospitals include all facilities operated
by federal, state, and city and local community governments. Regardless of whether a hospital is private or government operated, a significant percentage of the operating funds, in the form of payments for

services and support for government sponsored treatment programs, is public money. The reason that private hospitals pay nonphysician staff somewhat less is because of the economic realities of running such institutions rather than differences in qualifications and training of personnel, who are equal in these regards.

AVERAGE ANNUAL SALARIES OF ADMINISTRATIVE STAFF IN PRIVATE AND GOVERNMENT HOSPITALS (1978-79)

Position	Salary in Private Hospital	Salary in Government Hospital
Administrator	$49,100	$53,000
Director of Finance	$38,300	$37,900
Controller	$27,800	$29,900
Director of Personnel	$25,400	$27,000
Chief Pharmacist	$24,800	$25,000
Director of Public Relations	$23,200	$23,800
Director of Social Services	$22,500	$23,100
Training Director	$20,100	$21,800
Chief of Medical Records	$18,600	$16,600
Chief Admitting Officer	$15,300 to $19,400 (all hospitals)	
Social Worker (MSW)	$16,700	$15,500
Laundry Manager	$16,700	$14,700
Chaplain	$16,000	$15,100
Chief Medical Librarian	$15,800	$15,100
Director of Volunteer Services	$14,500	$15,300
Director of Outpatient Department	$12,500 (all hospitals)	

Hospital nurses are the largest group of nurses, both registered and practical, and they not only provide skilled bedside care, but also assist in surgery and perform essential medical treatment and functions under the supervision of the doctors. The responsibilities and duties of nurses are manifold and varied, and the skill and morale of a nursing staff to a great degree sets the whole tone of a hospital community. Nurses often feel that the degree of responsibility they have warrants better recognition and income, and this can be a heated subject. The salaries of hospital nurses are shown below, as well as the salaries of other nursing occupations.

AVERAGE ANNUAL SALARIES OF NURSING STAFF IN PRIVATE AND GOVERNMENT HOSPITALS (1978-79)

Position	Salary in Private Hospital	Salary in Government Hospital
Director, Nursing Service	$28,800	$28,800
Director, School of Nursing	$24,000	$26,000
Chief Nurse Anesthetist	$23,100	$22,800
Nurse, Supervisor	$17,500	$17,100
Head Nurse	$15,700	$15,600
Instructor, Nursing Service	$16,200	$15,100
Heart-Lung Machine Operator	$15,400	$14,300
Staff Nurse	$13,300	$12,800
Licensed Practical Nurse	$9,800	$10,000
Surgical Technician	$9,700	$9,700
Nursing Aide	$8,200	$8,700
Orderly	$7,600	$7,000

Many nurses work outside a hospital setting in jobs where their paychecks vary considerably depending on changing circumstances. For example, nursing homes are usually staffed with practical nurses making somewhat less than they would in a regular hospital, about $8,300 per year. The nurse supervisors are generally registered nurses, but once again making less, about $14,000 a year, than they would in hospitals.

Private duty nurses, who usually work through agencies, may be registered, practical or even nurse's aides, according to the requirements of the patient and doctor. They can work at home or in hospitals. Registered nurses on private duty make from $7 to $8 an hour; those with less training naturally earn somewhat less.

Community health nurses make house calls and do tests at home or in a community office. Their salaries can vary from $3.50 to $5.50 an hour. Home aides, once again, may have any qualifications required by the patient, but normally they are not, strictly speaking, nurses, but rather helpers, either temporary or permanent, for those who can afford them and/or the handicapped. They generally earn about $2.75 to $3.00 an hour.

The technical staff of a hospital performs tests, operates complex equipment and deals directly with patients. Some technicians carry out tests directly on the patient, such as X-rays and electroencephalograms. Other members of the technical staff work in the privacy of the laboratory, often under great time pressure, and never need see a patient. Some of the major jobs and average salaries are listed in the next table.

AVERAGE ANNUAL SALARIES OF TECHNICAL STAFF IN PRIVATE AND GOVERNMENT HOSPITALS (1978-79)

Position	Salary in Private Hospital	Salary in Government Hospital
Chief Medical Technologist	$18,200	$18,700
Chief Radiologic Technologist	$18,200	$18,600
Nuclear Laboratory Technologist Supervisor	$16,900	$15,400
Nuclear Laboratory Technologist	$12,900	$14,800
Medical Technologist	$13,600	$13,100
Radiologic Technologist	$11,400	$10,800
Electroencephalograph Technician	$9,500	$9,900

The therapeutic and dietary staff of a hospital is generally paid more than the technical staff, matching their qualifications, which are usually higher. Therapies dealing with speech, movement, hearing and so forth require special training and knowledge of the body and the emotional and the psychological problems of patients suffering from problems in these areas.

The importance of diet in medical treatment, once ignored, has received much greater recognition in recent years. Nutrition has become a much more commonly taught subject in medical schools. Food directors and dieticians are consulted about the proper foods for the needs of particular patients. Their broad but in-depth training, based on an increasing body of information, has won them greater status and higher salaries in the health care industry.

AVERAGE ANNUAL SALARIES OF THERAPEUTIC AND DIETARY STAFF IN PRIVATE AND GOVERNMENT HOSPITALS (1978-79)

Position	Salary in Private Hospital	Salary in Government Hospital
Food Service Director	$21,300	$22,700
Chief Physical Therapist	$20,000	$19,300
Chief Speech and Hearing Therapist	$19,300	$18,500

Chief Occupational		
Therapist	$17,000	$17,000
Audiologist	$14,800	$16,400
Speech and Hearing Therapist	$14,700	$13,800
Dietician	$14,200	$13,500
Physical Therapist	$14,000	$12,900
Occupational Therapist	$13,800	$12,600

Health care jobs are also found on the staffs of insurance companies, research labs, industrial firms and many other businesses. Below are listed a number of these full-time positions in both research and practicing medicine.

AVERAGE ANNUAL SALARIES OF OCCUPATIONAL AND INDUSTRIAL HEALTH-CARE STAFF (1978-79)

Position	Salary
Medical Director	$69,200
Research Medical Director	$58,500
Industrial Physician	$41,500
Director of Pharmacology	$35,500
Director of Microbiology	$29,100
Industrial Nurse	$17,200

Physicians are constantly prescribing drugs, and the cost of them is one of the great issues in the whole health care controversy. The question of generic vs. brand name prescription medicines is just one facet of the drug controversy. Certain frequently prescribed drugs, such as Valium (a tranquilizer) and Tagemet® (an antacid for control of ulcers), are enormously profitable for the firms that created, produced and marketed them, and a debate swirls around when the exclusive patent for the originating companies should expire. Regardless of the outcome of this debate, the pharmaceutical business is very lucrative. Here are five of the top companies with their principal officers, who are paid very high up on the scale of American executives in all businesses.

INCOMES OF TOP EXECUTIVES OF LEADING DRUG COMPANIES (1978)

Company and Executive	Total Income	1978 Net Profit (millions)
American Home Products		$348
William F. Laporte, Chairman	$830,000	
John W. Culligan, President	$650,000	

INCOMES OF TOP EXECUTIVES OF LEADING
DRUG COMPANIES (1978)

Company and Executive	Total Income	1978 Net Profit (millions)
Johnson and Johnson		$299
J. E. Burke, Chairman	$733,000	
D. R. Clare, President	$526,000	
Bristol-Myers		$203
Richard L. Gelb, Chairman	$651,000	
Herman Sokol, President	$496,000	
Bruce S. Gelb, Executive Vice President	$373,000	
Merck		$308
John L. Horan, Chairman	$418,000	
John L. Huck, Executive Vice President	$272,000	
Huskel Ekaireb, Executive Vice President	$263,000	
Eli Lilly		$278
Richard D. Wood, Chairman	$410,000	
Cornelius W. Pettings, Executive Vice President	$223,000	
A. Malcolm McVie, Executive Vice President	$203,000	

At the other end of the drug pipeline are neighborhood pharmacies and pharmacists. A full-time licensed pharmacist in a drug store, filling prescriptions and assuring a constant supply of necessary drugs, makes about $20,000 to $24,000 a year. However, many pharmacists are also general merchants, selling candy, toiletries, gifts, tobaccos, lighting fluids, razors, ointments, lipstick, general cosmetics, hair tints, prophylactics, hairpins, wash cloths, stockings and pantyhose, puzzles, games, vacation items from lotions to bathing suits, paperback books, clocks, jewelry and an infinity of other products of importance, curiosity or simple whimsy. These merchant-pharmacists make what profit their business acumen, store location and traffic will produce. The pharmacist deals with everything human, or as much as he can cram into his four walls.

Medicine is one of our most scientific and yet mystical professions. We read about doctors and hospitals, we admire their achievements, sue them when they fail us, and idealize and celebrate their battle against death and disease. Above all, society demonstrates its esteem for doctors by being extraordinarily generous; we may not pay doctors quite as much as basketball players or movie stars, but we pay them more than almost any other profession in America.

CHAPTER 9
Education

O VER 63 MILLION Americans were engaged, one way or another, in education as their primary activity in 1978-79. An estimated 59.3 million were students, another 3.3 million were teachers, and over 300,000 were administrative and other instructional staff members, including principals, college presidents, deans, supervisors, counselors and support people.

This means that nearly a quarter of the more than 218 million people in this country are directly involved with the educational process as students, teachers or in related jobs. This striking statistic reflects the importance that education has always had in America from the very beginning, economically, socially and culturally. For example, the percentage of the total population enrolled full time in education has changed relatively little over the years. In 1870, 19.7% of the total attended primary and secondary school and college, in 1920, 20.6%, and in 1975 the figure was 21.6%.

It has always been a fundamental belief in this land of immigrants that the education of our youth greatly influences the national character and the achievement of the entire society; creating a common heritage has always been a principal responsibility of the educational system. For this reason, educators in America have always been accorded great respect and social status; yet the fact is that education has generally been the lowest paying of all the professions. For example, in 1950 the average salary for all full-time workers in America was $3,262; for physicians in that year it was $13,150 and for educators it was approximately $5,980. Twenty-five years later, in 1975, the average salary for all full-time workers was $10,845; for physicians it was $58,440; and for teachers it was $11,890 in primary and secondary schools and about $15,000 for colleges and universities. Educational salaries, while always higher than the American average, have consistently lost ground, particularly and dramatically to medicine and law. (In 1978-79 physicians had a median income of $68,000 and lawyers earned a median of $32,000, while educators made a median salary of only $15,950.)

The reasons for this are many. There are nearly 10 times as many teachers as doctors or lawyers, and teacher qualifications are less demanding in terms of time and expense, for most positions. Also, unlike medicine and law, education is by and large a publicly financed activity, and its funds are limited by the political process. Furthermore, despite its acknowledged prestige, education is not viewed as particularly glamorous by the public; there are no teacher "superstars," no Dr. Kildares or Perry Masons of the classroom (let alone O.J. Simpsons to draw fans by the millions). Education is an essential, but commonplace, aspect of everyday life in America. Not profit-oriented by nature, it is paid for involuntarily by all citizens out of their taxes and thus receives relatively little in the way of special treatment, folklore or financial remuneration.

HIGHER EDUCATION

In 1978-79 over 11 million students were enrolled in schools of higher education. The faculty of these institutions numbered about one million, creating a ratio of 11 students to one faculty member. In 1870 approximately 53,000 students were enrolled in higher education with a faculty of about 5,200, or at a ratio of slightly over 10 to one. While the ratio of students to faculty has remained fairly constant (except in some large state systems where it has reached the level of 15 or 20 to one), the number of degrees in relation to population has increased strikingly in the past half century. In 1920 there were about 54,000 bachelor's, master's and doctorate degrees for a population of 106 million people. In 1976-77 there were a total of about 1.4 million such degrees for a population of about 212 million, a relative increase of almost 20-fold. The output of higher educational institutions in terms of degrees-granted may have risen greatly, but the salaries of the faculty and administrative staffs have by no means increased at a comparable pace.

Independent studies show that key administrative personnel in higher education are paid from one-third to one-half as much as people with jobs of similar responsibility in business. For example, Dr. Clifton R. Wharton, Jr. makes $57,650 as chancellor of the State University of New York (SUNY), which has 64 branches and approximately 340,000 students, 15,000 full-time faculty members and nearly 18,000 full-time administrative and support employees. SUNY is the largest state system in America, embracing all forms of public higher education within the state. California, by contrast, has three different systems. Dr. Wharton is responsible for medical schools, junior colleges, football coaches and teams, campuses, all types of facilities, faculties and courses of instruction. The budget for his operation in 1978 was $816 million. In private industry he would make a great deal more than his current salary, as would many presidents or chancellors of major universities in the country. (Dr. Wharton is responsible for about four-fifths the number of employees as American Home Products but he makes less than one-fourteenth the salary of its president, William Laporte.)

SALARIES OF PRESIDENTS OF SOME MAJOR UNIVERSITIES (1978)
(with approximate 1978 budgets where available)

Institution	President/ Chancellor	Salary
University of California, entire system (total 1978 budget $900 million)	David Saxon	$78,750
University of California, Berkeley	Albert H. Bowker	$67,500

SALARIES OF PRESIDENTS OF SOME MAJOR
UNIVERSITIES (1978)
(with approximate 1978 budgets where available)

Institution	President/ Chancellor	Salary
University of California, Davis	Dr. James H. Meyer	$64,000
University of California, Los Angeles	Charles E. Young	$67,000
University of California, Santa Barbara	Dr. Robert A. Huttenback	$62,500
University of Pennsylvania (1978 budget $320 million)	Martin Meyerson	$75,000
Princeton University (1978 budget $155 million)	William G. Bowen	$75,000
Rutgers University	Dr. Edward J. Bloustein	$50,800
State University of New York (1978 budget $816 million)	Dr. Clifton R. Wharton	$57,650

The ratio of administrative staff and faculty to students varies considerably from institution to institution. At Princeton and the University of Chicago, for example, the combined faculty and staff are about equal to the number of students. At California the ratio is about two to one (130,000 students, 60,000 faculty and staff), while at SUNY it is 10 to one (340,000 students, 33,000 faculty and staff). The lower administrative and support employees, including secretaries and maintenance people, are paid according to the going rate in their communities, or somewhat less, but the higher-ranking personnel (instructional staff) definitely receive smaller salaries than do their business counterparts, as the table below clearly shows.

SALARY COMPARISONS OF TOP EXECUTIVES IN
HIGHER EDUCATION AND PRIVATE BUSINESS,
BY SIZE OF ORGANIZATION (1977)

Positions*	Average Salaries ($) by Size of Organization		
	Small	Medium	Large
Chief Executive Officer (HE)	$34,600	$40,800	$50,050
Chief Executive Officer (B)	75,300	104,900	164,400

Chief Academic Officer (HE)	25,100	33,900	43,600
Chief Operating Officer (B)	68,000	93,000	140,900
Chief Planning Officer (HE)	20,100	26,100	30,400
Long-Range Planning			
Executive (B)	N. A.	39,600	43,800
Chief Business Officer (HE)	23,700	29,600	40,100
Top Financial Executive (B)	39,600	61,100	82,200
Treasurer (B)	37,600	45,700	54,000
Chief Student Life			
Officer (HE)	18,800	28,300	36,300
Top Industrial Relations			
Executive (B)	26,500	40,300	53,100
Chief Development Officer (HE)	22,700	26,700	33,100
Chief Public Relations			
Officer (HE)	14,700	20,200	31,900
Top Public Relations			
Executive (B)	N. A.	N. A.	39,900
Top Advertising			
Executive (B)	28,600	31,200	37,500
Admissions Director (HE)	16,600	21,000	26,200
Top Marketing Executive (B)	43,400	60,300	71,900
General Sales Executive (B)	36,300	42,000	55,100
Director, Computer Center (HE)	16,000	22,700	33,400
Top Electronic Data			
Processing Executive (B)	25,800	30,100	37,400
Controller (HE)	17,600	20,900	28,100
Controller (B)	27,300	39,400	49,200
Purchasing Agent (HE)	13,500	16,100	24,400
Top Purchasing Executive (B)	22,300	35,500	39,500
Dean, Arts and Sciences (HE)	19,200	30,300	40,100
Deans and Directors (Schools			
and Colleges) (HE)	18,400	26,800	35,800
Top Engineering Executive (B)	29,500	41,200	53,300
Top Research Executive (B)	32,200	41,400	54,900
Top Product Development			
Executive (B)	39,200	44,600	52,100

* (HE) higher education; (B) business.

The range of salaries for teachers in colleges and professional schools is broad, and yet the highest paid professors receive noticeably less than other people who have reached the top in most of the occupations discussed in this book, except for civil and public service.

Among the highest paid academics are the chairmen of departments at the medical schools in the New York State University system. If a chairman works full time on a calendar-year basis, without earning outside fees for medical services, he or she can receive in a few rare cases a top salary of $102,403 per year. If he retains the right to work for outside fees, his academic salary can go as high as $58,517. The salary limits for a full professor in the same schools are $96,063 without outside fees and $54,893 with fees in addition; once again the top is reached only in rare cases.

Medical schools are the best paying of all institutions in higher education. Below are listed the average compensation (salary plus benefits) for full professors and associate and assistant professors at seven medical schools across the country. The figures given are for the calendar year (12-month basis) 1978-79; they do not include chairmen of departments nor do they take into account fees that the teachers can and often do earn in outside practice.

AVERAGE ANNUAL SALARIES OF FACULTY MEMBERS IN SEVEN MEDICAL SCHOOLS (1978-79)

Medical School	Professor	Associate Professor	Assistant Professor
Johns Hopkins University	$57,900	$36,400	$29,900
Columbia University	$55,500	$39,100	$31,000
Stanford University	$53,000	N. A.	$30,400
Yale University	$51,800	$36,100	$25,000
University of Pennsylvania	$49,800	$35,400	$27,400
Harvard University	$47,500	$35,400	$28,700
University of Chicago	$46,500	$34,200	$27,400

Law school salaries run somewhat lower than those of medical schools, but full professors at the highest paying institutions, such as Harvard, Yale, Columbia and Chicago, receive between $51,000 and $57,000 per year, exclusive of fees earned for outside work. The same is true of the leading business schools, where the number of master's degrees conferred have doubled since 1970. However the very highest salaries at law schools rarely equal the figures for the medical schools in New York or elsewhere. It is evident from the previous chapters on the law and medicine that someone who is at the height of either of those professions could make many, many times over in private practice the salary of a full professor in one of the prestigious schools. But some do

both, such as Dr. Michael DeBakey, president of the Baylor College of
Medicine, Professor William Baxter of the Stanford Law School or
Walter Blum of the University of Chicago Law School, to mention a
few who make in outside practice three or four times over their faculty
salaries. In fact, many prominent physicians and, to a somewhat lesser
extent, lawyers teach and practice, deriving income from both activities. In some cases doctors and lawyers maintain separate offices for
their private practice; in the law schools this is frequent among those
specializing in tax law.

The salaries paid teachers in the regular college and university ranks
are lower than those in the professional graduate schools, considerably
lower at most institutions of higher education. However, the incomes
of significant numbers of teachers in many disciplines are supple-
mented by writing scholarly books, textbooks or other publications and
by outside teaching and consulting jobs. The range of salaries within
institutions and the profession in general is quite large. Within the
State University of New York, for example, the range extends from
$53,566 for a leading professor all the way down to $5,137 for a
teaching assistant, who is frequently responsible for the day-in and
day-out instruction of hundreds of students.

In this table are listed the average compensations (salary plus
benefits) of full professors, associate and assistant professors and
instructors in 17 institutions across the country. The number of men
and women holding the job of professor and instructor at various
institutions are shown in parentheses after the salary figures for these
positions to indicate the growing trend of hiring women in the universities and colleges.

AVERAGE ANNUAL COMPENSATION OF FACULTY MEMBERS
AT SELECTED INSTITUTIONS (1978-79)
(with number of men [M] and women [W] professors and
instructors)

Institution	Professor	Associate Professor	Assistant Professor	Instructor
American University	$31,100 (M-113, W-19)	$23,700	$19,200	$16,400 (M-7, W-7)
Alabama State University	$22,800 (M-17, W-0)	$20,600	$17,800	$14,900 (M-20, W-26)

AVERAGE ANNUAL COMPENSATION OF FACULTY MEMBERS
AT SELECTED INSTITUTIONS (1978-79)
(with number of men [M] and women [W] professors and
instructors)

Institution	Professor	Associate Professor	Assistant Professor	Instructor
University of California (Berkeley)	$38,200 (M-832, W-35)	$26,400	$22,200	N. A.
University of Chicago	$39,600 (M-381, W-14)	$26,800	$21,700	$18,800 (M-25, W-5)
Florida State University	$27,100 (M-329, W-33)	$20,300	$17,600	$14,600 (M-7, W-5)
University of Georgia	$30,300 (M-387, W-13)	$22,900	$18,900	$14,100 (M-57, W-5)
Harvard University	$44,300 (M-492, W-13)	$24,700	$20,400	N. A.
Jackson State University	$23,000 (M-29, W-15)	$21,900	$18,900	$15,600 (M-28, W-38)
New Mexico State University	$30,000 (M-376, W-62)	$23,300	$19,100	$14,400 (M-28, W-38)
New York University	$35,500 (M-376, W-62)	$25,400	$21,100	$18,000 (M-42, W-48)
Northeast Louisiana University	$25,300 (M-61, W-7)	$21,700	$17,600	$12,700 (M-8, W-31)
Princeton University	$39,100 (M-295, W-4)	$25,900	$19,500	$15,200 (M-34, W-5)
Rutgers University	$40,500 (M-404, W-53)	$29,100	$20,800	$16,200 (M-51, W-39)
Slippery Rock State College	$33,200 (M-97, W-8)	$27,400	$22,600	$17,500 (M-10, W-18)

University				
of Tennessee				
(Nashville)	$27,900	$21,700	$18,100	$15,100
	(M-19, W-0)			(M-3, W-11)
University				
of Wyoming	$29,600	$24,500	$20,300	$16,800
	(M-231, W-13)			(M-30, W-36)
Yale				
University	$39,200	$24,100	$18,100	$16,400
	(M-350, W-10)			(M-18, W-20)

Within faculties there is a range of salaries depending on the discipline taught. The average of all salary ranks in a number of disciplines at eight universities is presented to show the variation. The average salary shown is the average of the salaries of full, associate and assistant professors in each case. Not surprisingly, the more practical disciplines, those with immediate job applications after graduation, such as business and psychology, were more lucrative than areas such as English or philosophy. Average outside earnings apart from salary are also listed to emphasize this point.

AVERAGE ANNUAL SALARY IN NINE DISCIPLINES AT SELECTED UNIVERSITIES (1978-79)
(with average outside earnings)

Discipline	Average Faculty Salary	Average Outside Earning
Economics	$25,030	$2,883
Business	$24,684	$3,444
Engineering	$24,528	$1,685
Sociology	$24,325	$1,791
Biology	$23,264	$1,581
Psychology	$22,553	$2,345
Philosophy	$21,441	$997
English	$20,846	$1,477
Foreign Languages	$19,712	$1,291

There are also institutions that do not have faculty ranking, e.g., a junior college with less than a four-year curriculum and frequently with a vocational, instructional or practical purpose. The salary for full-time faculty members at such institutions is lower than those listed above. These institutions perform an invaluable educational service in society and are growing in enrollment and popularity by leaps and bounds. We have listed 14 of them here with the average faculty compensation and size.

AVERAGE ANNUAL COMPENSATION IN INSTITUTIONS WITHOUT FACULTY RANKING (1978-79)

School (State)	Average Compensation	Number of Full-time Faculty
Bank Street College of Education (New York)	$21,200	26
California Institute of the Arts (California)	$19,600	70
Fox Valley Technical Institute (Wisconsin)	$19,500	180
Enterprise State Junior College (Alabama)	$18,200	35
Hawkeye Institute of Technology (Iowa)	$17,100	111
Texas Chiropractic College (Texas)	$15,600	7
Ringling School of Art (Florida)	$15,500	19
Indiana Vocational Technical College (Indiana)	$15,400	29
National College of Business (South Dakota)	$14,000	28
Manhattan School of Music (New York)	$13,600	22
Muskegon Business College (Michigan)	$12,800	14
Katherine Gibbs School (Massachusetts)	$12,700	19
Bay State Junior College of Business (Massachusetts)	$12,300	15
Colorado Technical College (Colorado)	$10,100	18

ELEMENTARY AND SECONDARY EDUCATION

In 1978-79 the highest paid supervisor of schools for a major urban public school system was William Johnston of Los Angeles, who earned $62,797. The average salary for superintendents was $36,924. The highest paid high school principals in the United States were in

Anchorage, Alaska, where the salary was $44,900. The national average of the upper third of salaries for principals in the United States was: elementary $24,911; junior high/middle $26,554 and senior high $28,034.

The national average of the lowest third of salaries for principals was: elementary $16,917: junior high/middle $19,414 and senior high $21,231. The national average of the upper third of classroom teachers' salaries was $19,562, and the national average of the lowest third of classroom teachers' salaries was $10,062, ranging from $6,520 to $17,424. The midrange salary for classroom teachers was $14,982.

Below are salary figures for superintendents, classroom teachers (average) and principals of high schools (highest) in the public school systems of 15 cities across the country in 1978-79.

ANNUAL SALARIES FOR HIGH SCHOOL ADMINISTRATIVE AND TEACHING PERSONNEL IN SELECTED CITIES IN THE UNITED STATES (1978-79)

City and State Superintendent (Name) Salary	Classroom Teacher Average Salary	High School Principal Maximum Salary
Montgomery, Alabama (W.S. Garrett) $42,865	$13,038	$21,203
Anchorage, Alaska (Dr. John Peper) $53,000	$24,555	$44,900
Los Angeles, California (William J. Johnston) $62,797	$18,743	$32,344
San Diego, California (Thomas Goodman) $56,056	$18,052	$36,758
San Francisco, California (Robert F. Alioto) $49,000	$19,200	$30,175
Denver, Colorado (Joseph E. Brzeinski) $44,000	$18,795	$35,325
Miami, Florida (Dr. J. L. Jones) $54,600	$15,935	$34,666

ANNUAL SALARIES FOR HIGH SCHOOL ADMINISTRATIVE
AND TEACHING PERSONNEL IN SELECTED CITIES IN THE
UNITED STATES (1978-79)

City and State Superintendent (Name) Salary	Classroom Teacher Average Salary	High School Principal Maximum Salary
Hawaii (entire state) (Charles G. Clark) $42,500	$18,530	$32,586
Chicago, Illinois (Richard Martwick) $56,000	$17,800	$40,132
Boston, Massachusetts (Robert L. Wood) $50,000	$17,546	N. A.
Detroit, Michigan (Arthur Jefferson) $53,000	$18,511	$31,237
New York, New York (Frank J. Macchiarola, Chancellor) $59,000	$18,811	$36,750
Cleveland, Ohio (vacant) $44,500	$15,445	$31,950
Philadelphia, Pennsylvania (Michael P. Marcase) $50,000	$21,491	$35,760
Houston, Texas (Billy R. Reagan) $60,000	$13,904	$31,287

While private and public institutions of higher education pay within the same general range for faculty and staff, private secondary and elementary schools generally pay less than the public sector. In some cases the difference is striking, as the figures below reveal. The reasons for the lower pay levels in private schools are several: the schools in most cases have lower operating funds; they require lower qualifications from beginning teachers and only experience for advancement, rather than further education as in the public school system; and finally, in private boarding schools room and board is, of course, provided for the teachers.

SALARIES FOR BEGINNING TEACHERS IN PRIVATE SCHOOLS
(1978)
(no previous teaching experience)

School Type	Range	Median Salary
Girls' Day	$5,000-$9,750	$7,800
Girl's Boarding	$5,000-$9,000	$6,900
Boys' Day	$5,000-$10,900	$8,500
Boys' Boarding	$4,500-$8,400	$6,250
Coed Day	$4,500-$10,730	$8,000
Coed Boarding	$4,000-$10,270	$6,100

SALARIES FOR FACULTY MEMBERS IN
PRIVATE SCHOOLS (1978)

School Type	Median
Girls' Day	$10,200
Girls' Boarding	$9,443
Boys' Day	$12,250
Boys' Boarding	$8,550
Coed Day	$10,963
Coed Boarding	$9,040

MEDIAN SALARY FOR HEAD OF PRIVATE
COEDUCATIONAL SCHOOL, BY NUMBER OF PUPILS
IN SCHOOL (1978)

School	Median Salary
Coed under 101	
Day	$19,785
Boarding	$18,000
Coed 101-200	
Day	$21,100
Boarding	$20,000
Coed 201-350	
Day	$25,000
Boarding	$27,870
Coed 351-500	
Day	$26,500
Boarding	$26,950
Coed over 500	
Day	$31,000
Boarding	$30,465

As stated before, salaries for support personnel are usually set in line with the going rate of the area where the school district or school is located. However, in locales where the educational institution is the major source of employment, the salary levels tend to be lower. For example, a boarding school in a small rural town or a district high school that is the largest institution in an area can have a considerable negative influence on income levels. (This is also true at the higher education level where a large university is a major employer or where a small town survives largely because of the presence of such an institution.)

Listed here are some nationwide average salaries for administrative and other support personnel that have not already been discussed. These figures are for public secondary and elementary positions in 1978-79.

**ANNUAL AND HOURLY SALARIES FOR SELECTED ADMINIS-
TRATIVE AND SUPPORT PERSONNEL IN SECONDARY AND
ELEMENTARY SCHOOLS (1978-79)**

Position	Average Salary
Counselors	$17,698
Librarians	$15,727
School Nurses	$13,113
Secretaries/Stenographers	$7,772
Library Clerks	$6,449
	Salary per hour
Bus Drivers	$4.93
Custodians	$4.53
Teacher Aides:	
instructional	$3.77
noninstructional	$3.57
Cafeteria Workers	$3.48

FOUNDATIONS

There are 22,000 private foundations in the United States, and the 50 largest gave nearly $1 billion in grants during 1978. While the interests of major foundations are varied, one primary concern is to improve and broaden education. However, the foundations described in this section usually have other philanthropic activities, regardless of the degree of emphasis placed on educational support through grants and projects.

"Charity begins at home," as they say, and the rewards for those who dispense largess to education are substantial. Foundation officers have very handsome paychecks, including salary and benefits, usually far higher than those of the educators who work at the institutions receiving aid. Apparently, it is indeed better to give than to receive.

The selected income figures for the seven foundations shown below are based on the most recent statements available, which in general are for 1978. Changes in amounts and in the people in charge have occurred during the intervening time and allowance should be made for this.

ANNUAL COMPENSATION FOR HEADS OF SOME MAJOR FOUNDATIONS (1977-78)

Ford Foundation (1978): Assets $2,354,147,000.

Purpose: To advance the public welfare by trying to identify and contribute to the solution of important national and international problems. The Ford Foundation is the largest in assets and grants.

Post and Person	Employee Benefits	Salary
Chairman of Board		
Alexander Heard (part time)	$8,520	$28,394
President		
McGeorge Bundy (now Franklin Thomas)	$30,959	$117,090
Executive Vice President		
David E. Bell	$27,122	$100,590
Vice President*		
Roger Kennedy	$25,616	$93,334
Vice President		
Jon C. Hagler	$21,930	$92,490
Vice President		
Howard R. Dressner	$21,633	$77,090

*There are five other vice presidents whose salaries range from $67,500 to $81,078.

Johnson (Robert Wood) Foundation (1978): Assets $1,058,048,000.

Purpose: "Advancement of health in the United States...." The Johnson Foundation has the second largest assets of any private foundation in the U.S. In 1975 it was ninth highest in grants with $33,303,000 given.

ANNUAL COMPENSATION FOR HEADS OF
SOME MAJOR FOUNDATIONS (1977-78)

Post and Person	Salary
President	
David Rogers, M.D.	$96,724
Vice President	
Leighton E. Cluff	$70,999
Vice President	
Margaret E. Mahoney	$56,707
Assistant to President	
Walsh W. McDermott	$56,707

Lilly Endowment Inc. (1977): Assets $761,963,000.

Purpose: "To help maintain and strengthen those human institutions
...most likely to build and sustain...an open...and just society."

Post and Person	Salary
President	
Landrum R. Belling	$63,606
Vice President	
Robert A. Johnson	$58,590

Rockefeller Foundation (1978): Assets $739,889,103.

Purpose: "To promote the well-being of mankind throughout the
world."

Post and Person	Salary
President	
Richard W. Lyman*	$113,004
Vice President	
Ellsworth T. Neumann	$ 78,000
Associate Director	
Laurence Stifel	$ 62,667
Vice President	
Sterling Wortman	$ 78,000

*Appointed in 1980.

The Duke Endowment (1978): Assets $423,192,195.

Purpose: "To make provision in some measure for the needs of mankind along physical, mental and spiritual lines." The Duke Endowment
gives over $20 million a year in grants.

Post and Person*	Employee Benefits	Salary
Executive Director, Trustee		
Richard B. Henney	$1,695	$78,000

Secretary		
John F. Day	$2,315	$70,350
Treasurer		
Stewart Campbell	$2,295	$64,050
Assistant Secretary		
Ashley H. Gale	$2,143	$51,450
Investment Officer		
Frederich W. Bowman	$2,266	$60,350
Educational Affairs and Public Information		
Robert J. Sallstad	$7,366	$44,100

*The Duke Endowment has eight other officers or employees making over $30,000 a year. The endowment has 15 trustees, including Doris Duke. Except for Ms. Duke, who waives her annual fee, the trustees (including Mr. Henney, the executive director) each receive a fee of $63,737 per year. They meet 10 times a year to decide what grants will be authorized. The trustees, officers and employees of this foundation make collectively from salary, fees and benefits nearly $1.5 million a year, and their salaries and fees are proportionately higher than those paid by the other major foundations.

Carnegie Corporation of New York (1978): Assets $284,799,215.

Purpose: "The advancement and diffusion of knowledge and understanding among the people of the United States and certain parts of the British Overseas Commonwealth...."

Post and Person	Employee Benefits	Expense Allowance	Salary
President			
Alan Pifer	$22,536	$14,630	$108,562
Vice President			
David Z. Robinson	$16,794	$9,528	$81,170
Program Officer			
E. Alden Dunham	$13,292	$4,193	$54,655
Program Officer			
Frederick A. Mosher	$10,906	$13,962	$49,438

Rockefeller Brothers Fund (1978): Assets $182,391,632.

Purpose: "Interests include quality of life (religion, human values and cultural affairs) and education...."

Post and Person	Salary
Vice-Chairman, Trustee	
Dana S. Creel (part time)	$100,008
President, Trustee	
William M. Dietel (part time)	$85,008
Vice President	
Robert C. Bates	$58,167

The salaries of foundation officers are high in comparison to those of teachers, but not in comparison to many of the paychecks received in other professions, businesses and fields of endeavor. Education, like public service, yields relatively low financial rewards, but the importance of the profession for the general well-being of the country as a whole, and the subtlety and range of challenges in the work, draw many of the most talented and qualified people in the country. It is nevertheless ironic that those who make education their career usually earn less than their better students, that those who teach so often prosper less than the taught.

Part Four
BRASS TACKS JOBS

CHAPTER 10

Agriculture, Mining and Construction

TOGETHER, AGRICULTURE, MINING and construction accounted for nearly 10% of the national income of the United States in 1978, or $169 billion out of a total of around $1,746 billion. These essential and timeless industries cultivate and harvest the earth's natural resources, extract its mineral wealth and arrange its materials into homes, factories and offices. Throughout our history they have provided not only the basic necessities—food, shelter and clothing—but also employment and income for tens of millions of Americans. In fact, the nation's wealth rested, until very recently, predominantly on these basic industries.

AGRICULTURE

In 1880 the farm population of the United States was 21,973,000, or 44% of the total population; in 1970 it was 9,712,000, or only 3.3% of the population. As the farm population dwindled, so did the number of farms, from a high of 6,812,000 in 1935 to the present low of 2,680,000 in 1978. Similarly, total farm employment declined from 13,550,000 in 1910 to 3,350,000 in 1978. Meanwhile, the average size of an individually owned farm increased from 155 acres with a value of $31.16 per acre in 1935 to 446 acres with a value of $336 per acre in 1978. (The 1978 figures are for the farms in the East.) Farms are steadily becoming fewer, larger and less populated.

While the great majority of farms are still owned by individuals, the number of farms held by partnerships and corporations is increasing. This is particularly true in the West, where in 1978 over 23% of all farms were owned by corporations. Furthermore, 88% of all farms valued over $10 million are owned by corporations. The table below shows the average size of farms and type of ownership in the entire United States as compared with the West and the average value of farms by ownership.

AVERAGE FARM SIZE AND VALUE, BY TYPE OF OWNERSHIP (1978)

Ownership	Average Size U.S.	Average Size West	Average Value
Corporate	3,377.3 acres	6,938 acres	$857,000
Partnership	856.6 acres	2,136 acres	$285,000
Individual	446.8 acres	1,084 acres	$159,000

The continuously declining number of existing farms produce more and more agricultural goods, and every year agriculture accounts for a larger figure in the gross national income column. In 1935 gross farm income was $6 billion; in 1955 it was $14.5 billion; in 1976 it was $23.6 billion and just two years later it was $54.7 billion. Even adjusting for the declining value of the dollar, this represents an increase of nearly double in 38 years.

Although the income of full-time farm workers has also risen, it is still nowhere near that of other sectors in the American labor force. In fact the farmer income base has never come close to the national average for other occupations. The median annual income for all employees in agriculture was $5,488 in 1978, only 40% of the $12,800 median income for all U.S. industrial workers that year. This ratio has risen slightly in favor of agriculture over the years, but not substantially. In 1900 the average annual earnings for agricultural workers were $178 per year, or 37% of the $478 annual income of manufacturing workers. In 1940 the average agricultural income was $407, or 30% of the $1,432 earned in manufacturing; 20 years later the average agricultural earnings were $1,658, compared with $5,352 for manufacturing, again 30%. In 1970 agricultural workers earned an average $3,063, which was 38% of the $8,150 annual income for those in manufacturing.

Hourly farm wage rates further emphasize that agriculture is a tough way to earn your living. The average hourly wage for all hired farm workers in 1978 was $3.07, compared to $6.47 for all manufacturing workers. In that year the highest average wage paid in agriculture was the $4.39 per hour earned by supervisors. Comparable wage earners in manufacturing made much more; a supervisor in a machine tool plant, for example, made about $8.50 per hour.

Farm labor is mostly nonunion, unskilled and fluctuates in demand according to weather, seasons and numerous special agricultural techniques and conditions. In the related field of forestry, where there is a constant need for manpower due to the regularity of timber output, the average hourly wage in logging camps was $7.48 in 1978. This is true even though the per capita use of timber products in the United States (including firewood) has declined from 156.9 cubic feet in 1900 to 62.1 cubic feet in 1970. The per capita consumption of firewood has declined the most, from 63.1 cubic feet in 1900 to 2.6 cubic feet in 1970. (However, firewood use is growing again with the scarcity and rising cost of heating oil and other petroleum products.) Only pulp products, mainly packaging materials, paper and newsprint, and lumber (softwood and hardwood) for veneers and plywoods have increased substantially in recent years.

In contrast to the plight of farm workers, the proprietors of farms, whether individuals, partnerships or corporations, are prospering as the size of farms increases, as mechanization becomes virtually omnipresent and as small uneconomical farms are absorbed into larger holdings. In fact, when the acreage is large enough, great wealth can be amassed from agriculture, whether the owner is one person or an agribusiness corporation.

Income figures for specific farm owners are difficult to obtain, but the information on farm incomes listed on 1975 tax returns is very revealing. That year there were about 2.6 million individual returns declaring farm incomes up to $40,000 and a substantial number declaring a loss. Another 310,000 returns stated gross farm incomes between $40,000 and $100,000 for the year, and 111,800 returns declared gross farm incomes of over $100,000.

The same technological and mechanical advances that have increased farm size have diminished the farm population and the need for human labor. They have also created the vast farm implement and machinery business, revolutionized the fertilizer and feed industry and promoted the growth of a huge corporate farm structure, known as agribusiness. The end result has been an enormous increase in production, albeit, in the opinion of many, at a sacrifice in the quality and taste of food products.

Farming today is truly big business. Some of the major agribusiness firms, their principal agricultural product and the names and incomes (salaries plus bonuses) of their top management people are shown below. These firms of course have other business interests as well as agriculture.

INCOMES OF TOP EXECUTIVES OF AGRICULTURE-RELATED BUSINESSES (1978)

Type of Business Company and Executive	Total Income	1978 Net Profit (millions)
Farm Machinery		
International Harvester		$187
Archie R. McCardell, President	$1,907,000	
Brooks McCormick, Chairman	$436,000	
Deere		$265
William A. Hewitt, Chairman	$584,000	
Ellwood F. Curtis, Vice-Chairman	$434,000	
Robert A. Hanson, President	$334,000	
Caterpillar Tractor		$566
Lee L. Morgan, Chairman	$345,000	
Robert E. Gilmore, President	$263,000	
Chemicals		
Du Pont		$786
I.S. Shapiro, Chairman	$843,000	
E.R. Kane, President	$672,000	
R.E Heckert, Senior Vice President	$509,000	
Dow Chemical		$575
Earl B. Barnes, Executive Vice President	$507,000	

C.B. Branch, Honorary Chairman	$417,000	
Celanese		$112
John D. Macomber, President	$430,000	
John W. Brooks, Chairman	$360,000	
Food Processing		
Ralston Purina		$155
R. Hal Dean, Chairman	$1,035,000	
Warren M. Shapleigh, Vice-Chairman	$621,000	
Borden		$136
Augustine R. Marusi, Chairman	$649,000	
Eugene J. Sullivan, President	$472,000	

MINING AND PETROLEUM

Oil, natural gas and coal in various forms are extracted from the earth to feed the ever growing appetite of modern industrial society. As these three major energy sources become more scarce, they are discussed obsessively, worried about, sought for and even threaten to result in war. Without them, the modern world would collapse or be so altered as to utterly change the nature of its economy.

Other essential products of mining are ferrous and nonferrous ores and stone, which are fashioned into the materials that are required to construct the buildings, manufactured goods, transportation systems and other vital elements of the economy. Yet, despite the central importance of mineral and petroleum products, the number of people employed actually mining and drilling for them is surprisingly small. Together, the mining and petroleum industries had only 623,000 employees in 1970, roughly one-sixth as many as agriculture. By 1978 the number of employees had risen to 850,000, of which 405,000, or about one-half, worked for petroleum and natural gas companies. The latter figure is about the same as the number of physicians, a comparison indicative of the small size of this labor force.

It is interesting that the number of actual production workers (as distinct from total employees) in the mining and petroleum industries declined from 871,000 in 1947 to a low of 455,000 in 1971. After that year the number began to rise due to increased coal production and oil exploration efforts, and by 1978 there were 628,000 production workers, accounting for over 70% of the total employees in these fields. The same year management made up 8%, professional and technical workers 12% and clerical and kindred workers the rest of this work force. Approximately one-half of these workers belonged to unions, but in most cases the earnings of union and nonunion workers were comparable. The 1978 average earnings for all workers in all of these categories are presented below. These averages exclude nonsalary benefits, including medical and unemployment insurance, vacations and pensions, which may add 20 to 35% to the total wage value. Such benefits are frequently available to both union and nonunion employees.

AVERAGE EARNINGS IN MINING AND PETROLEUM OCCUPATIONS (DECEMBER 1978)

Occupational Category	Average Hourly Wage	Average Weekly Work Hours	Average Weekly Earnings
Bituminous Coal and Lignite Mining	$9.79	41.2	$403.35
Coal Mining (general)	$9.77	41.1	$401.55
Copper Ores Mining	$9.01	43	$387.43
Iron Ores Mining	$8.93	42.9	$383.10
Metal Mining (general)	$8.76	42.2	$369.67
Crude Petroleum, Natural Gas and Gas Liquids Extraction	$8.27	41.5	$343.21
Oil and Gas Extraction (general)	$7.27	45.1	$327.80
Oil and Gas Field Services	$6.90	46.6	$321.54
Nonmetallic Minerals (except fuels) Mining	$6.51	44.4	$291.71
Crushed and Broken Stone Mining	$6.31	45.1	$284.58

Production workers in the above occupations earn surprisingly good wages, certainly higher than the national average and often higher than those of teachers. It's only fair to add that most of these workers are not employed 52 weeks a year. Seasonal fluctuation, however, is less here than in agriculture and construction.

The average wages or salaries of miners have always been somewhat higher than those of industrial workers, usually double the average agricultural wages, and slightly more than wages in construction trades. In 1900 the average annual income of mining workers was

$479; over the next 50 years it rose to $3,460 and by 1970 reached $9,262. Just nine years later, in 1979, the average climbed to $16,437.

Since the days of John D. Rockefeller, "big oil" and the men who run it have been the object of criticism and controversy. Today, as the price of oil and the profits of the oil companies continue to rise at unprecedented rates, people both in and out of government are scrutinizing the financial records of the major oil firms more than ever before. A corollary of this scrutiny would be to examine just how much some of these firms pay their top management people. Despite the extent of their economic influence, executives of the major oil companies are not the highest paid group in American business. Nevertheless, they do very well, as the following table shows. Incomes listed are for salaries plus bonuses.

INCOMES OF THE TOP EXECUTIVES OF 10 MAJOR OIL COMPANIES (1978)

Company and Executive	Total Income	1978 Net Profit (millions)
Mobil		$1,100
Rawleigh W. Warner, Jr., Chairman	$935,000	
William P. Tavoulareas, President	$801,000	
Texaco		$852
Maurice F. Granville, Chairman	$812,000	
John K. McKinley, President	$483,000	
Exxon		$2,800
C. C. Garvin, Jr., Chairman	$768,000	
H. C. Kauffmann, President	$507,000	
Union Oil of California		$382
Fred L. Hartley, Chairman and President	$804,000	
Claude S. Brinegar, Senior Vice President	$316,000	
Ray A. Burke, Senior Vice President	$295,000	
Atlantic Richfield		$804
Robert O. Anderson, Chairman	$720,000	
T. F. Bradshaw, President	$610,000	
Louis F. Davis, Vice-Chairman	$537,000	
Continental Oil		$451
Howard W. Blauvelt, Chairman*	$550,000	

INCOMES OF THE TOP EXECUTIVES OF 10 MAJOR OIL COMPANIES (1978)

Company and Executive	Total Income	1978 Net Profit (millions)
Ralph E. Bailey, Deputy Chairman*	$377,000	
John E. Kircher, Deputy Chairman	$334,000	
Gulf Oil		$791
Jerry McAfee, Chairman	$549,000	
James E. Lee, President	$440,000	
Shell Oil		$814
John F. Bookout, President	$538,000	
Sun		$365
H. Robert Sharbaugh, Chairman	$427,000	
Theodore A. Burtis, President	$399,000	
Standard Oil of California		$1,100
H. J. Haynes, Chairman	$377,000**	
J. R. Grey, President	$270,000**	
G. M. Keller, Vice-Chairman	$270,000**	

*Howard W. Blauvelt retired on April 2, 1979, at which time Ralph E. Bailey became chairman.
**1978 bonuses not included.

Three of the major mining corporations with their net profits and the incomes (salaries plus bonuses) of their top executives are listed below. There are many other huge industrial corporations that are directly dependent on the mining and petroleum industries for much of their business, but because they are so diversified in manufacturing and distribution, they are included in the chapter on industry.

INCOMES OF TOP EXECUTIVES OF THREE MINING CORPORATIONS (1978)

Company and Executive	Total Income	1978 Net Profit (millions)
Kaiser Aluminum and Chemical		$146
Cornell C. Maier, Chairman and President	$500,000	
Ira R. Davidson, Vice President	$220,000	
Reynolds Metals		$118
David P. Reynolds, Chairman	$399,000	
John E. Blomquist, Executive Vice President	$334,000	

Kennecott Copper		$5
Frank R. Milliken, Chairman	$385,000	
William H. Wendel, President	$306,000	

CONSTRUCTION

Construction work is one of the most volatile occupations in the United States. Weather, the fluctuations of the economy, and the availability of capital, equipment and materials all influence the amount of construction work available at any given time. While the national average hourly wage for all construction workers in December 1978 ($8.91) was higher than that for all mining workers ($8.05) and all manufacturing workers ($6.47), the average annual wage ($14,392) was lower than in either mining ($16,437) or manufacturing ($15,099).

In 1978 there were approximately 3.9 million people employed in contract construction. An additional estimated 1.6 million workers, either self-employed or employed directly by federal, state or local governments, built and repaired the nation's highway system. The contract construction industry itself consists of general residential and industrial construction, special trades such as plumbing, electrical and air conditioning contractors, and heavy construction—dams, bridges, roads, etc. Three out of four construction employees are blue-collar workers; 12% of the remainder are management and the rest are clerical or kindred workers.

The number of construction workers in the United States has risen slowly but steadily, from 3.5 million in 1970 to the present 3.9 million. Their earnings have gone from an average of $593 per year in 1900 to $3,333 in 1950, $9,137 in 1970 and to $14,392 at present. Fifty-five percent of construction workers are in skilled crafts and special trades— bricklaying, plumbing, carpentry and so forth. This is the highest proportion of skilled craftsmen in any industry, which partially accounts for the high average hourly wage compared with other major segments of the economy. Laborers and semiskilled workers—truck drivers, welders, etc.—account for the rest. Most of the 12% who are managers are self-employed.

Many construction workers are unionized, particularly in the crafts. In 1978 the number of unionized workers totaled about 2.95 million, or more than two-thirds of the industry's work force. Union and nonunion wages are roughly equivalent, although nonmonetary benefits may be higher for union members.

Finally, it must be remembered that by putting in overtime workers in construction can substantially raise their incomes. This is particularly true among craftsmen, who can work in small groups or alone. The average salaries listed here are for all construction workers regardless of union status and excluding the value of benefits.

AVERAGE EARNINGS IN CONSTRUCTION
OCCUPATIONS (DECEMBER 1978)

Occupational Category	Average Hourly Wage	Average Weekly Work Hours	Average Weekly Earnings
Electrical Work (electrician)	$10.65	38.7	$412.16
Plumbing, Heating and Air Conditioning	$9.60	38.2	$366.72
Special Trade Work (general)	$9.55	36.5	$348.58
Masonry, Stonework and Plastering	$9.32	33.8	$315.02
Nonresidential Building Construction	$8.99	36.4	$327.24
Painting, Paperhanging, Decorating	$8.89	35.3	$313.82
Heavy Construction (except highway)	$8.55	39.7	$339.44
Carpentry and Flooring	$8.44	36.0	$303.84
Roofing and Sheet Metal Work	$8.27	32.2	$266.29
Highway and Street Construction	$8.24	41.2	$312.30
Residential Building Construction	$7.76	33.7	$277.03

A supervisor of construction and maintenance work earns an average annual salary of $24,000 when he is in charge of 20 or more people. A supervisor of carpentry, masonry or painting earns an average of $22,300 a year when he supervises a similar number and an electrician supervisor earns an average of $24,300.

Here are four of the major building materials and contract construction corporations in the country with the incomes (salaries plus bonuses) of their top executives.

INCOMES OF TOP EXECUTIVES OF FOUR MAJOR BUILDING MATERIALS AND CONSTRUCTION CORPORATIONS (1978)

Corporation and Executive	Total Income	1978 Net Profit (millions)
Boise Cascade		$136
John B. Fery, Chairman	$413,000	
Jon H. Miller, President	$281,000	
Turner Construction		$3.6
W. B. Shaw, Chairman, President and CEO*	$228,000	
U.S. Homes		$30
G. R. Odom, President and CEO	$225,000	
Weyerhaeuser		$413
George H. Weyerhaeuser, President	$417,000	
Charles W. Bingham, Senior Vice President	$250,000	

*CEO: Chief Executive Officer.

The construction business has grown rapidly in the United States to become one of the major contributors to the nation's income, outpacing agriculture, mining, all manufacturing industries taken separately, all of transportation, communications and utilities and all services taken separately, including even health care. Construction is also one of the principal and most accurate indicators of the state of the national economy. Citizens invest in new homes and commercial construction when business is prospering. When it is not, the number of new construction starts is one of the first things to falter. So while the incomes of construction workers may be among the very highest, they are also among the least secure.

CHAPTER 11
Industry and Manufacturing

A MERICANS HAVE ALWAYS had a love-hate relationship with "big business." To many, industry is synonymous with free enterprise, wealth, power, and the growth of the United States into the greatest industrial and economic force in the history of the world. To others, industry is synonymous with greed, unchecked power and riches, social injustice, pollution and every other evil imaginable. Even those who basically take a benign view have always harbored a certain amount of suspicion and skepticism about industry, with its history of huge trusts and monopolies, "robber barons," labor wars, strikebreaking, pitched battles with unions and grim industrial landscapes. Most of us find the salaries of business managers and executives almost as intriguing and aggravating as those of sports superstars and entertainment figures. Sometimes, although rarely, corporate executive earnings equal or, even more rarely, exceed those of the heroes of the playing field or the silver screen.

For example, from 1928 to 1933 G.W. Hill of the American Tobacco Company declared that he had earned $785,000 in salary. During the same period, but only revealed by a later congressional investigation, he had also gotten $3,181,120 in "other compensation." In an even more blatant case, E.G. Grace of Bethlehem Steel announced that he had received $12,000 per annum in salary from 1928 to 1930. It was later uncovered that during the same period he had received $2,470,789 in "other compensation." Of this total, $1,623,753 was for the year of the great crash—1929—alone. Since in those days the dollar was worth a little over four times what it is now, both Messrs. Hill and Grace were definitely in the superstar category, higher than Chaplin then and higher than Arnold Palmer now, even higher than Steve McQueen now.

Today the income tax structure, the watchful public eye, the power of the labor unions, federal regulatory commissions, alert stockholders, the realities of the marketplace and even public opinion have curbed the salaries—or at least the take-home pay—at the top of industry. The following lists show 25 of the highest paid executives in industry in 1978, the average salaries of other executives and then for comparison the salaries of some of the most powerful labor union leaders in the country. As can be seen in the chart on the next page, top executive earnings by no means always reflect the sales and size of the company that is paying them. This listing includes executives of several companies that do not fall into the manufacturing category in order to give a picture of the top money makers in all of corporate America.

Compensation for top executives—and some middle-level people— often combines salary, bonus and various types of performance payments. There are also other "perks" that cannot be shown in dollars and cents. While they do not equal those of the President, they do frequently include company transportation, company counsel on preparation of personal income tax returns, company meals and related expense account perks such as company-paid vacations.

The average compensation, according to amount of sales and type of product, for chairman of corporations who are also the chief executive officers (CEOs) varies widely, as illustrated in the list on p. 182.

25 TOP CORPORATE EXECUTIVE EARNERS (1978)

Executive	Company	Total Compensation (Salary Plus Bonus and Other Payments)	1978 Corporate Sales (millions)	Profits (millions)
1. David Mahoney, Chairman	Norton Simon	$2,037,000	$2,429	$116
2. Archie R. McCardell, President	International Harvester	$1,907,000	$6,664	$187
3. Harry J. Gray, Chairman	United Technologies	$1,683,000	$6,265	$234
4. T. A. Wilson, Chairman	Boeing	$1,227,000	$5,463	$323
5. M. T. Stamper, President	Boeing	$1,215,000	$5,463	$323
6. Willard F. Rockwell Jr., Chairman	Rockwell International	$1,165,000	$5,669	$177
7. Edwin A. Gee, President	International Paper	$1,109,000	$4,150	$234
8. Elton H. Rule, President	American Broadcasting	$1,107,000	$1,784	$128
9. William A. Marquard, President	American Standard	$1,099,000	$2,111	$101
10. Henry Ford II, Chairman	Ford Motor	$1,056,000	$42,784	$1,589
11. R. Hal Dean, Chairman	Ralston Purina	$1,035,000	$4,058	$155
12. Philip Caldwell, Vice-Chairman and President	Ford Motor	$1,030,000	$42,784	$1,589
13. Robert Anderson, President	Rockwell International	$1,020,000	$5,669	$177
14. J. Edward Lundy, Executive Vice President	Ford Motor	$999,000	$42,784	$1,589
15. Thomas A. Murphy, Chairman	General Motors	$975,000	$63,221	$3,500
16. Rawleigh Warner, Jr., Chairman	Mobil	$935,000	$36,684	$1,100
17. Elliott M. Estes, President	General Motors	$925,000	$63,221	$3,500
18. Frank T. Cary, Chairman	IBM	$892,000	$21,076	$3,111
19. C. Peter McColough, Chairman	Xerox	$870,000	$5,902	$465
20. W. O. Beers, Chairman	Kraft	$865,000	$5,670	$184
21. Edward G. Harness, Chairman	Procter & Gamble	$852,000	$8,100	$512
22. Richard L. Terrell, Vice-Chairman	General Motors	$850,000	$63,221	$3,500
23. Irving S. Shapiro, Chairman	Du Pont	$843,000	$10,584	$786
24. William F. Laporte, Chairman	American Home Products	$830,000	$3,277	$348
25. Fred L. Hartley, Chairman & Pres.	Union Oil of California	$804,000	$6,340	$382

182

AVERAGE COMPENSATION FOR CHAIRMEN/CEOs (1977-78)

Sales (in millions)	Durable Goods	Nondurable Goods	Wholesale and Retail Trade	Utilities
$50 to $100	$120,800	$102,200	$102,000	$85,200
$100 to $200	$152,200	$146,300	$115,600	$99,800
$200 to $500	$207,500	$171,300	$137,800	$154,300
$500 to $1,000	$266,000	$247,500	$159,900	$192,000
over $1,000*	$385,500	$353,500	$276,000	$252,000

*The average total compensation for petroleum corporation chairmen and chief executive officers with sales of $1 billion and over is $334,600.

Companies that pay their top executives a bonus, which include about 70% of all large industrial enterprises, pay about 23% more in total compensation than those who don't. Bonus-paying companies with sales of over $5 billion pay their top executives an average of $499,400 a year, and one-quarter of them pay the top man, in combined bonus, salary and performance payments, over $627,400 a year. (This puts them in the range with top basketball players.)

In small companies with sales of $10 million or less, the high average salary for the chief executive officer is between $62,200 and $78,100 in durable goods and slightly less in nondurable goods industries.

Below are some average salaries for chief executive officers of medium-sized companies in nonmanufacturing businesses. These are the average salaries for the position of chief executive officer only and include bonuses to give total compensation. The majority of the companies are in the $50 to $100 million sales range except where noted.

AVERAGE ANNUAL COMPENSATION FOR CEOs IN MEDIUM-SIZED COMPANIES (1977-78)

Type of Company	Average Annual Total Compensation
Durable Goods	
Nonferrous Metals (over $100 million)	$229,200
Glass and Allied Products	$212,000
Iron and Steel Foundries (over $50 million)	$181,400
Iron and Steel Producers (over $200 million)	$173,500
Tools and Hardware	$155,200
Electrical Equipment	$141,200
Office Machinery and Equipment	$126,800
Fabricated Metal Products	$124,400

Aerospace	$119,500
Light Machinery	$117,700
Heavy Machinery	$114,800
Furniture Manufacturing	$111,500
Instruments and Allied Products	$110,400
Transportation Equipment	$105,500
Building Materials and Equipment	$102,100
Automotive Parts and Accessories	$95,900

Nondurable Goods

Drugs and Medicines ($200 million to $500 million)	$247,000
Publishing (over $100 million)	$202,100
Paper and Allied Products (over $100 million)	$188,900
Textiles-Apparel (over $100 million)	$179,400
Textiles-Fashion (over $100 million)	$178,900
Printing (over $100 million)	$177,800
Cosmetics and Toilet Preparations (over $100 million)	$165,500
Food, Beverage, Tobacco and Kindred Products ($200 to $500 million)	$149,500
Leather and Leather Products	$135,700
Rubber and Allied Products	$125,400

Others*

Airlines and Transportation (over $200 million)	$217,600
Insurance (over $500 million)	$183,100
Finance Companies (over $100 million)	$179,200
Utilities-Public, Communications (over $100 million)	$165,700
Airlines and Transportation ($100 to $200 million)	$126,400
Banks and Trust Companies ($1 billion to $2 billion)	$118,500
Utilities-Gas and Electric ($200 to $500 million)	$115,400
Petroleum, Crude Oil and Natural Gas	$100,000
Retail Trade	$98,800
Wholesale Trade	$98,400
Construction	$94,600
Life Insurance ($500 million to $1 billion)	$76,500
Banks and Trust Companies ($100 million to $300 million)	$69,400

Note: Many of the above figures are based in part on studies made by the American Management Associations Executive Compensation Service.

*Under this category are found salaries for executives in businesses that are covered in other chapters. However, to present a consistent, comparative view of total executive compensation in American companies, they are included here.

The number of workers involved in the manufacturing of both durable and nondurable goods has changed very little in the past 25 years. In 1955 there was a total of 16,882,000 employees, of which 13,228,000 were production workers. In 1979 the total number was 20,744,000, of which 14,887,000 were production workers. Salaries and wages of production workers, however, rose significantly during that period. In 1955 the average hourly wage was $1.85 and the average weekly income was $75.30. In April 1979 the average hourly wage was $6.55 and the average weekly income was $271.17.

Going further back, the annual average income for a manufacturing worker in 1940 was $1,432; by 1970 it had climbed to $8,150 and nearly doubled over the next nine years, reaching $15,099 in 1979.

Approximately 9.7 million manufacturing employees, or 46%, were members of unions in 1978, representing a very slight increase over the 44.3% who were union members in 1970. A list of leaders of major unions and their salaries in 1977 follows. These are the latest figures available for all union leaders, and allowance must be made for changes in the past year. For example, after the late George Meany's retirement in 1979, Lane Kirkland assumed the leadership of the AFL-CIO at a salary of $110,000 a year.

The list ot top union leaders' salaries included on the next four pages does not take into account one important factor in the incomes of some union executives. It is possible for one man to hold a number of jobs in different local unions. Perhaps the highest paid union leader using this technique is Harold Friedman. He is president of a local of the Bakery and Confectionary Workers Union, as well as a local of the Teamsters Union. In addition, he has a position on the national executive board of a bakery union. His combined income from these three jobs is $337,182.

Since it is not illegal to hold paid office simultaneously in several unions, many labor leaders have done so to increase their incomes.

The paychecks for workers in industry are as varied as the almost innumerable different tasks and jobs they perform. Listed on p. 189 are a selection of jobs, their average hourly and weekly earnings and the average hours a week worked in December 1978. The figures are averages for the jobs, whether union or not, and once again the value of benefits are not included, nor is overtime computed. In some cases annual salary for supervisory or technical jobs is also included.

HOW MUCH THE TOP LABOR LEADERS WERE PAID IN 1977

Union and Leaders	Salary	Allowance	Expenses	Total
AFL-CIO				
George Meany, President	$90,000	$—	$921	$90,921
Lane Kirkland, Secretary-Treasurer	$60,000	$—	$11,583	$71,583
AFL-CIO Building Trades Dept.				
Robert Georgine, President	$56,058	$14,600	$7,311	$77,969
AFL-CIO Industrial Union Dept.				
Jacob Clayman, President	$55,000	$—	N. A.	$55,000
Auto Workers				
Douglas Fraser, President	$49,929	$—	$21,333	$71,282
Emil Mazey, Secretary-Treasurer	$46,731	$—	$5,573	$52,394
Bricklayers				
Thomas F. Murphy, President	$48,558	$18,250	$3,870	$70,579
John T. Joyce, Secretary	$43,186	$18,750	$7,761	$69,198
Carpenters				
William Sidell, President	$66,250	$8,380	$858	$75,488
William Konyha, First Vice President	$55,650	$10,175	$2,596	$68,421
Clothing & Textile Workers				
Murray H. Finley, President	$50,000	$—	$11,111	$61,111
Jacob Sheinkman, Secretary-Treasurer	$50,000	$—	$9,220	$59,220
Communications Workers				
Glenn F. Watts, President	$52,335	$—	$10,634	$62,969
Gus Cramer, Executive Vice President	$40,955	$—	$18,708	$59,663
Electrical Workers (IBEW)				
Charles H. Pillard, President	$77,500	$—	$2,998	$80,498
Ralph A. Leigon, Secretary	$67,500	$—	$8,092	$75,592
Electrical Workers (IUE)				
David J. Fitzmaurice, President	$34,461	$—	$6,836	$41,297
George Hutchens, Secretary-Treasurer	$28,102	$—	$7,968	$36,070

HOW MUCH THE TOP LABOR LEADERS WERE PAID IN 1977

Union and Leaders	Salary	Allowance	Expenses	Total
Hotel, Restaurant Employees				
Edward T. Hanley, President	$87,500	$22,780	$16,671	$126,951
John Gibson, Secretary-Treasurer	$74,500	$22,780	$19,777	$117,057
Iron Workers				
John H. Lyons, President	$64,242	$25,970	$10,143	$100,355
Juel D. Drake, Secretary	$48,216	$25,020	$3,190	$76,426
Laborers				
Angelo Fosco, President	$100,000	$—	$9,776	$109,776
W. Vernie Reed, Secretary-Treasurer	$95,000	$—	$13,483	$108,483
Ladies' Garment Workers				
Sol. C. Chaikin, President	$62,400	$—	N. A.	$62,400
Longshoreman (ILA)				
Thomas W. Gleason, President	$60,000	$14,000	$1,948	$75,948
Machinists				
William W. Winpisinger, President	$50,000	$—	$11,709	$61,709
Eugene Glover, Secretary-Treasurer	$51,000	$—	$7,055	$58,055
Maritime Union				
Shannon J. Wall, President	$78,470	$5,200	$7,728	$91,398
Mel Barisic, Secretary-Treasurer	$53,803	$5,200	$6,886	$65,889
Meat Cutters				
Patrick E. Gorman, Chairman	$72,609	$—	$17,083	$89,692
Harry Poole, President	$67,401	$—	$8,975	$76,376
Sam Talarico, Secretary-Treasurer	$59,116	$—	$38,494	$97,610
Mine Workers				
Arnold Miller, President	$45,880	$—	$20,593	$66,473
Oil, Chemical, & Atomic Workers				
A. F. Grospiron, President	$45,160	$1,575	$14,875	$61,610
A. C. Sabatine, Secretary-Treasurer	$39,140	$1,253	$19,976	$60,369
Operating Engineers				
J. C. Turner, President	$94,050	$30,100	$6,004	$130,154
Russell Conlon, Secretary-Treasurer	$66,357	$20,200	$4,305	$90,862

Painters				
S. Frank Raftery, President	$62,099	$14,560	$10,671	$87,330
Robert Petersdorf, Secretary-Treasurer	$46,574	$14,560	$26,535	$87,669
Plumbers				
Martin J. Ward, President	$66,000	$34,370	—	$100,370
Joseph A. Walsh, Secretary-Treasurer	$55,000	$28,870	$825	$84,695
Postal Workers				
Emmet Andrews, President	$58,000	$—	$12,000	$70,000
Railway & Airline Clerks				
Fred J. Kroll, President	$70,000	$—	$34,378	$104,378
D. A. Bobo, Secretary-Treasurer	$47,000	$—	$19,157	$66,157
Retail Clerks				
William H. Wynn, President	$110,000	$13,000	N. A.	$123,000
Thomas G. Whaley, Secretary-Treasurer	$66,000	$10,400	N. A.	$76,400
Retail, Wholesale Union				
Alvin E. Heaps, President	$48,413	$—	$14,409	$62,822
Rubber Workers				
Peter Bommarito, President	$36,374	$—	$7,036	$43,410
Seafarers				
Paul Hall, President	$109,108	$—	$16,591	$125,699
Service Employees				
George Hardy, President	$69,628	$—	$11,207	$80,835
Anthony Weinlein, Secretary-Treasurer	$57,151	$—	$6,647	$63,798
Sheet Metal Workers				
Edward J. Carlough, President	$62,500	$26,950	$576	$90,026
Edward F. Carlough, President emeritus	$62,500	$23,200	$550	$86,250
David S. Turner, Secretary-Treasurer	$57,500	$27,700	$—	$85,200
State, County & Municipal Employees				
Jerry Wurf, President	$68,959	$7,200	$5,346	$81,505
William Lucy, Secretary-Treasurer	$54,960	$5,760	$3,965	$64,685
Steelworkers				
Lloyd McBride, President	$75,000	$—	N. A.	$75,000

HOW MUCH THE TOP LABOR LEADERS WERE PAID IN 1977

Union and Leaders	Salary	Allowance	Expenses	Total
Frank McKee, Treasurer	$55,000	$—	N. A.	$55,000
Lynn Williams, Secretary	$55,000	$—	N. A.	$55,000
Teachers (AFT/UFT)				
Albert Shanker, President	$71,050	$—	$27,236	$98,286
Teamsters				
Frank E. Fitzsimmons, President	$156,250	$3,660	$9,543	$169,453
Ray Schoessling, Secretary-Treasurer	$125,000	$3,660	$4,407	$133,067
Transportation Union (UTU)				
Al H. Chesser, President	$66,369	$—	$2,876	$69,245

AVERAGE WAGES IN SELECTED MANUFACTURING
PRODUCTION JOBS (1977-78)

Occupational Category	Average Hourly Wage	Average Weekly Hours	Average Weekly Earnings
All Manufacturing	$6.47	41.4	$267.86
Manufacturing (durable goods)	$6.92	42.3	$292.72
Furniture and Fixtures	$4.86	40.1	$194.89
Mattresses and Bedsprings	$5.15	37.9	$195.19
Stone, Clay and Glass Products	$6.57	42.2	$277.25
Glass Containers	$7.03	41.7	$293.15
Cement, Hydraulic	$8.98	42.4	$380.75
Pottery and Related Products	$5.41	39.8	$215.32
Primary Metal Industries	$8.56	42.5	$363.80
Blast Furnace and Steel Products	$9.82	41.8	$408.51
(Plant of Factory Manager)	($36,000 per year median salary)		
Primary Nonferrous Metals	$8.97	42.0	$376.74
Nonferrous Rolling and Drawing	$7.67	43.5	$333.65
Aluminum Sheet, Plate and Foil	$9.31	43.8	$404.05
Fabricated Metal Products	$6.62	42.2	$279.36
Metal Cans and Shipping Containers	$8.39	42.9	$359.93
Screw Machine Products	$5.83	43.1	$251.27
Machinery, except Electrical	$7.13	43.6	$310.87
Engines and Turbines	$8.49	43.4	$368.47
Internal Combustion Engines	$8.69	44.1	$383.23
Farm Machinery and Equipment	$8.14	43.8	$351.53
Industrial Trucks and Tractors	$6.94	42.8	$297.03
Machine Tools, Metal Cutting Types	$7.64	46.1	$352.20
General Industrial Machinery	$7.10	42.8	$303.88
Electric and Electronic Equipment	$6.10	41.3	$251.93
Household Appliances	$6.07	40.6	$246.44

AVERAGE WAGES IN SELECTED MANUFACTURING
PRODUCTION JOBS (1977-78)

Occupational Category	Average Hourly Wage	Average Weekly Hours	Average Weekly Earnings
Radio and TV Receiving Equipment	$5.61	38.8	$217.67
Telephone and Telegraph Apparatus	$7.07	39.5	$294.11
Radio and TV Communication Equipment	$6.81	42.9	$292.15
(General Supervision)	($24,200 per year median salary)		
Engine Electrical Equipment	$8.23	42.6	$350.60
Motor Vehicles and Equipment	$9.03	46.2	$417.19
Motor Vehicles and Car Bodies	$9.56	47.2	$451.23
Aircraft and Parts	$7.95	43.6	$346.62
Guided Missiles, Space Vehicles and Parts	$7.88	44.8	$353.02
Engineering and Scientific Instruments	$6.28	43.8	$275.06
Medical Instruments and Supplies	$5.11	40.5	$206.96
Watches, Clocks and Watchcases	$4.63	39.7	$183.81
Meat Packing Plants	$7.30	42.1	$307.33
Dairy Products	$6.05	41.5	$251.08
Canned Specialties	$6.06	42.2	$255.73
Grain Mill Products	$6.61	45.0	$297.45
Bakery Products	$6.23	38.9	$242.35
Confectionary Products	$4.98	38.9	$193.72
Beverages	$7.17	40.8	$292.54
Tobacco Manufacturers	$6.32	38.8	$245.22
Cigarettes	$7.58	39.2	$297.14
Textile Mill Products	$4.48	40.8	$182.78
Apparel and Other Textile Products	$4.07	35.8	$145.71
Paper and Allied Products	$6.79	43.4	$294.69
Printing and Publishing	$6.68	38.2	$255.18
Book Printing	$6.17	40.3	$248.65

Chemicals and Allied			
Products	$7.28	42.3	$307.94
Drugs	$6.61	42.2	$278.94
Paints and Allied Products	$6.50	41.6	$270.40
Petroleum and Coal Products	$8.86	43.8	$388.07
Petroleum Refining	$9.50	43.3	$411.35
Leather and Leather Products	$4.01	37.1	$148.77
Railroad Transportation	$8.27	45.1	$359.75
Transportation and Public			
Utilities	$7.83	40.2	$314.77
Wholesale and Retail Trade	$4.80	33.1	$158.88
Finance, Real Estate and			
Insurance	$5.07	37.1	$184.04
Banking	$4.33	36.3	$157.18

The days of John D. Rockefeller, G.W. Hill, E.G. Grace and the other titans of industry may have passed in the United States. Yet, vast fortunes still can be made, although no longer can one man or family virtually corner a vital natural resource or economic function, be it oil, railroads, communications or whatever. In other parts of the world, notably the Middle East in recent years, this seems still possible, but not in America with all its taxes, regulations and other safeguards.

Nevertheless, the top managers of the largest and most productive industrial complex in history earn a great deal. They earn far more than the production workers, but the unique aspect of American industry is that even the workers earn a great deal. The wealth that stems from all the industrial productivity, while by no means shared democratically, still benefits all the citizens who contribute to it more extensively than ever before.

While the system does not work perfectly, or even very well most of the time, it works as well or better than any that have gone before it. That is as high praise as can be given to any instrument which allocates the limited wealth of a complex, contentious and vociferous society, one that demands more in the way of consumer goods and material well-being as it gets more. This society also seeks complete economic security, but that industry has never given, nor ever will as long as the premium is placed on expanded output and continued growth.

CHAPTER 12

Merchandising and Selected Services

NOWHERE HAS THE growth and vitality of the American economy been more evident than in the fields of merchandising and services. Once goods have been produced by industry, a vast network of trade enterprises brings them to the consumer's attention, sells them and then finally delivers them.

Millions of people are employed in marketing and services; the latter category alone employed over 13.4 million workers in 1978. One of the most efficient aspects of American business is its ability to make products known and available throughout the entire nation in a very short period of time. Whatever the product—a refrigerator, hula skirt, a frozen pizza or a pre-planned vacation—or its quality, the marketing sector can present it to the consumer in the most attractive way possible and put it at his fingertips almost overnight.

MERCHANDISING

In 1978 wholesale and retail trade generated about $262 billion of the national income and employed 20.5 million people, or 22% of the total industrial work force. In 1950 these two sectors of the economy accounted for $51 billion of the national income and employed 10.7 million people. During the same period the average worker's individual income in these trades rose almost fivefold, from $3,045 in 1950 to a combined wholesale and retail average of about $14,700 in 1978. Wholesale employees generally earn more than those in retail, particularly in sales jobs. For example, the highest paid wholesale sales people in paper and paper products can earn a salary (plus bonus or commission) of over $80,000.

In both retail and wholesale trade about 23% of the employees are engaged directly in sales, and their incomes vary to a significant degree according to what they are selling. In the wholesale trade, for example, sales supervisors or sales managers earn incomes, combining salary and incentive (bonus or commission), that vary widely according to product sold.

MEDIAN ANNUAL INCOMES OF SELECTED SALES SUPERVISORS (1979-80)

Product	Median Income (salary plus incentive)
Paper	$45,900
Apparel	$42,200
Computers	$41,300
Fabrics	$39,300
Major Household Items	$36,500
Chemicals	$36,400
Publishing and Printing	$31,600
Tools and Hardware	$29,800
Ethical Pharmaceuticals and Surgical Supplies	$28,600
Automotive Parts and Accessories	$28,200
Food Products	$25,000

In the retail business the incomes of sales people also vary according to the product sold. At Bloomingdale's in New York City, to take a famous but low-paying example, all the sales people coming on the job in 1978 started at $122 per 37½ hour week, or about $3.25 an hour.

(This was well under the national average of $4.17 per hour, which was paid to a person with some experience, or the $5 or $6 an hour paid by some department and general retail stores such as Saks Fifth Avenue in New York.) The base weekly wage at Bloomingdale's then increased to $135 a week after 18 months, or $3.60 an hour. In addition to salary, every salesperson earns from 5% to 6% of gross sales as a commission, depending on the department. The best departments for sales income are ready-to-wear clothing and furniture, where a salesperson can be making $20,000 or more after a relatively short time and over $40,000 with years of experience and finely honed selling skills. Yet someone can work in the button department for years and still make less than $12,000.

Other jobs in the retail trade can pay much more. Buyers for large discount department stores are among the better paid, earning from $18,000 as an assistant buyer to $27,000 a year with experience. They can go much higher depending on the product line and the retailer. For example, there are buyers at Bloomingdales who earn above $60,000 a year, and in the furniture or apparel business, some top buyers can make $80,000 or even over $100,000 a year, depending on the skill and talent of the individual.

Another crucial aspect of retailing is promotion, including advertising and public relations. At most large retailers and companies with retailing divisions, the person in charge of promotion is a vice president who makes $70,000 a year or more. Retail trade promotion at department stores is handled by artists, who earn a median of $22,900 and $30,000 as supervisors or directors, and copywriters, who can reach a median of $18,900 and rise to $28,000 as supervisors. Exhibit and display experts are paid an average of $21,100 at the top level, but they can make as much as $28,000 as supervisors. Photographers for advertising and sales promotion begin at an average salary of $14,200 and can make at least $20,400 on a supervisory level. Media buyers, i.e., those who purchase or place space ads in newspapers or buy time on radio or television, begin at an average of about $16,000 with experience and can reach $28,000 to $32,000 at the managerial level.

The average total compensation of top managers in retail and wholesale trade operations, including department stores, general merchandise chains and grocery and drug chains, closely follows sales volume figures, as this breakdown shows.

COMPENSATION OF CHIEF EXECUTIVE OFFICERS IN WHOLE-SALE AND RETAIL TRADE (1978)

Company Sales Level	CEO Total Compensation (salary plus bonus)	
	Wholesale	Retail
$1 billion and over	$285,000	$267,000
$200 to $500 million	N.A.	$142,000
$100 to $200 million	$134,500	$122,000
$50 to $100 million	$101,000	$105,000

The chief executive officer of R.H. Macy's, Edward S. Finkelstein, earns $500,000 a year in total compensation. The flagship store of the Macy's chain in New York grossed about $250 million in sales for 1979 under Finkelstein's supervision. Edward R. Telling, chairman of the largest retail chain of all, Sears Roebuck and Company, earned $563,000 in 1978. Sears Roebuck made a net profit of $922 million in that year.

Advertising, an essential part of general merchandising, has grown enormously in the United States in the last 25 years. In 1955 the total advertising expenditure for all media was $9.1 billion. It reached $15.3 billion in 1965; in 1975 it was $28.2 billion and in 1978 it was $43.8 billion.

Advertising expenditures are closely related to general economic prosperity. In 1880, $200 million was spent on advertising. This figure rose yearly to a peak of $3.4 billion in 1929, when it dropped with the crash, falling to a low of $1.3 billion in 1933. Advertising spending then began a slow uneven climb until the 1950s, when its rise became constant.

In 1978 the top three advertising spenders were Procter and Gamble with $554 million, Sears Roebuck with $417.9 million and General Foods with $340 million. That year the largest media expenditure for advertising, $12.7 billion, went to newspapers; television was next with $8.9 billion. In 1980 the price for one minute of advertising time during the Superbowl was $450,000—$100,000 more than in 1978 and $250,000 above what the same minute cost in 1976. Sixty seconds of advertising time for the 1979 World Series went for $250,000. Normally, a minute of TV prime time network advertising costs about $60,000 and the price is steadily rising.

Just as the costs and expenditures for advertising have grown by leaps and bounds, so too have the incomes of those in this volatile field.

Below are listed six of the highest paid advertising executives in 1978 and their agencies.

INCOMES OF TOP ADVERTISING EXECUTIVES (1978)

Executive	Agency	Total Income
Paul Foley, Chairman and Chief Executive	Interpublic Group of Companies	$545,059
Arthur W. Schultz, Chairman and Chief Executive	Foote, Cone & Belding	$508,115
Edward H. Meyer, Chairman, President and Chief Executive	Grey Advertising Inc.	$423,000*
Don Johnston, Chairman and Chief Executive	J. Walter Thompson	$399,742
John E. O'Toole, President	Foote, Cone & Belding Communications	$391,619
Bruce Crawford, President and Chief Executive	BBDO International Inc.	$324,113

*Estimated.

In 1978 about 195,000 people worked in advertising, including those employed directly by an agency, the advertising departments of many varied businesses, the media and other related organizations. Ad agencies are heavily concentrated in New York, Chicago and Los Angeles, but other forms of advertising employment, particularly in industry and the media, are more widespread. Salaries for advertising workers vary according to size of agency or company and the type of work, but the jobs generally pay far more than do comparable slots in book publishing and somewhat better than jobs in journalism or in any of the media. Management supervisors, who hold the top middle-management positions, can earn from $50,000 to $60,000. Account supervisors earn from $35,000 to $45,000, and account executives reach about $25,000 a year. Executive art directors can earn $40,000 and up. Salaries for senior copywriters range between $15,500 and $22,000, with copy chiefs reaching $28,000. Research directors can make $26,000 to $29,000 a year. Creative supervisors can go as high as $50,000 and top creative directors can make up to $150,000 or $200,000 a year. However, it must be remembered that advertising is in a constant state of flux, and salaries vary from agency to agency and moment to moment.

Modeling has become a very lucrative adjunct to advertising in recent years. The current top superstar, Cheryl Tiegs, has a contract for $1.5 million over five years for the use of her lips, eyes and face by the Noxell Corporation, maker of Cover Girl cosmetics. Her hair is under contract to Bristol-Myer's Clairesse hair coloring for another substantial sum. She also appears on television for Olympus cameras. All this combined with other work, increasingly on TV, earns her about $1.5 million a year. Several years ago Margaux Hemingway kicked off the era of superstar models with a five-year, $1 million contract.

Some print models earn from $750 to $1,500 a day for posing, and a few have gone as high as $2,000 a day (Cheryl Tiegs in *Time* magazine in March 1978 announced that $2,000 was her minimum daily rate.) Furthermore, working on the basis of residuals, models are now paid each time a picture of them is used. Formerly, $600 for a day of posing would be the total fee, but now one day's work can bring from $6,000 to $15,000 over a period of time if the pictures are reprinted. Male models are receiving greater fees and residuals as well, particularly in print advertising, where they can make up to $750 or $1,000 a day with residuals.

In television advertising, the minimum pay scale for one day's work is $250 plus 13 weeks' residuals. But some models who have established selling personalities can make $7,000 to $10,000 per commercial and with residuals up to $30,000 for one television commercial.

The average annual income for successful models is about $55,000 a year, but a number make $200,000 to $250,000. If she can last for 10 years, a top model will gross $3 million and earn $750,000 in income for her agency. There seems to be no end to the upward spiral for models, and they help lead the trend of general affluence among those in the merchandising industry.

TRANSPORTATION SERVICES

Beginning with the inventor of the wheel, whose income went unrecorded, transportation has been a varied and profitable service for some and drudgery for others. Perhaps the lowest paid are urban messengers, who take envelopes, packages or whatever else that can be carried by hand from one location to another within a city, traveling by foot, bicycle, motorscooter, public transport or on rare occasions taxi. The Mobile Messenger Service of New York, for example, paid its messengers $2.00 per trip in 1979, and the average employee completed about 10 to 13 trips a day.

Subway train operators in San Francisco earned $1,825 a month in 1978, and with overtime their average salary was $25,100 a year. In Boston the same operators made $1,614 a month, in Washington $1,600 and in New York $1,494. Engineers for passenger locomotives averaged $29,500 in 1978. In general, the over one million people working in motor vehicle ground transportation and related public services that year were well paid, making an annual average salary of $16,118. Unfortunately the quality of passenger service was often not on the same level as these salaries, although the hardships of poor service cannot easily be measured in terms of dollars and cents.

Taxi drivers have the reputation of being hardy entrepreneurs with colorful personalities and a highly developed sense of independence. Whether this is true or mere folklore depends on the experience of the individual passenger, but taxi drivers do set their own hours more than most people, and consequently their earnings depend on the amount of time they are willing to work. Many drivers for large commercial fleets work only two, three or at the most four days a week, and they split their take with the management. Such drivers can earn between $35 and $60 a day for themselves, combining their share of the meter income and tips, which of course they keep entirely for themselves.

A taxi cab license, or medallion, is expensive, costing about $70,000 in New York, $45,000 in Boston, $40,000 in Chicago and $35,000 in Philadelphia, to give a few examples. Drivers who own their cabs outright, or more usually through bank loans, tend to work longer hours, keep all the meter fares, but pay all expenses such as gas, maintenance and insurance. Nevertheless, by working 12 or 14 hours a day, six days a week, some cab drivers earn as much as $600 to $750 a week after all expenses. Some have been known to make even more, either by working virtually all the time or by renting out their cabs part of the time.

Air transportation has expanded because of technical improvements that have resulted in lower fares and larger markets and the capital investments needed to reach these new markets. In 1930 there were a total of 1,782 airports in the United States, 640 of which were equipped with lighting for nighttime landings. The number of pilots, both commercial and private, that year totaled 15,000. By 1976 there were 13,770 airports in operation, of which 4,362 were equipped for night landings. In that year there were 744,000 pilots, of whom 45,000 were airline pilots and 188,000 others flew commercially.

The average salary of a jumbo passenger jet pilot is about $62,000 a year, based on the mandatory allowable maximum of 85 flying hours a month. Some senior pilots with supervisory responsibilities or exceptional experience can make $90,000 to $100,000 a year. Number two pilots average $42,000 a year and number three pilots $32,000. Pilots who fly for private businesses as opposed to airlines generally make somewhat less; the average for chief pilots on business jets is about $52,000. Test pilots, who assess the quality of new planes, make around $50,000 a year.

Flight attendants earned about $1,250 a month in 1978. With experience and greater responsibility their salaries can go to about $21,000 to $23,000 a year. They generally fly no more than 80 hours a month, but they have ground duties as well. A major benefit for these employees is the discounts they receive on airline tickets for their personal use; sometimes they pay only 10% of the face value of the ticket.

FOOD SERVICES

In a large city, a diner or diners can usually find a quality restaurant in the upper middle price range that has a seating capacity of about 65 people, which is considered small to medium sized. On a good day such a restaurant would serve one lunch sitting and two groups for dinner, or about 200 people. The gross for this number of meals and accompanying drinks would be in the range of $4,000. If the establishment maintained the same level of business on a reasonably consistent basis year-round, it would gross about $1 million a year. (This assumes a revenue ratio of about 70 to 30 for food and liquor.)

The chef at this restaurant, where all food is prepared to order, earns between $30,000 and $35,000 a year, making him one of the best paid in his profession. (Some chefs at nationally famous restaurants or hotels that have more than one dining room can make $50,000 a year or more.) His cook makes about $18,000 to $21,000 a year. But these figures are the high average; most of the more than 1.2 million chefs and cooks who worked in this country in 1979 made considerably less.

Our hypothetical restaurant requires four waiters, who get about $120 a week in salary and a share of the combined tips, totaling between $425 and $475 a week in take-home pay. The headwaiter will make more, perhaps $28,000 to $30,000 a year with salary and tips. (The headwaiter at a famous restaurant can make as much as the chef or even more, going as high as $75,000 or $80,000 a year.) The bartender is paid $180 a week and makes another $150 to $180 in tips. Busboys get about $120 in salary and a modest portion of the tips, adding up to about $185 to $210 a week. The dishwasher and handy-man make about $175 a week. Supervising the entire staff is the manager, who, if he is not the owner, can make from $30,000 up to $50,000 or even $75,000 a year plus incentive pay, depending on the characteristics of the restaurant.

The restaurant's food costs total about 30% of the gross, or $300,000 a year, and the payroll about 20%, or $200,000 more. Rent is another 10 to 15% and overhead (including $1,000 a month for laundry and $200 a month for dishware) takes an additional 10% of the total. The after-tax profit of this operation is about $130,000 a year, which goes to the owner or owners. However, as any owner will tell you, the hours are endless and the problems unrelenting. But the food is good, the customers come back, and the life is lucrative and gratifying.

Outside these posh surroundings, bartenders make roughly the same regardless of the establishment, which is about $275 to $360 a week. Certain locations, of course, are better for tips than the average $30 to $45 a day, just as some bartenders are more appealing to the customers and make more for that reason. In bars where there are more than one bartender, or a number of shifts, they "cut the cup" for their share of the tips.

A coffee shop runs on the principle of marking up the cost of all food by 50% and serving as many customers as possible. A counterman or waitress can make $150 a week in salary plus $20 to $30 a day in tips, while a short order cook gets a weekly salary of $200 to $250.

The food and restaurant business is booming in America and more and more people are eating out, just as they are spending more generally for goods and services. In this way the wealth of the productive sphere of the economy is consumed and returned through expenditure to further encourage production. When the economy works well, it builds on itself and rechannels its buying and spending power into producing goods to keep the circle going. When it is not working, the balance is broken and there are more goods than consumers or more consumers than goods. Either way merchandising and services falter along with the whole economic structure. Many Americans have seen both situations in their lifetime, although that number is getting smaller, and much has been learned from the experience of economic depression. The trend of activity at the retail store, including the attitudes of the consumer, is one of the most sensitive and instantaneous barometers of good times and bad because of the number of people and dollars involved.

CHAPTER 13

Finance, Insurance and Real Estate

V IRTUALLY EVERY CITIZEN and organization uses financial and insurance services, and from time to time almost everyone in our
highly mobile society deals with real estate agents.

Approximately 4.7 million people worked in finance, insurance and
real estate in 1978, and together they accounted for $122 billion, or
about 12%, of the national income. The overwhelming majority were
white-collar workers, many of whom held jobs unique to their particular fields, such as bank tellers or claim representatives in insurance
companies. Generally, however, pay scales in the three industries at all
but the top levels were low compared with other occupations, and even
the company presidents earned less than their counterparts in manufacturing or the media and of course less than most basketball players.

The proportion of managers to other workers is unusually high in
the three industries, far exceeding that of other sectors in the economy.
This can partly be attributed to the large amount of work carried on at

branch locations of financial institutions and the small and often autonomous offices that represent the main insurance organizations and, to a lesser extent, real estate businesses at the local level.

Insurance and real estate differ from banking in the size of their respective sales forces. About 40% of real estate employees are sales people, which is about six times higher than the average in American business. Sales people make up 30% of the employees in insurance companies. Finance, however, requires relatively few sales people, somewhat less than the national average for all industry.

Despite the differences in the character of their work forces, finance, insurance and real estate together perform the function of underwriting, securing and evaluating the daily transactions of goods and services that are an integral component of the economy. Because their role is so pivotal and affects the well-being of so many, these sectors and the people that run them are constant sources of controversy. In a sense, the three industries are the purest form of capitalism and as such symbolize strength and security in good times. During hard times, however, they can often provoke a feeling of outrage at the seeming injustice of their operating policies, leading sometimes to deep social unrest.

FINANCE

The number of banks of all types in the United States has fluctuated dramatically over the years because of the country's changing financial requirements and the impact of government regulatory actions. Overall the number has declined in the past 50 years, while assets have risen. At the end of 1978 there were 14,712 banks with total assets of $1,176 billion. The earliest reliable figures show that in 1834 there were 506 banks with total assets of $419 million. By the turn of the century, there were 13,053 banks with assets of $11.3 billion. In 1930 there was a total of 24,273 banks with assets of $74 billion. (This was the heyday of the small bank, so many of which failed during the depression.) After that the total began to drop and by 1960 there were 14,019 with assets of $282 billion. In a sense, banks are similar to farms in that they have decreased in number but grown larger and wealthier.

A whopping 25% of all bank employees are officers, starting with president, then vice president, treasurer, comptroller, branch manager, loan officer and others. In the past these jobs were often filled by people who had worked their way up from the lowest jobs in the bank, but today the more frequent route for bank officers is through management training programs.

Clerical employees with little or no previous experience make about $600 a month as secretaries, bookkeepers, proofers, file clerks and data processing clerks. With experience, a supervisor in this area can reach about $900 a month, but that is generally the limit.

Tellers with no previous experience begin at approximately $550 to $600 a month and go up to $850 or $900 a month. A teller supervisor is paid about $925 a month. After many years of experience, a head teller could eventually be promoted to assistant cashier at a top salary of $1,200 to $1,500 a month. Assistant cashiers manage the work of all the tellers, audit the cash vault, control cash flow and keep the receipt and transmittal of cash running smoothly. Cashiers, who are often vice presidents, and cashier managers are responsible for this entire aspect of banking and earn from $28,000 to $40,000 a year.

Newly graduated BAs are often given a starting job in customer service. They open accounts for customers and can handle small loan requests among other things. They start at about $750 to $900 a month and after gaining some experience go on to other departments of the bank.

Management trainees with MBAs are paid an average of $1,100 to $1,250 a month. Once they have successfully completed two or three years of training, they become junior officers working in the various areas of the banking business: auditing, accounting, operations, loans, marketing etc.

As officers in these departments, they are paid between $16,000 and $18,000 a year, depending on length of service and ability. After three years (or about five or six years after entering a training program), they can become assistant vice presidents in one of the departments and earn up to $23,000 a year or more at that level.

Branch managers are paid between $21,000 and $28,000 depending on the size of the main bank and the branch. Some, but not all, are vice presidents and at very large and important branches they can make $35,000 and over. Generally, vice presidents in charge of major departments of a bank, such as loans, operations, investments etc., can make from $35,000 to $45,000 a year. An executive vice president can go from $60,000 at a medium-sized bank to well over $135,000 at a larger bank. Bank presidents or CEO's range in salary from $60,000 a year at smaller banks to more than $225,000 at banks with assets over $2 billion. Of course, the top executives at the biggest banks make considerably more than that, as the following list demonstrates. Incomes shown are for salaries plus bonuses.

INCOMES OF TOP EXECUTIVES OF BANKS OR BANK HOLDING COMPANIES (1978)

Organization and Executive	Total Income	1978 Net Profit (millions)
Citicorp		$482
Walter B. Wriston, Chairman	$609,000	
BankAmerica		$514
A.W. Clausen, President	$525,000	
Manufacturers Hanover		$182
Gabriel Hauge, Chairman	$465,000	
Security Pacific		$133
F.G. Larkin, Jr., Chairman	$460,000	
J. P. Morgan		$267
Walter H. Page, Chairman	$410,000	
Chemical New York		$124
Donald C. Platten, Chairman	$383,000	
Chase Manhattan		$197
David Rockefeller, Chairman	$373,000	
First Chicago		$131
A. Robert Abboud, Chairman	$371,000	
Continental Illinois		$169
Roger E. Anderson, Chairman	$370,000	
Western Bancorporation		$167
J.J. Pinola, Chairman	$302,000	

Independent accountants and accounting firms play a very important role in the financial world and the rewards in this field can be significant. The nation's largest accounting firm—Peat, Marwick— received a total of $673.8 million in fees for the fiscal year ending in June 1979. The firm distributed $189 million of this amount to 1,633 active partners, each of whom averaged about $116,000. This was a very high average for a partner at a large accounting firm. The chairman of the company, Thomas L. Holton, made income in excess of $900,000 for the year.

General accounting executives with banks or business firms make less than this. The overall average for salaried accountants is $22,000 a year, but an accounting manager (chief accountant), usually, though not always, a vice president at a bank, can expect to earn an average of about $36,000 a year.

Tax accountants and cost accountants working for companies or banks range in salary from $24,000 to $26,000 a year on the average. Tax accountants who are self-employed or who are partners in groups specializing in tax work can earn much more depending on the number of their clients and the complexity of the work. Some make as much as $95,000 a year in successful practices.

Securities analysts and investment experts, or stockbrokers, play another key role in the nation's financial system. One of the top earners in 1978 was John K. Castle, managing director of the Donaldson, Lufkin and Jenrette brokerage firm in New York. He was a dramatic example of the shrewd and successful broker whose financial judgment led to a very lucrative year. As head of the company's investment banking operations, Mr. Castle's handling of mergers, acquisitions and capital ventures earned him $434,423, or nearly double the salary of Richard H. Jenrette, the firm's chairman and CEO, who earned $234,692 in the same year. However, the successful securities analyst normally makes less than this, whether working for a private firm or self-employed, earning an average of about $45,000 to $60,000 a year. A securities investment manager working at a medium-sized bank makes in the range of $33,000 to $38,000 per year.

However, in discussing this or any other occupation where an individual can earn according to his independent ability and effort, it must be remembered that incomes will vary widely. Great fortunes have been made by outstanding people, many of whom have gone on to found their own firms. The names of Morgan, Lehman, Harriman and others are synonymous with financial success. New financial wizards and entrepreneurs rise to the top every year by making fortunes for themselves or others whether the market goes up or down.

Top executives at the big brokerage houses do almost as well as bankers. James Davant of Paine Webber made $381,000 in 1978. Robert Fomon of E.F. Hutton made $393,000, and William M. Witter of Dean Witter Reynolds made $199,000.

INSURANCE

There are almost 2,000 life and nearly 3,000 casualty insurance companies in the United States. Large insurance companies generally have a home office and a network of regional offices and sales branches spread throughout the country. The three major kinds of insurance are life, property-liability and health. While some companies specialize in one type of insurance, the biggest firms generally offer most of the different categories.

Almost one-half of the 1.8 million people working for insurance companies in 1978 had clerical jobs. Their average weekly salary was approximately $192 a week. The lowest earners were file clerks, making about $135 a week, while executive secretaries averaged about $255 a week. The average weekly hours were low, about 37, but income could be supplemented by working overtime in many of the jobs.

Actuaries who have passed two levels of exams earn a starting high average of $13,000 a year. Thereafter, they receive merit raises for each level of exam they pass leading to membership in the Society of Actuaries. Associates of that organization received an average salary of $18,700 in 1978, and fellows of the society with years of experience averaged about $45,000 for the year.

Claims representatives are paid less than actuaries. The average salary for the 165,000 adjusters and examiners in 1978 was $15,200. Claims supervisors earned an average of $19,500 a year. "Inside adjusters," those who work from the office by telephone, made less, about $11,500, than those who saw people in the field. Underwriters averaged from about $16,000 to $19,000 with some experience. Senior underwriters went to $22,000 and supervisors as high as $26,000.

There were about 490,000 insurance agents and brokers in the United States in 1978. These people try to sell policies that are the most acceptable to a wide range of clients, individuals, groups, companies or other organizations, and to maintain relationships with clients in order to adjust their policies to meet changing needs in the future. The average income for insurance agents on a salary plus incentive basis in 1978 was about $36,500 a year. Self-employed agents, who can sell the policies of a number of companies or run their own company, frequently earn much more, going as high as their skills and energy allow them. An income of $90,000 and over is possible for such people. Even small storefront agencies have been turned into multi-million dollar enterprises over the years.

The incomes (salaries plus bonuses) of the top executives of some major insurance companies are listed below. The figures show that the top salaries in insurance are about equivalent to those of people in banking firms of comparable importance but lower than those in the manufacturing sector. The next lower range of insurance executives, principally those in life insurance, earned from $35,000 to $55,000 in 1978, which is again equivalent to comparable banking jobs and somewhat less than manufacturing.

INCOMES OF TOP EXECUTIVES OF SELECTED INSURANCE COMPANIES (1978)

Company and Executive	Total Income	1978 Net Profit (millions)
Travelers		$372.2
Morrison H. Beach	$540,000	
INA		$211.4
Ralph S. Saul	$515,000	
Aetna Life and Casualty		$517
John H. Filer	$514,000	
St. Paul		$126.5
Carl B. Drake, Jr.	$338,000	
American International		$190
Maurice R. Greenberg	$320,000	
Colonial Penn		$69.4
John J. MacWilliams	$300,000	
Kemper		$70.3
James S. Kemper	$230,000	
Lincoln National		$154.5
Ian M. Roland	$221,000	
American General Insurance		$149
Harold S. Hook	$220,000	

REAL ESTATE

Real estate brokers who belong to the National Association of Realtors are designated "realtors," and real estate agents who are members of the organization are called "realtor-associates." This distinction is an attempt to bring some order to an industry that has many licensed agents, many part-time employees, many real estate practitioners with uncertain credentials, and a good deal of confusion and disputes. One broker referred to the business as a "form of psychiatry— you see the client at his most vulnerable, looking for or getting rid of his home. It is a time of great emotional turmoil."

About 500,000 people sold real estate full time in 1978, and the number of people who were licensed to sell was over 1.5 million. Most real estate firms are relatively small; in fact many brokers run an office of their own and hire agents to work for them as independent sales people on a contract or some other arrangement involving commission on sales. The commission is normally 6% of the selling price of the property, but this varies slightly from area to area and according to the size of the transaction. It is increasingly rare for agents to be direct employees of a broker or agency, and many agents work only part time.

Agents employed by large urban brokers receive a salary to carry them, but their main income still comes from commissions. People who work exclusively in real estate management, usually for large firms, receive a salary in the range of $25,000 a year and up, according to their responsibility for larger properties or more apartment and commercial buildings. They rarely deal directly with potential clients concerning units in large buildings, but they do act as agents to promote and complete rental negotiations.

Brokers are independent business people who not only sell real estate, but also rent and manage properties, arrange for financing of transactions, institute title searches, advertise real estate opportunities, manage their own offices and attend to other business as well. Some, for example, are also lawyers or combine real estate and insurance work.

Most real estate brokers and agents sell residential property, but many also deal with commercial and industrial properties. The latter types of transactions are also handled by large firms specializing in such work. In any case each type of real estate work requires its own expertise. Because of the decided entrepreneurial quality of the real estate broker's work, it is difficult to establish ranges of income. During a prosperous economic period, brokers in favorable locations who are energetic, good with clients and wise enough to hire skillful agents can make $200,000 or more a year. Commercial brokerage firms can gross in the millions. On the other hand, some brokers are satisfied to work completely alone, even part time merely to supplement their income. In 1976 the average real estate broker made about $27,000 on a nationwide basis, according to estimates of the National Association of Realtors. This, however, is a very approximate figure.

It is possible to be more specific about agents. Average annual earnings from commissions by full-time real estate agents in 1978 were approximately $18,000. However, agents working less than 30 hours a week earned much less, around $4,500 a year. Experienced full-time agents made over $40,000 a year in 1978. In certain areas during real estate boom periods, such as Southern California in 1978-79, they have averaged over $150,000 a year.

The real estate market has been very profitable in the past 20 years, earning a splendid return on investment and higher incomes for both brokers and agents. The most successful have been those who constantly keep an eye on the social and economic patterns and trends of the area where they work as well as the country as a whole.

But since land values reflect the economy very closely, the same people are among the first to suffer in a recession. When there is less money to invest, property values and transactions decline just as banks fail, retail trade falls off and construction slows. When all is booming, the banker, builder, broker is everyone's best friend, aiding in every possible way the consumption of more and more of the good things of life. During periods of tight financing, however, these same people can quickly become the most unpopular members of society. Then they personify troubles: the foreclosing banker, the tardy builder, the litigating merchant, the evasive real estate broker who attempts to negotiate a sale for half the price of the purchase.

Real estate profits can be large and very rapid in comparison to many other business ventures. But the price of success is the risks that must be taken whether by an institution or an individual, and the knowledge that losses can be just as great and come just as quickly as the profits.

Part Five

JOBS WITHOUT PAYCHECKS

CHAPTER 14

Heirs and Entrepreneurs

NOT EVERYONE IN America lives by the paycheck. Some are born lucky and simply cash their dividend checks, trust payments and other forms of inherited income. Others create their own fortunes and pay themselves what they choose from their own earnings. Either way, whether in the past or present, each wealthy family has usually had one entrepreneur, or a whole line, who amassed enough money to care for themselves and all related to or connected with them, none of whom have had to work. Of course, many of them do work and some hold extremely responsible jobs, but it is by choice rather than necessity.

The two wealthiest families in the United States are the du Ponts and the Mellons, each of which are worth between $3 and $5 billion dollars and have interests in various financial, manufacturing and other enterprises that are interconnected with a substantial portion of the American business world. The next seven are the Rockefellers, the Gettys, Daniel Ludwig (an individual), the Fords, the Hunts, the Pews, and the Pritzkers, all of whom are worth at least $500 million and some over $1 billion. Add to this another 10 families or individuals, including Ray Kroc, the Kleberg family, the Phipps family and S. I. Newhouse, all worth over $400 million, and you have a list of the very richest of the rich in America.

There are at least another 40 to 50 families or individuals holding assets worth between $200 and $400 million. These include John Dorrance of the Campbell Soup empire, the Kennedys, Ernest Gallo of wine fame and John Hay Whitney of the Vanderbilt and Whitney fortunes. The others in this category comprise a who's who of American history, business and high society.

Most are members of families that began making their fortunes by creating or producing some of the most well-known and widely purchased consumer items on today's market. Walter Annenberg, for example, put together the publishing group that turns out *TV Guide* and *Seventeen* magazine. De Witt Wallace, whose fortune is estimated at over $300 million, is the publisher of *Reader's Digest*. Doris Duke is part of the family that founded the American Tobacco Company. Joyce Hall and his son Donald, worth more than $200 million, are members of the family of the man who created Hallmark Cards. Other wealthy families include: the Chandlers of California, whose communications conglomerate includes the *Los Angeles Times*; the Lilly family of Indiana, whose members are heirs of the pharmaceutical firm Eli Lilly and Co.; and the Stuart family, heirs of the Carnation Company. In other words, most founders of great American fortunes were merchants, farmers or publishers with new ideas; generally they were entrepreneurs who created commercial empires from extremely small beginnings. The du Ponts are a striking exception to this pattern; the family was already wealthy when it migrated to America from France in 1799.

How heirs spend the money amassed by entrepreneurial forebearers varies immensely. The Kennedys have used the power and opportunities provided by their fortune for political advancement, while the Mellons, with much more wealth, have been active in philanthropy but have shunned politics. The Rockefellers, whose name is synonymous with the negative side of capitalism, have been perhaps the most aggressive in using their fortune (through philanthropy) for the public benefit.

Other heirs have used their inherited wealth to further increase their families' commercial holdings. One of the sons of H. L. Hunt has used his annual income of nearly $300 million to invest heavily in the silver market. The Fords have continued active management of the huge automotive conglomerate, and there are power struggles among them for control of the firm even now.

Wealthy American families and individuals also reflect different ethnic backgrounds. The Mellons, Rockefellers, Hunts and Fords are of Anglo-Saxon origin, and the du Ponts originally came from France. The Pritzkers are a Jewish family that earned its fortune through real estate, the Hyatt Hotels and manufacturing enterprises. Other Jewish families and individuals of enormous wealth include S. I. Newhouse, who died in 1979, the Bronfmans, the Crowns, Walter Annenberg and others. The Gallos are Italian and the Pappas family and the Spyros Skouras family are Greek. John H. Johnson, founder of the Johnson Publishing Company, and the family of the late Cilian B. Powell, owner of the New York *Amsterdam News,* are black, as are Henry G. Parks, owner of the meat products company, and A. Maceo Walker, president of the Universal Life Insurance Company.

Not surprisingly, many wealthy families are from Texas, and most of them made their money during the past half century or so. The great Texas fortunes were not all built on cattle or oil, however. For instance, Texan Theodore Lay was the founder of Frito-Lay. Other wealthy Texans include the Duncan family, founders of Duncan Foods (now owned by Coca-Cola). One member of the family, John, founded Gulf and Western Industries; another, Charles, is currently secretary of energy. Dr. Denton Cooley is both a world famous heart surgeon and a successful real estate entrepreneur. Although Texas has more than its share of multimillionaires, similar lists could be drawn up for families from other states and regions of the country.

The millionaires' club, however, is much less exclusive than it used to be. Moreover, the flood of new members as a group is more widespread and more recently self-made. They have been helped by general economic prosperity and, even more, by the inflation that has made a million dollars a more easily obtainable, if less impressive, goal. In 1979 there were an estimated 520,000 people with assets of $1 million or over. This is a 15% increase from just the year before, when there were about 450,000 millionaires; it is more than a four-fold increase over the 121,000 millionaires the government counted in 1969. New York State is first with 51,031 millionaires, California second and Illinois third. The highest density of millionaires is in Idaho, which has 26.5 per one thousand people, and the lowest is in Wyoming, whose 84 millionaires produce a density of 0.19 per thousand people.

Some of these new millionaires are entrepreneurs with a great future ahead of them. Many have made their money because of increasing land values or in the real estate business. Others have invested wisely, and still others have risen up the corporate ranks and continue to receive paychecks. Some have succeeded in the professions. Only a few of them, however, will go on to join the ranks of the entrepreneurial multimillionaires who have created their own fortunes and established financial empires in a relatively short time. These entrepreneurs are shrewd, money oriented and immensely hardworking people who prosper in the American system, where tax rates are high but not as severe as in many European countries, and where freedom of action is less constrained by government regulations, however onerous they may seem to us. For these people, as for the inheritors of great wealth, the size of their paycheck has little effect on their own incomes, since they can write any check they want out of their own bank accounts.

Here some of the more recent self-made multimillionaires are listed along with the source and size of their fortunes.

TEN MULTIMILLIONAIRE ENTREPRENEURS
AND THEIR FORTUNES

Entrepreneur	Source	Amount (millions)
Charles D. Koch	Koch Industries (chemicals, oil)	$500 to $700
Marvin Davis	Davis Oil (exploration and production)	$300 to $500
Loren M. Berry	L. M. Berry and Co. (advertising)	$200 to $300
Harry B. Helmsley	Helmsley-Spear (real estate)	$200 to $300
Samuel Lefrak	The Lefrak Corp. (real estate)	$200 to $300
Edward Carey	Carey Energy Corp. (oil)	$150 to $200

Frank Perdue	Perdue Inc. (chicken processing)	$75 to $100
Irwin Jacobs	Jacobs Industries Inc. (diversified investments)	$50 to $75
Patrick McGovern	International Data Corp. (computer software)	$50 to $75
Samuel N. Regenstrief	Design and Manufacturing Co. (dishwashers)	$50 to $75

Many entrepreneurs begin at the very bottom of a trade or occupation and work up to a position of wealth and dominance. Although only a few of those who try complete the climb, they are numerous enough to make it the archetypical American success story. Modern-day Horatio Algers include R. David Thomas, founder of Wendy's hamburger chain, who began a barbecue restaurant when he got out of the Army after the Korean War. In 1978 his company's sales totaled $185 million. Billy Joe Pevehouse of Adobe Oil started out working for oil companies after earning a degree from Texas Tech on the G. I. bill. With $20,000 he saved from these jobs, he started Adobe, whose sales are now around $70 million a year.

An imaginative entrepreneur can build an empire based on what seems to be the most mundane and insignificant thing. Rory Fuerst started a company called Tred 2, Inc. after he noticed the number of young people walking around San Francisco in tennis shoes with worn out soles. With $37 he bought some rubber soles, glue and implements to repair tennis shoes and went into business. Following much trial and error, he hit on a method of replacing the old soles with new ones and managed to convince the Bank of America to invest in his company.

Few Horatio Alger tales can top Fuerst's. In additon to his repair business, Fuerst began creating and producing new tennis shoes. Tred 2 now has three plants in the United States and two Canadian affiliates turning out about 100,000 pairs of tennis shoes a month. Annual sales for the company, which Fuerst now jointly owns with a few others, exceed $10 million.

There are numerous other tales of entrepreneurs who have made it big in recent years through imagination and hard work. Some build financial empires that will last long after their lives are over. Some are in publishing, such as Ralph Ingersoll, Robert Howard (both of whom have communications groups named after them) and John Wolfe of the Columbus *Dispatch*. Others are involved with energy exploration and production, such as Edwin Cox of the Cox Oil Company and Mary Hudson Vandergrift of the Hudson Oil Company. Still others are in real estate and finance, such as Thomas J. Flatley of Flatley Enterprises, a Boston real estate development firm, and Joseph Albritton of the Perpetual Corporation, a Texas communications and banking group. All of these people are individually worth over $50 million.

To some entrepreneurs, long-term growth and the building of an enduring business are of no interest. They are excited and motivated by a quick turnover, a speculative profit, or simply the idea of making a fast buck by gambling everything on a sudden and potentially lucrative investment. One such entrepreneur is Boston attorney Harold Staviasky, who obtained the United States recording rights for a record album of songs by Pope John Paul II, some sung by the Pope and others composed by him. The recording was manufactured in America by Infinity Records and released around the time of the Pope's visit to America in 1979. The first sales were very brisk, and it has continued to sell in department and chain stores, confirming Staviasky's judgment in obtaining the rights in the first place.

Another field for big earners is dolls and toys. In 1978 Star War toys grossed over $100 million and in 1979 Harvey Rosenberg sold more than $1 million worth of "Gay Bob" dolls at $18 each.

Killings in stocks, commodities or precious metals are the open or secret ambition of nearly every investor. Some phenomenal sums have been made recently on gold stocks, gold and gold funds. Perhaps one of the best investment funds in this area over the last 10 years was International Investors, Incorporated, which rose by 535.7% between December 31, 1969 and December 31, 1979. For the year 1979 alone, Strategic Investments, Incorporated, another gold fund, rose by 149.9%. In straight stocks, those who brought the First Mississippi Corporation, a chemical and fertilizer manufacturer, in December 1969 for $1.37 a share were able to sell it 10 years later in November 1979 for $25.00 a share.

A classic entrepreneurial undertaking is exploring for lost treasure; it requires individual effort and skill and a vast amount of preparation and work. The outcome can be a huge success, as in the case of Burt Webber. In 1979 Webber apparently succeeded in laying claim to $40 million worth of 17th century Spanish treasure sunk off the coast of the Dominican Republic.

In a similar case Mel Fisher, president of Treasure Salvors, Inc. has been coordinating a search over the past 10 years for treasure contained in a Spanish galleon, *Nuestra Senora de Atocha*, sunk off Key West over 200 years ago. The passengers on the ship were apparently smugglers and so far over $24 million worth of gold coins, gold and silver bars and other valuables have been recovered. The *Atocha's* manifest listed 800 gold bars, 896 silver bars, and 250,000 gold and silver coins worth in total several hundred million dollars today. But Fisher's treasure recovery operation has been the subject of law suits launched by the state of Florida. He has won one case that went to the Supreme Court, getting $2.3 million of the first $24 million in treasure, but other suits are pending the recovery of more of the smuggled riches. Besides spending $500,000 in legal fees, Fisher lost his son and daughter-in-law on one dive for the treasure.

Gamblers are entrepreneurs only in the sense that they are willing to take risks for instant rewards. Some do not even risk very much to gain a great deal, taking their chances on lotteries and slot machines, unless, of course, they have been pouring money into them for years. The "largest payout in Las Vegas slot machine history" took place in 1979 when Noreen Singer won $295,000 playing a $3 machine. This supplanted the former "biggest payout in Las Vegas slot machine history," the $275,000 won by James Schelich in 1978 on another $3 machine.

Heirs and entrepreneurs are two of the most close-lipped groups about their incomes and wealth. This is partly because they are under government scrutiny for tax reasons, and partly in reaction to the constant curiosity of a public that envies their success and resents them for being born rich or for making money far more successfully than the average person can.

By the same token, an heir who is having trouble quickly becomes the subject of great and not particularly sympathetic media attention, as in the case of Patty Hearst. On the other hand, when an entrepreneur fails or his business falters, he soon falls from the public eye. The "Gay Bob" dolls and the resold tennis shoes are news now, but hundreds of similar gimmicks, devices and toys are gone and forgotten.

Entrepreneurs are envied for their success, but the rigors and risks they undergo to gain that success are ignored. Gamblers for the most part live on dumb luck and are of interest to no one when they lose. Heirs are not dependent on regular paychecks by virtue of their birth and entrepreneurs by virtue of their hard work, but the casualty rate for both is often high.

CHAPTER 15
Crime and Sin

THAT SUPERSTAR OF criminals Al Capone was estimated to have grossed over $100 million dollars during the Prohibition year of 1927 from his various illegal undertakings: production and sale of liquor, gambling establishments, dog tracks, "protection" rackets, extortion, prostitution and so forth. Even if the figure is exaggerated and the overhead (including the cost of labor) was high, it still makes Capone one of the great earners of all time and worth more than a whole league of professional basketball players. It also indicates the earnings potential that has existed for criminals in America's past. Today the potential is higher still and growing all the time.

The annual "take" from crime of all kinds is over $100 billion. More than one-third of this money stems from ordinary crimes against business. For example, burglary, robbery, shoplifting, employee theft, bad checks, credit card fraud and arson account for as much as $35 to $40 billion a year. The victims of these crimes suffer in roughly the following proportions: retailing 35%, services 25%, wholesale and manufacturing about 15% each, transportation 10% and arson victims 10%.

Another $50 billion or more in criminal profits are derived from major crimes, including illegal gambling, narcotics, loan sharking, hijacking and assorted other vices. These activities are usually associated with organized crime, but obviously independent operators take a good share of the action and income. Independent entrepreneurs are even more in evidence in personal crimes involving what might be described as "gainful sin," that is, prostitution, pornography and other types of sexual exploitation for money. Although highly publicized and profitable in individual cases, crimes against people for gain, such as kidnapping, blackmail, hostage taking and murder for money, are actually a minor factor in the total crime take.

Crime is very big business in the United States, currently employing an estimated 500,000 "career criminals." They have a large and diversified range of enterprises in which to engage, and the turnover in some of them is staggering. During 1978, between $75 and $85 billion changed hands in illegal gambling, from numbers rackets to bets on professional football and other popular sports aside from horseracing. The profits from such transactions are very high and naturally not declared or subjected to taxation. The Internal Revenue Service, however, estimates that about $800,000 per hour is bet in the United States, and other sources put the amount of net profit from illegal betting over $12 billion a year. This is a much higher percentage of profit out of total revenue than that of the great majority of legitimate businesses in the country.

Illegal gambling is the largest single source of criminal income, but other crimes are also increasing, although they still have a less impressive profit margin. Arson, in particular, has grown at a rapid rate in recent years, with losses in arson-caused fires rising from about $74 million in 1965 to over $2 billion in total property and related losses in 1978. Fires intentionally set to collect insurance have become a major threat to the insurance industry.

Robberies, burglaries and larcenies are also rising at a brisk pace. In 1975, 4,180 banks were reportedly held up; in that year bank robbers made off with about $25 million in cash and negotiable securities. In 1979 there was a much publicized wave of bank robberies that increased the amount of money stolen to nearly $40 million. According to the FBI, the average "take" from a bank robbery is $4,000, compared to $400 for other armed robberies. Reports of all types of property theft, including automobiles, went from 719,000 in 1957 to 4.8 million in 1979. In 1977 the number of incidences of these crimes were reported as follows: robbery 404,850, burglary three million, larceny-theft 5.9 million.

One category of property crime, shoplifting, accounted for nearly $8 billion in losses to retail stores of all types in 1978. Professional shoplifters sometimes turn over their stolen goods to fences for about 25% of the actual value. At other times they return the merchandise to the very stores from which they were lifted for a 100% refund. Another lucrative aspect of professional shoplifting is, ironically, instituting civil lawsuits against stores for false arrest. Damages settlements from such suits can be sizable. Careful studies of shoplifting in the past decade show that a highly skilled and experienced practitioner could average about $30,000 in 1971 and about $53,000 a year in 1978.

These figures, as well as all other crime income statistics, are by nature only informed estimates. Reliable figures are difficult and sometimes impossible to obtain. Both criminals and law enforcement authorities exaggerate their estimates; the criminal generally downplaying success to avoid more attention, the lawmen inflating it to dramatize the problems they are facing. Income estimates are likely to be more accurate for individual criminals than they are for large organized groups. In fact, reports on the wealth and profits of "the mob" vary so much as to be of little help. For example, the recent mob superstar Meyer Lansky is credited with running a crime empire that has gained him a personal worth variously estimated at figures between $150 million and $300 million. Because the spread for such figures can be so great, it is better to discuss crime profits on a more modest, manageable level both for major offenses and for commercial vice.

ILLEGAL GAMBLING

The day-to-day core facet of illegal gambling is the unglamorous but extremely pervasive numbers racket. This racket grosses an estimated $14 to $15 billion a year with a total profit margin of about 40%, before and after taxes of course. It has been estimated that almost 60% of all adults living in the inner city play the numbers at least occasionally.

The numbers runner is the low but indispensable man in this business. His job is to accept bets in homes, bars, pool halls, barber shops, work places or wherever else there are gamblers. For his work the runner receives about 20% of all bets handled, and on an average day that would be about $500. Thus, a runner can make about $100 a day. As an independent entrepreneur, his annual income depends on the number of hours and days he works, but the average runner can earn about $25,000 a year. The numbers collector oversees a group of runners and so he makes more, perhaps as much as $70,000 a year on the average.

NARCOTICS

Narcotics is considered much more dangerous and more socially unacceptable than gambling and is far more closely scrutinized by law enforcement officials. For the most part, it is dominated by members of organized crime, who are active in all phases of drug traffic—obtaining, distributing and selling. According to the Drug Enforcement Administration, it costs about $28,000 a year to maintain the habit of a drug addict, and there are an estimated 110,000 to 160,000 such addicts in the United States. Besides addicts there are an estimated 10 million marijuana users in the country. Although the efforts to control marijuana are relatively weak, considerable profit is still made from its sale.

But the real money is in hard drugs, where the process of diluting heroin or other narcotics and the continuous price markups along the route from grower to consumer make the ultimate profit enormous for everyone involved. An original investment of $300,000 for nearly pure heroin obtained in Mexico or elsewhere can earn the wholesaler $1 million after the drug has been cut and broken down into small packages. The heroin then goes to a supplier, who recuts it, repackages it and makes another $500,000 on the shipment. Finally the drug is diluted again, put into smaller packages and sold on the street, gleaning the pusher an additional $300,000 profit per kilo sold. At this point the heroin is about one-fifteenth of its original strength. Everyone, from original importer to final pusher, can make hundreds of thousands of dollars a year, although most of it is shared with the overall organization. Of course, because of the nature of the work, a person in narcotics may be on easy street one day and in jail the next.

LOAN SHARKING

Loan sharking is another illegal enterprise where organized crime predominates. Fast loans at stupendous rates of interest make for great profits, although sometimes considerable violence must be used to ensure repayment. Most states' usury laws limit interest rates to 1.5% monthly, or an annual total of 18%. Loansharks charge 20% a week on short-term loans and 15% per week on longer-term transactions. Thus a one-year loan of $10,000 will cost the borrower $17,800. Loansharks, who share their profits with the mob in return for its protection and the use of its musclemen, can make over $175,000 a year on the average.

HIJACKING AND INDUSTRIAL THEFT

Hijacking is another widespread and profitable crime. Whole truckloads or boxcar loads of goods are often stolen by hijackers and sold to fences for redistribution into the market. Hijacking profits depend on the size of the theft and the number of accomplices, which can be many. The rewards of success are great and incomes of over $100,000 a year on a continuous basis are possible.

On a somewhat smaller scale, industrial theft can also produce substantial profits. Rather than by the truckload, individual manufactured items can be removed from the production line in a quiet and occasional manner. This can add up if the product is, for example, a TV set retailing at $550. If a hundred sets were pulled off the line for "testing" every three months, the thief and his accomplices might net as much as $60,000 in one year, or even more if they can sell the goods without a fence. This form of theft is common with products ranging from books to bulldozers, with the elements of profit and risk rising as the value of the product increases.

AUTO THEFT

There were 968,000 reports of auto theft in the United States in 1978, and this profitable crime continues to increase every year. A competent auto thief generally gets about one-quarter the value of the car from a fence or a car salesman who directly handles stolen vehicles. A thief turning over 20 cars a year for resale can make an average of

$20,000 to $25,000 a year, and this is often a handsome supplement to a salary earned in some legitimate phase of the automobile service business.

FRAUD AND CON GAMES

Fraud, "con" games and scams of every description are very common elements of crime in this country. The number and variety of frauds and con games are enormous. They can range from stock certificate swindles and complicated bankruptcy frauds to simple cons employed by panhandlers to get money. Some involve counterfeit securities, others include orders placed for goods that are delivered but never paid for, phony gambling establishments that take bets but never pay off, and even gypsy fortune tellers who urge their clients to turn over their money in order to remove the root of evil.

It has been estimated that some highly talented con men moving in prosperous circles make over $200,000 in an exceptional year and can easily make $50,000 in an average year.

Panhandlers with a tale to tell (as distinguished from mere beggars who earn $20 to $30 on a good day) can be consummate professionals and earn princely sums at their trade. One of the most famous was Yellow Kid Weill who made an estimated $8 to $15 million in his lifetime, traveling leisurely around the country. However, he died in a poverty ward like so many of his kind.

Fraud by gypsy fortune tellers is frequently perpetrated by a family whose members lure potential victims, gain their confidence and convince them of the sincerity of the teller. Faith healers, sellers of miracle medicines, exorcists and the like abound. The successful ones can earn $20,000 or $30,000 a year, and sometimes much more.

KIDNAPPERS AND HIT MEN

In 1532-33 the conquistador Francisco Pizarro kidnapped the ruler of the Incas and held him for a ransom approximately equivalent to $120 million in modern currency. This record sum dwarfs the highest paid in modern times, when two businessmen were kidnapped in 1975 by political terrorists in Argentina and returned for $60 million. Kidnapping has not been very successful in recent years in the United States because of the efficiency of the FBI in handling this crime, which is so abhorrent to society. Most recent attempts have failed, usually because the kidnapper is seized when the ransom is handed over or soon afterwards.

Murder for pay is one of the most dramatized of all crimes in America, and "hit men" have been depicted in movies and literature for years. Ironically, hit men who operate for organized crime do not receive high financial rewards for their work as a rule. The average is $2,000 or $3,000 for a murder, but the real profit for the hit man is the position he gains in the mob by executing someone. Promotion in the syndicate is based on loyalty and trust and a killing proves that loyalty and cements the trust. Bodily damage inflicted on recalcitrant debtors, employees who do not contribute their full share or even enforcers who overstep their bounds is even less profitable; $500 would be a good average pay for an assault.

Of course, independent hit men and specialized or unusually difficult jobs can earn greater pay. In some cases a professional murderer can command $75,000 for a job, but this is a figure that defies independent verification and statistical averaging.

COMMERCIAL VICE

Prostitutes and pimps intrigue the public even more than hit men, and popular literature in America is filled with fictionalizations of their lives, interviews with those in "the game" and even scholarly studies of their social backgrounds and roles.

Because figures on the number of arrests vary over such a broad range, it is hard to say whether vice for pay is increasing faster than the population or not. Most likely it is not. According to FBI figures, there were 311,000 arrests of females for prostitution in 1973 and 392,000 in 1977. There were 94,000 men arrested for prostitution in 1973 and 177,000 four years later, according to the same source. Assuming that these figures are accurate, then the number of male prostitutes has either increased sharply or they are being apprehended more often. During the same period the number of female arrests increased, but not much more than the growth in population. In any case, experience shows that the number of arrests has little or nothing to do with controlling the incidence of prostitution; in fact, pimps and prostitutes look upon payment of fines as simply one more overhead item in their business.

Prostitutes differ in how they go about their profession as much as they do in their incomes; they can be straightforward street walkers, work bars of varying class and clientele, be independent call girls or members of a call girl group controlled by a pimp or they can be managed by a madam. Independent call girls can earn $50,000 a year, getting from $200 to $500 for a night's work. (They also sometimes travel to pleasant places in their work and receive gifts as side benefits. One pimp was offered the weight of his girl in pure heroin as the price for her companionship for a week.)

Some call girls share their earnings with a pimp who helps manage their financial affairs and acts as their protector on the job and companion during their leisure time. Pimps with three to five stylish and successful call girls can make as much as $300,000 a year and even more, although the overhead is high.

Prostitutes who work in brothels, or at a lower economic and performance level, such as in massage parlors, must also split their take, giving half or even two-thirds of their earnings to the management. Prostitutes who work out of bars usually charge from $25 to $50 per client. If they handle 10 or 15 clients in one night, sharing the proceeds with their pimp plus a percentage for the bartender or owner of the bar, they will come away with not much more than $175 or so for their work. This is moderate pay for what can be dangerous work.

Streetwalkers generally have pimps who take care of their housing, clothing, health and legal expenses and even their dental bills. A streetwalker charges a fee of $20 to $50 per client and usually earns from $200 to $300 a night. If a pimp has three streetwalkers in his stable, he can gross over $3,000 a week, and if the girls also steal wallets, watches etc. from the clients, the income can be much higher, as much as $500,000 a year or more after expenses. However, this represents pimping at an unusually lucrative level compared to the rewards of ordinary street prostitution, and the life is often short and uncertain. Violent encounters with competitors, jail sentences, the police and operators of the omnipresent drug traffic are always threats. The rise from the ghetto to the Cadillac, flashy clothes and great power over a few people can be swift, but the fall to a jail sentence and the permanently damaging effects of that experience can be just as quick.

Commercial vice has as many variations as does the human imagination. Peep shows, pornographic magazine and movie houses, sex shows and exhibitions and sexual apparatus businesses run the gamut from legal-but-harassed to quasi-legal to outright indictable. The actors in pornographic movies generally earn from $150 to $300 per performance, unless they become "adult screen" superstars such as John Holmes or Georgina Spelvin. They are then paid several thousand dollars for a cinematic performance. The movies themselves, if successful, usually do well to gross $50,000 in total, but *Deep Throat* and *The Devil in Miss Jones* have been reshown for years. *Deep Throat* has grossed over $50 million worldwide and is still playing.

Regardless of the nature of the work, criminals seek more than anything else to avoid prison sentences. Nevertheless, the prison population in state and federal institutions increased from 166,133 in 1950 to 263,291 in 1976 and continues to rise annually. The number of prisoners in county and municipal jails, usually for shorter sentences, is much larger still.

However, if worse comes to worse, and a criminal ends up in jail, it does not necessarily mean that his money-making days are over or even suspended. Organized crime leaders have administered the activities of their mobs from a jail cell, and prisoners have perpetrated great cons and scams on those outside the walls. In the Greenfield, Mass. House of Detention during the early 1970s, inmates secured the loan of an extremely valuable stamp collection under the guise of holding a stamp exhibition for rehabilitative purposes. The stamps were replaced by fakes and the real ones disappeared; later they were fenced out of the country.

Other prisoners in recent years have engaged in a particularly profitable and innovative con. By filing false income tax returns, the prisoners receive illegal refund payments from the federal government. The General Accounting Office in 1979 explained that the prisoners managed this by obtaining new Social Security numbers using fictitious names. In 1976 inmates at the California Men's Colony in San Luis Obispo filed 70 false returns based on this simple method and received over $55,000 in refunds before the scheme was detected. And there is no reason not to believe that this new practice goes on in prisons throughout the country.

This chapter is a testament of sorts to the devotion of Americans to the principle of free enterprise, entrepreneurship and the unrelenting quest for greater income. It proves that whenever there is money to be made, be it through a legitimate paycheck, commission, merit or performance award, hidden bonus or even fraudulent rebates and crime, the drive to achieve is also there. Nothing, not even the confines of prison, will stop the entrepreneur from taking advantage of the situation, turning challenges and obstacles into financial gain. Sometimes this passion is for work that is far from admirable, but it is always there. Society can only hope that it will be used in ways that enrich the public at large as well as the individual entrepreneur.

Index

248 PAYCHECKS